CLEAR MORAL
OBJECTIVES

To Cathie,
With best wishes! Thanks
for a great blurb!

Be Logical,

Lyn Woolley

11-14-03

CLEAR MORAL OBJECTIVES

Lynn Woolley

SUNBELT EAKIN Austin, Texas

FIRST EDITION
Copyright © 2003
By Lynn Woolley
Published in the U.S.A.
By Sunbelt Eakin Press
A Division of Sunbelt Media, Inc.
P.O. Drawer 90159
Austin, Texas 78709-0159
email: sales@eakinpress.com
website: www.eakinpress.com
ALL RIGHTS RESERVED.
1   2   3   4   5   6   7   8   9
1-57168-811-0

Library of Congress Cataloging-in-Publication Data
Woolley, Lynn, 1949–
    Clear moral objectives / Lynn Woolley.
        p.   cm.
Includes bibliographical references and index.
    ISBN 1-57168-811-0 (alk. paper)
    1. Conservatism–United States. 2. Political planning–United States.
I. Title
JC573.2.U6W66   2003
302.52'0973–dc21   2003008820

To Tyler Ryan Oglesby—
May you learn to love books as much
as your father does.

CONTENTS

ACKNOWLEDGMENTS

The author wishes to thank Missy Stebbins, Lou Ann Anderson, and Jodie Woolley for proofreading the text and for making valuable suggestions to improve its clarity. Thanks also to Bob Moos of the *Dallas Morning News* for being the first editor to publish my columns. And a special "thank you" to New York talk show host Barry Farber, who planted the seed for this book. Barry, you're one of the all-time greats.

Photography by Bob Smith, Accurate Image, Waco, Texas.

INTRODUCTION

We live in a strange world where up is down, black is white, and right is wrong. In today's world, nothing is as it seems, and few things seem to be called what they really are. Racial preferences, for example, are known by the pleasing term "affirmative action," and the right of a woman to end a pregnancy by destroying her unborn baby is known simply as "choice."

Did we say "baby"? The term used by radical feminists and others on the left is "fetus." It's easier to exercise "choice" over a "fetus" than over a baby.

It's been said that a picture is worth a thousand words, but that's not true. As any member of NOW will tell you, if the word "baby" is substituted for "fetus" in any discussion of abortion rights, the pro-abortion side is likely to lose. By the way, that term we just used, "abortion rights," was popularized by the Left and picked up by the media. It has a high sound to it, as if it was plucked from the Constitution itself. But the "rights" mentioned are nothing more than the right to kill the unborn child.

The practice of using such words and forming them into pseudological arguments is known in political circles as "spin." When spin is successful over a period of time, it becomes virtual truth to those who have done the spinning and those who want to believe.

At that point, such a "truth" may enter the culture and become sacrosanct. We refer to that as "political correctness."

In advertising and marketing, similar methods are used, though on a much less brutal scale. Here, we call it "positioning." Words in advertising copy and in radio commercials—or combined with images on television—create lasting impressions that can lead to huge sales and profits. All the major brands have used positioning campaigns. Coca-Cola is still the "Real Thing" years after that campaign ended. Tylenol became a world-class brand using doctors in its commercials and promising "it won't upset your stomach like aspirin can." And Miller Lite gave you "everything you always wanted in a beer—and less."

Light beer may, in fact, be the best example of how words position a product in the minds of consumers. It is simply beer with fewer calories. So why don't they call it "diet beer"? Simple. Beer drinkers are not embarrassed to belly up to the bar and order another light beer. But few of them want anything to do with diet beer.

The power lies in how it's said. A smart marketing executive who knows how to use positioning concepts understands that the battle for brand loyalty is played out inside the minds of prospective buyers. The product or service isn't really positioned; it is what it is. Soap is a personal hygiene product. Beer is an alcoholic beverage. Pepsi is a soft drink. So the advertising must penetrate that tough exterior and get inside the head of the person it is designed to reach.

Soap becomes more than just soap. It becomes "Dove"—one-quarter moisturizing lotion—enhancing beauty. That sells to women. Lava contains pumice. It'll clean those greasy, manly hands. Both products are soap, but their positions are very different. Similarly, the people who market Pepsi look for ways to differentiate their product from Coca-Cola.

In the battle for discount-store loyalty between two similar giants with similar names, Wal-Mart defeated Kmart with just a few words: Always Low Prices.

Positioning campaigns work best when the same concept is used over and over for years—perhaps even for decades. And so it is with political spin. Some schools of thought even hold that the bigger the lie, the easier it is to believe. Everyone knows that if the lie is repeated over and over by enough people in enough places, eventually it will be accepted as truth.

President Bill Clinton understood the concepts of spin, positioning, and the Big Lie. He used them all to his advantage.

In the area of spin, the Clinton war-room team had no peers. "The Ragin' Cajun" James Carville, Paul Begala, Lanny Davis, and a host of others appeared on network and cable TV night after night to explain away all the Clinton foibles from Whitewater to Monica Lewinsky. Clinton's troubles were usually the fault of "extremists in the Republican Party," or "an out-of-control independent counsel." (It didn't seem to matter whether the IC was Robert Fiske, Kenneth Starr, or Robert Ray. Whoever it was, he was always partisan and always out of control.)

The Clinton spin machine also told us that Republicans wanted to let little children go hungry, keep the elderly from getting their prescriptions, destroy Social Security, and let Medicare wither on the vine.

From a positioning standpoint, Mr. Clinton carefully crafted his image to become the president who cared. "I feel your pain" was an oft-quoted Clintonism that pretty well summed up how he wanted his followers to think of him, and how most of them did. Images of Clinton tearing up during speeches are still fresh in the minds of people who followed his career. Who could forget Clinton sobbing at a moment's notice when he spotted a television camera that was focused on him after the Ron Brown funeral?

Then there was the Big Lie. "I didn't have sex with that woman" is a line that will go down in history. Mr. Clinton said it to the nation on television, to his staff in private, and presumably to Mrs. Clinton while dodging a few flying lamps and vases. Many of the American people bought the story, and almost all the staff signed on to it—at least officially.

Mrs. Clinton is positioned as "the smartest woman in the world," so it's hard to believe that she might have believed the story. But in a calculated effort to hold on to power, she told a national television audience that the truth was there for anyone who was willing to go and find it. Of course, she was referring to the Vast Right Wing Conspiracy, another major component of the Big Lie.

As it turned out, the truth was indeed out there. A semen-stained blue dress belonging to "that woman" turned up, and the president's lies were exposed. But Mr. Clinton's spin machine was so strong and his positioning was so ingrained (he was the nation's first black president, you'll recall) that Republicans on the Hill were scared to death of him.

He was impeached, all right. But when the case went to the Senate for trial, senators who were sworn to uphold the Constitution failed to convict and remove Mr. Clinton. The reason had nothing to do with pictures. In fact, most of the pictures worked against Mr. Clinton's interests. There were pictures of him pointing at the camera during the "I didn't have sex" speech on TV. There were pictures of him testifying about the meaning of the word "is."

What mattered most was words. Mr. Clinton had so branded the Republicans as "extremists" and so positioned them as "partisan" that they were literally afraid to remove him from office. After all, Mr. Clinton was just trying to "do the job the American people had elected him to do." What's a little perjury; what's a bureaucratic snafu here and there when the President of the United States cares so deeply?

During the Clinton years, up was truly down and right and wrong just merged into a single concept. Clinton could get away with anything. Sex in the Oval Office; perjury; ransacking the files of a just-deceased legal advisor; selling the Lincoln Bedroom; selling pardons. Such is power of words in the hands of a master—even words that are untrue.

Imagine, then, the power of truth.

President Ronald Reagan shocked the world when he called the Soviet Union an "evil empire." People all over the world gnashed teeth and pulled hair: how could he say that?

It was absolutely true. People in the old USSR were certainly repressed.

There were no free elections. *Izvestia* carried little if any truth. The Soviets were always eyeing some neighbor with aggression on their minds.

Everyone knew that the Soviet Union was evil, but until Mr. Reagan came along, no one would say it. Ah, but once he said it, and once the shock wore off, people began to recognize the evil and talk about it. The Soviets felt the pressure not only of the Reagan military buildup, but of words. Powerful—and this time truthful—words that packed a bigger punch than any missile ever could. These words fueled a major shift in world opinion.

Several factors contributed to the decline of communism and the fall of the Berlin Wall, but it was Mr. Reagan and his impassioned plea to the Soviet leader—"Mr. Gorbachev, tear down this wall!"—that made the policy crystal clear.

So why is it that conservatives can't seem to come together and articulate a clear policy based on truth? They seem to worry more about political goals—holding on to the White House, maintaining a majority in Congress—than they do about issues that affect the future well-being of the United States of America.

They talk about a "big tent" philosophy of everything goes, and anyone with any viewpoint is welcome. But what can be accomplished by a political movement that is so undefined that real core values are practically nonexistent?

Former Defense Secretary Caspar Weinberger once said that the Cold War was won only after the United States finally defined a clear moral objective—when President Reagan first made the "evil empire" comment.

More recently, in a Reaganesque moment during his first State of the Union address, President George W. Bush referred to Iran, Iraq, and North Korea as an "axis of evil." Once again, the world let out a collective gasp. How could the American president say such a thing? Leaders of the three named countries reacted angrily.

But Mr. Bush was simply being blunt, clear, and truthful.

It's not as if he had let the cat out of the bag. Everyone knows that those three nations are potential adversaries of the free world. But once Mr. Bush made that statement flatly and clearly, the pressure was on.

There are other issues that deserve to have such clarity—such truth—applied to them. The American people know and understand little about the size of government, having been told for years that budget increases are actually "cuts." Many people fail to realize how simple life could be if the IRS could just be identified as what it really is.

Family matters, diversity and multiculturalism, language, national security, education, morality, religion, a reaffirmation of the Constitution and the Bill of Rights—these are issues that should be discussed in clarity and in truth. And so, we're going to make some declarations in this book. Perhaps they won't echo around the world as Reagan's "evil empire" or Bush's "axis of evil" did, but they will be powerful nonetheless.

These are the core values. These are the things that matter.

These are clear moral objectives—and if men and women of good faith will work to see them accomplished, they will do more than just help a political party to win elections; they will keep America great.

CHAPTER 1

Preserve the Right to Life

We must declare that life is our most precious possession and without it there can be no freedom, no liberty, and no justice.

In our most precious documents, life comes even before liberty. And yet, in today's "every child a wanted child" society, the answer to the problem of an unwanted child is simple: kill it.

To understand this frame of mind, you should first realize that the entire language of abortion is fraudulent. "Pro-choice" was a stroke of brilliance on someone's part—a term that actually means to support "a mother's right to have her unborn child killed" but expresses that position in a very positive and palatable way. Following that lead, major newspapers decided a few years ago to utilize the equally high-sounding term "abortion rights" to refer to the pro-abortion movement.

Even the term "abortion" is a weasel-word. It actually refers to the ending of a pregnancy before birth, resulting in the death of the unborn child. But nowhere in any of these terms do you see the words "death" or "kill" actually used. That would be too harsh; it would have a negative connotation, and the language of abortion supporters must be positive. After all, we're talking about women's rights here.

It's not uncommon for someone who's pro-abortion to make a statement such as: "A woman should have the right to terminate her pregnancy." But a pregnant woman is also an expectant mother. So if we substitute real words for politically correct terms, we could express the statement this way: "A mother should have the right to kill her unborn baby."

In no other political or moral argument are words so important as they are in the abortion issue. When we refer to the baby as a "fetus," we have replaced the warm image of a newborn, perhaps being cradled in its mother's arms, with a harsh, clinical, and even disgusting image of something growing in the womb like a parasite.

"Fetus." Was there ever a worse-sounding word?

And if the newspapers could agree on "abortion rights" for one side of this issue, what would they call the other side? "Anti-abortion," of course. In much of the media, these terms have replaced "pro-choice" and "pro-life," making the abortion side seem positive and leaving the life side saddled with a negative.

So let's be clear.

Abortion, as we will use the word, means to purposefully prevent a child in a normal pregnancy from being born by killing it. Of course, there are valid arguments in favor of abortions—usually centering on rape, incest, or endangerment to the life of the mother if the pregnancy should come to term. But for our purposes, we're talking about abortion on demand; abortion for convenience' sake; abortion as birth control. And, as defined in the famous *Roe v. Wade* decision—abortion as part of a woman's right to privacy.

A landmark decision

Roe v. Wade changed everything. Since the mid-1800s there had been laws in the United States to limit or prevent abortions. But in 1973, the Supreme Court ruled that in most cases, states may not prohibit a woman's right to have an abortion during the first six months of her pregnancy.

The case sprang from a legal challenge brought by a Texas waitress, styled in the lawsuit as "Jane Roe." She sued the Dallas district attorney, Henry Wade, saying that she was denied her right to an abortion under state law. Specifically, the Court ruled that Ms. Roe's right to privacy—that is, to go behind closed doors and have her baby removed from her body—had been violated under the Fourteenth Amendment and other sections of the Bill of Rights.

Furthermore, the Court ruled that a fetus is not a living person, though the justices were concerned about "viability." They eventually decided that the baby could live outside the womb at about seven months. That's twenty-eight weeks. But they weren't really sure that the baby wouldn't be viable as early as twenty-four weeks. Viability was important because the fetus might be a living person at that point.

The justices set up new rules for the states, based on the three trimesters of pregnancy. During the first trimester, the states were now prevented from interfering at all with a woman's decision to end the pregnancy. In the second trimester, the states could regulate abortion only for purposes of protecting a woman's health. In the final trimester, the states were allowed to regulate abortions, but even then, if the woman's health were in question, she could still obtain a legal abortion.

The Supreme Court's decision mentioned both the "life and health" of the mother, and that brings us back to the language of abortion once again. Doctors may agree on a circumstance—rare in the extreme—in which a woman's life may be in danger from a pregnancy. But what about her "health"?

The Court's decision gave the abortion-on-demand crowd everything it wanted. It got free and open abortions during the first six months, and all it needed after that was to find a doctor who would state for the record that a pregnancy might damage the health of the woman. It might cause her to have headaches or mental anguish or cause her to break out in a rash. It really didn't make a lot of difference, because, combined with the privacy ruling, the language about "health" opened the door for abortions right on through the third trimester.

There is even a grisly procedure known as "partial birth abortion" (the medical term is "intact dilation and evacuation"), in which a baby who is almost free of the womb can be legally destroyed. Abortion doctors get away with this because of the "health of the mother" language.

How it's done: the gruesome details

It's important to understand just how an abortion is performed—and there's no way to make it sound pleasant. So here are the methods that "providers" use to end a pregnancy.

Abortion is easiest, of course, during the first trimester, when the baby is still in his or her early stages of development. The abortionist simply removes the baby using suction, then scrapes the wall of the uterus. This is known as "suction curettage" or "vacuum aspiration."

It gets messier during the second trimester. The baby is better formed and looks more like a human being, and suction doesn't work as well. The abortionist has several choices.

He may choose a method known as "dilation and evacuation." The baby is dismembered inside the womb and brought out piece by piece to be placed in a container for disposal. Another method involves injecting a salt solution into the fluid that surrounds the unborn child. That kills the baby and causes it to be dispelled from the mother's body. The final method is a simple injection of prostaglandin drugs, shot into the amniotic fluid surrounding the baby. The drugs cause contractions that expel the baby.

It's all neat and simple. A woman is pregnant one moment, not pregnant the next. It's only grisly if you watch it happen, or if you see the little head, the little arms and legs in the disposal container. In many cases, no one has to know. But what if the pregnancy goes too far, into the fourth month and beyond, and yet the expectant mother decides that she wants to be rid of the baby?

In such cases—ranging from four and a half months to nine months into the pregnancy—the woman may consider having a partial birth abortion (PBA). This procedure is accomplished by extracting most of the child from the uterus and through the birth canal—feet first—leaving just a few inches of the head still inside. Then, with the baby not quite born, the abortionist plunges surgical scissors through the child's skull. The baby is surely dead by this point, but to make sure, a suction catheter is inserted and the child's brain is taken out.

Views from the Left

You may be sick at your stomach by now, or asking, "How does the pro-abortion crowd justify such a hideous procedure?" The truth is that many on the Left have hardened their hearts for two very important causes: profitability and radical feminism. Let's be clear. Abortion is profitable to those who provide it; it has become an industry. To the radical Left, it has become a cause—almost a religion. And when it comes down to the repulsiveness of it all, the Left simply doesn't care.

In 1996, Congress passed a bill to ban partial birth abortions. President Bill Clinton promptly vetoed the bill, and Congress failed to override the veto. The president, who lied about Monica Lewinsky and so many other things during his administration, lied about this, too, saying that the procedure was used on "a few hundred women every year" whose fetuses are "about to be born with terrible deformities." A presidential spokeswoman, Mary Ellen Glynn, said the president would be happy to sign a bill banning PBAs if they were being used for elective purposes.[1] He was lying about that, too.

As it turns out, PBAs are not rare—certainly not in the neighborhood of five hundred per year, as claimed by Planned Parenthood. And it turns out that more than a few doctors utilize it. The *New York Times* quoted an anonymous gynecologist at a New York teaching hospital: "Of course I use it, and I've taught it for the last ten years. So do doctors in other cities."[2]

The Greater Austin Right to Life newspaper *Life Matters* looked at two abortionists, Dr. Martin Haskell of Ohio and Dr. James McMahon of California, with three thousand PBAs between them as of the 1995 article. Dr. McMahon claimed that his "nonelective" abortions were for such things as maternal depression, but Dr. Haskell admitted that 80 percent of his PBAs were purely elective.

The *Wall Street Journal* ran a story about a newspaper in Bergen County, New Jersey, that reported on an abortion clinic in Englewood. The clinic claimed that it used partial birth abortions in about half of the three thousand abortions it did between weeks twenty and twenty-four. When the paper approached Planned Parenthood about this, it was told that the five-hundred-per-year number referred only to abortions beyond twenty-four weeks.[3] In other words, when it came up with the misleading figure of five hundred PBAs per year, Planned Parenthood was only counting late-term abortions performed on what it mockingly referred to as "Gerber Babies" because those are the babies that pro-lifers depict in their literature. It was a parsing of words worthy of Clinton himself.

Perhaps the most startling revelations about partial birth abortions came from a very prominent abortion rights supporter named Ron Fitzsimmons. His story broke in February 1997 when he was executive director of the National Coalition of Abortion Providers in Alexandria, Virginia, a group of about two hundred abortion clinics. Tired of all the false claims, Fitzsimmons stated flatly that he had lied when he said PBAs were performed rarely and only to save the life of the mother or to abort malformed fetuses.

But Fitzsimmons wasn't becoming a pro-lifer. He said he had "no apologies" for the procedure—just for his lies and the fact that he waited a year and a half to come clean. He now placed the number of PBAs each year at three to four thousand out of a total of about 1.3 million abortions nationwide. Prior to Fitzsimmons, no prominent abortionist or pro-abortion organization had come forward to tell the truth about these numbers.[4]

Of course, this now meant that Congress had more ammunition to override the veto or resubmit the legislation. And President Clinton, who promised to sign a PBA ban only if it could be shown that the procedure was being used on an elective basis, was now obligated by his own words to sign such a bill. In reality, the issue was already decided. Republicans in Congress had satisfied a core constituency by submitting the bill, and Clinton had pleased a core constituency by vetoing it. The political world was functioning normally.

Radical feminism: the core constituency of abortion

The beliefs that women should receive equal pay for equal work, that they should have the right to vote and serve in public office, and that women should not be discriminated against because of gender is known as "feminism." The belief that there is no physical difference in men and women, that women need men only as sperm donors (and then only out of absolute necessity to keep the species alive), that pregnancy can be seen as a disease, that any sexual contact with a man is rape, that a "fetus" is a parasite, and that abortion should be available on demand—paid for by public funds—is known as "radical feminism."

Rush Limbaugh takes heat for referring to members of the radical feminist movement as "Femi-Nazis," but he's right about their extremist views.
Radical feminists don't believe in dehumanizing the Jewish people as Nazi
Germany did; they believe in dehumanizing their own offspring.

The National Organization of Women (NOW) claims to be the nation's
largest women's rights group. But NOW and its membership—such as former group president Patricia Ireland and her replacement, Kim Gandy—are
really focused on the task of making sure that no fetus goes unaborted, if
that's what a woman desires.

This is the agenda that Ms. Gandy put forth upon the occasion of her
election as president of NOW: stop conservative appointments to the
Supreme Court and the federal bench and persuade more women to run for
office. In other words, Ms. Gandy doesn't want the country to seat any federal judge who might be protective of an unborn child—especially Supreme
Court justices. And she wants more (liberal) women to be elected to office
to make sure that conservative judicial nominees are rejected—as in the
2002 rejection of Judge Charles Pickering as an associate justice to the 5th
U.S. Circuit Court of Appeals—and that *Roe v. Wade* is never challenged.

Even though there were racial overtones during the confirmation debate, Judge Pickering was tossed out by the Democrats on the Senate
Judiciary Committee for one reason: he didn't satisfy the radical feminists on
the abortion issue. Pickering, in effect, served as a test case for NOW and
the rest of the radical Left. If they could get Pickering turned away, then no
pro-life candidate ever need apply for a Supreme Court nomination.

Senate Minority Leader Trent Lott, threatening to retaliate, said the
Democrats had established a litmus test. "That is the message: 'You send up a
pro-life conservative man of faith for the Supreme Court, and we will take care
of him or her.' That's what it's really all about."[5] Lott did not attempt to hide
his anger. "I'm not going to let go of it for a long time," he said while threatening to block a nomination to the FCC by Majority Leader Tom Daschle.[6]

Columnist Robert Novak shared the opinion that the borking of Judge
Pickering was all about the abortion issue—not race. Take the case of
Senator John Edwards, who wants to be president and therefore was obligated to oppose Judge Pickering. "Pickering flunks the abortion test," wrote
Novak, "and Edwards cannot risk his hopes of the 2004 presidential nomination by offending the feminist lobby."[7]

President Bush was not happy about the situation and accused the
Democrats of using judicial appointments to engage in "ideological battles." Just
prior to the committee's vote, the president called Judge Pickering a "respected
and well-qualified nominee" and asked the committee to send the nomination
to the full Senate.[8] That wasn't about to happen; at least three conservative

Democrats had announced their intentions to vote for confirmation or to strongly consider it—and that meant the Democrats had to kill the nomination in committee, and that Senator Daschle had to prevent a full Senate vote.

Over time, the controversy died out as usual, only resurfacing with the appointment of another highly qualified but conservative judge to fill a still-open slot on the 5th U.S. Circuit bench. This time, the president's choice was Texas Supreme Court Justice Priscilla Owen. It was déjà vu all over again.

This time, pro-abortion forces were upset about some Texas cases in which teenaged girls were trying to obtain abortions without their parents' consent. The cases had come before the Texas Supreme Court because of a 1999 parental notification law that provided some exceptions in which young girls could bypass their parents and go to a judge. But the law said that only a "mature and sufficiently well-informed teenager" could bypass the parental notification.

What did the legislature mean by this? Judge Owen's interpretation of the clause was that a minor girl should have to demonstrate to a judge that she was aware of the religious, social, and philosophical implications of abortion.

That was all New York Senator Charles Schumer needed to oppose Judge Owen. "Let there be no confusion. I have absolutely no objection to a woman—minor or otherwise—taking religious considerations into account when weighing the serious question of whether to exercise her constitutional right to choice," he wrote. "My concern is that you appear to have attempted to write into law something that the legislature decided not to put there."[9]

In her reply to Schumer, Judge Owen stated that the legislature had not narrowly defined the terms "mature" and "well-informed" and so she had turned to the Supreme Court, which by that time "had given considerable guidance on the extent to which a state could ensure that a minor was 'mature' and 'well enough informed' to consent to an abortion without the knowledge of either of her parents."[10] Judge Owen explained that her opinions were based on Supreme Court language suggesting that the courts could indeed consider religious, social, and philosophic issues. That did not satisfy the liberals on the Judiciary Committee.

Nor did it satisfy the radical feminists. "In almost every case concerning reproductive rights decided by the [Texas Supreme] Court during her tenure," wrote Kate Michelman, president of the National Abortion and Reproductive Rights Action League, "Owen has sought to restrict a woman's right to choose."[11]

As he had done for Judge Pickering, Mr. Bush stood with Judge Owen in a show of support. But again, it wasn't enough. The Owen nomination was defeated by a 10–9 vote—entirely along party lines—in the Judiciary Committee, the same vote tally that had doomed the Pickering nomination.

Mr. Bush again expressed his anger at the Democrats, telling supporters at a Kentucky fundraiser that the Owen defeat was "bad for the country, it's bad for our bench, and I don't appreciate it one bit, and neither do the American people."[12] Some Republicans hinted that Judge Owen's name might be resubmitted, even though—for now—the nomination was dead.

These rejections defined the litmus test that will be in effect when Mr. Bush names his first Supreme Court nominee. Short of conservative majorities in the Senate and on the Judiciary Committee, the president will have to get tougher with the Democrats if he wants to get his nominations to go through. Unless the president can bring himself to speak with clear moral authority and back it up with strong actions, he can forget naming a conservative to the High Court, and certainly no one who is pro-life.

You may be thinking that the all-out battle to keep conservative judges off the bench is nothing more than protecting a hard-fought judicial victory for women. After all, in the words of Sarah Weddington, the radical feminist lawyer who argued *Roe v. Wade* back in 1973, it was a "right-to-privacy case filed on behalf of all women 'who were or might become pregnant' and who wanted to be able to choose from all options ... including abortion."[13] Sure, just a little privacy case. Well, let's take a look at some current thought within the ranks of the movement.

Eileen L. McDonagh, a professor of government at Radcliffe College, is author of a book called *The Abortion Deadlock: From Choice to Consent* (Oxford University Press). Her op-ed piece in the *Austin American-Statesman* is a perfect example of radical feminist thought.[14]

She begins by mentioning the twenty-fifth anniversary of *Roe v. Wade* but quickly segues into one of the basic tenets of radical feminism, that taxpayers (even those who are pro-life) should have to pay for poor women to have their abortions. She blasts the 1977 decision upholding the Hyde Amendment, prohibiting the use of taxpayer money for most abortions. To Ms. McDonagh, government should be the source of funding for abortions, and she decries the fact that thirty-three states have no public assistance for pregnancy termination. She mentions that one in five women seeking an abortion can't get one. (Translation: one of five women who want an abortion can't find a way to make someone else pay the bill.)

After completing her tirade about access to abortions, she gets to her real point: a woman should have the right not just to abortion on demand but the right to "consent to pregnancy." You read this correctly; Ms. McDonagh believes that pregnancy is a "condition" that leads to a fetus. And the woman must consent to the massive transformation within her body that the fetus will bring about. Stay with us here; it gets better.

The changes brought on by this fetus, she explains, are nothing short of extraordinary. Hormones go on the rise; a woman's blood supply is rerouted to serve the fetus; a new organ, the placenta, is grown; blood plasma and cardiac volume increase 40 percent; heart rate increases 15 percent! And these things, she screams, are just a few examples of changes in a normal pregnancy.

For good measure, she adds that a medically abnormal pregnancy can render a woman crippled for life or put her into a coma.

So from a legal standpoint—and this is where Ms. McDonagh's ranting gets pretty silly—she claims that the fetus is doing harm to the woman, assuming the woman is not a consenting host. She reminds us that the law recognizes that all people are entitled to consent to what is done to their bodies by private parties. Without that consent, the woman is legally harmed.

You'll notice that the first time she mentions the unborn child as something other than a "fetus," she calls it a "private party." This is about as radical as it gets. The baby is not human in her eyes; it has no rights, and yet she is willing to grant it enough status to in effect be sued, found guilty, and executed. All this "logic" is offered in relation to a woman who has been impregnated by a consenting male, because later, she talks about rape and incest.

The idea of the mother as a victim and the unborn child as a criminal wreaking all sorts of damages to her body is the key to Ms. McDonagh's thesis in this column—but even so, it is situational. She goes on to say that if the woman consents to the pregnancy, it is joyous, but if she does not, she is seriously harmed. So, magically, all the bad effects of the pregnancy go away if the woman suddenly decides she wants to be pregnant.

Understand that Ms. McDonagh is not talking about nonconsensual sex. She is talking about nonconsensual pregnancy. She means that if a woman has consensual sex—protected or not—and she gets pregnant but doesn't want to be, then she has the right to kill the invading fetus. Here's how she puts it: "A woman who seeks an abortion is not merely exercising her right to choose what to do with her own body, but also her right to refuse to consent to what a fetus does to her body."

Coming full circle, Ms. McDonagh contends that the woman then has the full rights of a "patient" to stop the harm through obtaining an abortion. And what's more, since the government spends public funds to protect people from harm, the Constitution's equal-protection guarantee mandates that the government must pay for the abortion.

In Ms. McDonagh's world, there would be no-fault, no-cost abortions for every woman. It's hard to imagine that Ms. McDonagh was once a vicious little fetus herself.

Four doctors and a survivor

As the controversy over partial birth abortion was raging in late 1996, four doctors decided that they couldn't take the lies anymore and so they went public. The doctors—Nancy Romer of Wright State University and Miami Valley Hospital in Ohio; Pamela Smith of Chicago's Mt. Sinai Medical Center; Curtis R. Cook of Butterworth Hospital, Michigan State College of Human Medicine; and Joseph L. DeCook, a fellow of the American College of Obstetricians and Gynecologists—said they simply wanted to set a few things straight. [15]

Just before their op-ed piece came out in the *Wall Street Journal*, President Bill Clinton had vetoed the Partial Birth Abortion Ban Act. Clinton had surrounded himself with women who had had PBAs and whose lives or health were supposedly saved by the procedure. The House of Representatives was about to vote on an override.

The doctors felt that members of Congress needed some additional information, minus the spin. These doctors were all experts in pregnancy and delivering babies—dealing with it on a daily basis. They were frank and to the point.

They began by pointing out that the PBA supporters had been changing their stories to fit the emerging facts. First, the National Abortion Federation and other groups claimed that there was no such procedure. When that was proved wrong, they claimed that the procedure was done only to save the mother's life. Then the nation's top PBA provider was caught on tape saying that 80 percent of the procedures were elective. So they talked about anesthesia, telling the American public that it wasn't the procedure but the anesthesia administered to the woman before the PBA began that actually killed the baby. This, too, was false.

The four doctors mentioned Bill Clinton by name, saying that he was a part of the misinformation process. They quoted Clinton as having said that if mothers who opted for PBAs had delivered their children naturally, the women's bodies would have been "eviscerated" or "ripped to shreds." Clinton claimed that these women would never have been able to bear more children. The four doctors called these claims completely false.

Now here's the key statement from the *WSJ* column: "Contrary to what abortion activists would have us believe, partial birth abortion is never medically indicated to protect a woman's health or her fertility." The doctors went on to say that the exact opposite is true. The procedure can have a devastating effect on a woman's body, including her immediate health and her future ability to have children. The doctors wondered why there had been no media reports that one of the five women who appeared with Clinton at the vetoing ceremony had experienced five miscarriages since her PBA.

But President Clinton and most of the members of Congress ignored the doctors, just as they ignored the testimony of a then nineteen-year-old girl named Gianna Jessen. Miss Jessen's story was told in the *Washington Times*. The young girl was a victim of a botched abortion, seven and a half months into her seventeen-year-old mother's pregnancy.[16]

"I am the person she aborted," Miss Jessen said. Her legs were twisted from the effects of the saline solution that was intended to kill her. She described four surgeries and years of therapy as she learned to walk. "I am happy to be alive. Every day, I thank God for life," she said.

Miss Jessen was speaking to a hearing called by Representative Charles T. Canady of Florida. But of the thirteen members of the House Judiciary Subcommittee on the Constitution, only two showed up: Mr. Canady and fellow Republican Henry J. Hyde.

Miss Jessen explained that her cerebral palsy was caused by the concentrated salt solution used in the botched attempt to kill her. She explained that she lingered between life and death for three months and was finally adopted, and that she has met other abortion survivors. One little girl, two-year-old Sarah, whom Miss Jessen had met was blind and had cerebral palsy, too. The abortionist had injected Sarah in the head.

At the same hearing, a Harvard law professor, Mary Ann Glendon, explained that *Roe v. Wade* doesn't provide a constitutional right for PBAs. "Roe says nothing about the killing of a baby during delivery," she said. She said that in Texas, where *Roe v. Wade* originated, there is still a law untouched by the Supreme Court that outlaws the killing of a child.[17]

There was some—but not much—media coverage of this hearing. It was emotional, yet factual. It provided empirical evidence of the brutality of abortions. It contained the moral clarity so often lacking in today's "spin" society. And it had absolutely no effect on the mainstream media, the majority of the members of Congress, and President Bill Clinton. The radical feminist constituency is simply too important.

The politics of abortion

It's widely known that former Vice President Al Gore was once pro-life. What isn't so widely known is that many of the liberal icons of today's political world have also had their attitudes adjusted. In fact, abortion has long been a bouncing ball that follows the tide of current group-thought or polling.

Take a look at a seminal editorial that appeared in the *Wall Street Journal* about litmus tests and how one exists in the Democratic Party too—as the late governor of Pennsylvania, Bob Casey, discovered when he was barred from making a pro-life speech at the 1992 Democratic National Convention.

But the meat of the editorial is contained in a few terse quotes that speak for themselves.

Here they are:

"I am opposed to abortion and to government funding of abortions. We should not spend state funds on abortions because so many people believe abortion is wrong."—Governor Bill Clinton in a 1986 letter to Arkansas Right to Life.[18]

"Life is the division of human cells, a process that begins with conception ... The [Roe] ruling was unjust and it is incumbent upon Congress to correct the injustice."—House Minority Leader Richard Gephardt in 1977.[19]

"[I have a] deep personal conviction that abortion is wrong and [voted to amend the Civil Rights Act to define the word 'person' to] include unborn children from the moment of conception."—former Vice President Al Gore in a 1984 constituent letter.[20]

"Human life, even at its earliest stages, has a certain right which must be recognized—the right to be born, the right to love, the right to grow old."— Senator Edward Kennedy in a 1971 letter.[21]

"What happens to the mind of a person, and the moral fabric of a nation, that accepts the aborting of the life of a baby without a pang of conscience? What kind of a person, and what kind of a society will we have 20 years hence if life can be taken so casually?"—Jesse Jackson in a 1977 article.[22]

And yet, these views don't work in today's narrow-minded Democratic Party. Each of these men has cast aside his "deep" convictions in favor of core constituencies, political ambitions, and votes. The Republicans are only nominally better.

There is a pro-choice minority inside the GOP, forcing what is often known as a "wedge issue"—one where a president such as George W. Bush can hardly win. Mr. Bush is pro-life. He is of the camp that believes abortion should only be legal in cases of rape or incest, and when the mother's life is at stake. Mr. Bush has even embraced the Republican Party pro-life plank, which contains no exceptions.

But there is a group of "fiscal conservatives" who are not at home in the Democratic Party, and they have migrated to the GOP, bringing their more liberal social views with them. They believe in "a woman's right to choose." Mr. Bush believed—perhaps correctly—that he would need a coalition of the social conservatives (examples include Dan Quayle, Pat Robertson, Dr. Laura Schlessinger, and Dr. Alan Keyes) and the fiscal conservatives (examples include Homeland Security Secretary Tom Ridge, former EPA Director Christy Todd Whitman, and Secretary of State Colin Powell) in order to beat Al Gore.

And so the advisors told Mr. Bush what consultants tell radio talk show hosts: avoid the abortion issue whenever possible. That means that while Mr. Bush eked out a win in the closest election in United States history, he was unable politically to make abortion an issue. That means no leadership, no educating the masses from the bully pulpit, no forward movement toward protecting the unborn, and no representation for people like Gianna Jessen.

In the name of politics, all morality on this issue has been abandoned by the Democrats and moral clarity has been sacrificed by the Republicans.

Sarah and Jane: going in opposite directions

"Jane Roe" of *Roe v. Wade* is really Norma McCorvey. No longer wishing to remain anonymous, she's gone public with her current views on abortion, and they are shocking to the abortion-rights community. In 1995 she announced that she now believed that some abortions were wrong.

In January of 1996, at the twenty-third anniversary of the landmark decision, she stood on the steps of Dallas City Hall and proclaimed, "I believe that all abortions are wrong." As if to accentuate her 180-degree change of heart, she read from a poem: "All I did was give my baby away so that other women could tear theirs apart. For this, I will never be able to look You [God] in the face without shame."[23]

It is a fact that many women who have abortions later have regrets, descend into deep depression, or feel shame. Many wonder what their babies would have become—what kind of men or women. Would they have made some great discovery, or lived a simple life at home with children of their own?

It seems unlikely that these types of thoughts occur to Sarah Weddington. Her book *A Question of Choice* instructs women to be ever vigilant, to make sure that there is never again a time when abortion is not legal. She wrote in an op-ed piece: "The issue is not whether I or anyone else is for or against abortion. The issue is: Who should make the decision about abortion in response to a pregnancy: the government, strangers, or the woman involved? I still say, 'The woman.'"[24]

Ms. Weddington was not present at the congressional hearing when young Gianna Jessen spoke. And if she had been there, she would not have been moved. Her heart is hard and her mind is locked. She and Norma McCorvey are now walking down different paths.

The United States should protect its unborn

This issue is going to need a miracle, a movement, a transfiguration. But it has to begin somewhere—most likely in the hearts and minds of those who are willing to see abortion for what it really is: the killing of unborn human beings.

The Left has done its job well. It has planted and nurtured a general belief among the American public that abortion is some sort of right and that "right to life" means federal agents in the bedroom and in the doctor's office. It has also planted another seed—that any politician, Democrat or Republican, who aspires to high office had better be one of two things: pro-abortion or very quiet. This especially applies to judges who want appointments to the federal bench.

The real victim is the truth. As history goes, it's not much of a loss when some individual politician loses a race. No one candidate is indispensable, even if he may think so. But what kind of an impact on the future of our country could even a losing candidate make if he championed the cause of life? Perhaps another candidate would be brave, and then another. Of course, we have pro-life people in high office, including President Bush. But few serious candidates make the pro-life plank a major part of their campaigns.

However, let's give credit where credit is due, because Mr. Bush has not been entirely silent on this issue. In February 2002, the Bush administration announced that it will make embryos and developing fetuses "unborn children" eligible for a government health-care program. Under this plan, the unborn child would be eligible from the moment of conception. Administration officials were careful to say that this has nothing to do with establishing the rights of a fetus, but rather was designed to get more prenatal care to low-income women.[25]

It was a baby step in the right direction, and it was severely criticized by radical feminists, who charged that this could lead to a reversal of *Roe v. Wade*. The administration replied that detractors must be against prenatal care. The radical Left also opposes a White House proposal that would make it a federal crime to harm a fetus during an assault on the mother. But then, that's why they're called "radical."

The radicals' hearts will never change, but many thinking people across America will support life if they come to know the truth. That's why the language of abortion must change. We shouldn't call a tough abortion law "restrictive," as the major networks will do. Let's call it "protective." Let's stop using the word "fetus" and such oxymorons as "abortion rights."

With today's medical technology, most young mothers know the sex of their child soon into the pregnancy. Many of these young parents go ahead and name the child while it's still in the womb, making it virtually impossible to even consider an abortion.

General Electric has even come up with a new ultrasound method that provides color pictures of the unborn child. Cal Thomas writes that GE's television commercial might lead to a turning point in the abortion battles: "[The commercial] shows the face of a woman as she reacts to seeing her baby for the first time. We also see her husband, an unusual twist on television. Over the song 'The First Time Ever I Saw Your Face,' an announcer says, 'When you see your baby for the first time on the new GE4D Ultrasound system, it really is a miracle.'"[26] With pictures such as these, the word "fetus" is inadequate. With pictures such as these, hearts and minds will be changed.

That's the power of truth. That's the power that must be used to establish moral clarity in this most divisive of issues.

CHAPTER 2

Reduce the Size of Government

We must declare that government should be kept as small as possible while maintaining a safety net for the deserving poor.

L et's be perfectly clear: the appetite of U.S. senators and representatives for increased government spending is insatiable. Democrat or Republican—it doesn't matter. Whether it's "for the children" like a daycare program, or for senior citizens like a pharmaceutical benefit, or just a simple bicycle trail in some small town, Congress will spend as much money as there is.

Sometimes, members of Congress find sweeping ways to spend money, instituting programs that affect people's lives and take away the need for personal responsibility. Such programs are almost always permanent, and after a while, the American people become dependent on them, making big government more entrenched than ever. We call this "the entitlement state" and sometimes refer to it as "the nanny state."

More often, wasteful government spending comes in smaller packages—little stuff for senators and representatives to take home to the people in the district. This type of wasteful government spending is usually hidden away in some large appropriations bill. It may be the result of some back-and-forth back scratching; one member of Congress agrees to put in something for another member in return for a quid pro quo. We call this type of spending "pork barrel" or simply "pork."

Many members of Congress, as well as many past presidents, have embraced both types of spending. You hear them talk about it all the time, but they rarely ever say "Let's spend!" Instead they talk in code words and say things like "We need to invest in America." That means "spend." They will go on and on about the need to fix Social Security and Medicare and "investing" in infrastructure. Some correctly talk about rebuilding the military and building a missile defense shield. Great! Some of these things really are needed. However, there are many aspects of government spending that Congress would just as soon not talk about.

For example, government hardly ever reduces spending, no matter how unnecessary, nor does it ever cut back on a bureaucracy, no matter how bloated. The motto of most government agencies is "Use it or lose it," and that provides the impetus for finding new and creative ways to keep budgets high.

Politicians and bureaucrats have even invented a new definition for the word "cut" so that the word can be safely integrated into government-speak about spending proposals. So now, a "cut" refers to a two-step process in which (1) someone proposes a massive amount of increased spending for some project, and then (2) Congress reduces the amount of the increase. That way, the project gets considerably more money but Congress can say the budget was "cut."

Congress knows exactly what it's doing, and so do the American people. Organizations as formal as the Grace Commission and as entertaining as the *Golden Fleece Awards* have pointed it out. The watchdog group Citizens Against Government Waste (CAGW) publishes a "Pig Book" each year to catalog the waste. The group also bestows the dubious honor of "porker of the month" on some spendthrift bureaucrat or member of Congress.

When the big surpluses started to materialize after the Clinton tax hikes, the Democratic leader in the Senate, Tom Daschle, couldn't wait to get his hands on it. Senator Daschle proposed splitting up the surplus three ways. He wanted to dedicate a third of it to deficit reduction, a third to tax cuts, and a third to new government spending.[1] Mr. Daschle was quite serious about that final third of the surplus, but did he really mean what he said about deficit reduction and tax cuts?

Senator Daschle has been among the loudest critics of George W. Bush's $1.35 trillion tax cut, routinely charging that the cut benefits the "wealthiest one percent of Americans." Following the September 11, 2001, attacks, Mr. Daschle outlined an economic plan that contained new government spending and took the opportunity to blast the Bush tax cut: "The tax cut failed to prevent a recession; it probably made the recession worse," he told a crowd at the Washington headquarters of the Center for National Policy.[2]

In fact, Senator Daschle has publicly challenged the Republicans' position that American taxpayers can spend their own money more wisely than the government. In his home state of South Dakota, Daschle was participating in a televised town hall meeting when he was asked by a firefighter about equipment shortages. Daschle answered that only government can solve the problem. "I really defy someone to say you can spend that money in fire protection or law enforcement better if you were doing it yourself than if you did it collectively," he told the group. "That, in essence, is what's lost with this mentality that you can spend it all better than the government can."[3]

Mr. Daschle was using a false analogy, as the Left often does. Of course it is proper for government to do certain things that individual citizens can't do, and purchasing major equipment for firefighting is one of them. But Mr. Daschle's comment insinuated that government can always, or at the very least usually, spend money more wisely. That opinion, shared by other big spenders like Bill and Hillary Clinton, Senator Edward Kennedy, and Senator Robert Byrd, is easily disputed. No one can waste money as efficiently as the government.

Mr. Daschle is a recognized master of waste. Oliver North noted in his column that Mr. Daschle has earned a lifetime rating of 11 percent from CAGW and in December 2001 was named their "porker of the month."[4]

So what has Mr. Daschle done to reduce wasteful government spending since then? Nothing at all; he's done just the opposite. In a *Washington Times* column, Rush Limbaugh noted that Mr. Daschle recently proposed a whole bevy of new programs—$75 billion for additional farm subsidies, $15 billion to bail out the railroad retirement system, and $15 billion for some of Senator Byrd's projects. In addition to that, Mr. Daschle is a champion of the proposed prescription-drug entitlement, a major transfer of wealth that could cost $200 billion over a decade.[5]

As we proceed to demonstrate how government flushes so much of your money down a hole, think of Senator Daschle's money pie in a different way. With just a tiny bit of government restraint on spending, we could have applied a third to debt reduction and two-thirds back to the American people as a tax cut. As we're doing this, we could match the tax cuts dollar for dollar with spending cuts. That's C-U-T-S as defined by your Webster's Collegiate Dictionary.

When it became apparent that President Bush's tax cuts were going to pass, Democrats suggested a trigger mechanism whereby the tax cuts would be halted if the projected surpluses failed to materialize. Here's a better idea: How about a trigger mechanism that would force commensurate cuts—real cuts—in spending if the surpluses fizzle?

Washington's bipartisan pastime: spending your money

So you thought most government spending would be folded into the War on Terrorism following September 11? Wrong. Take a look at some sample headlines from newspapers around the country—all *after* 9/11:

"Lobbyists pounce on anti-terrorism cause."—"Spending brings political parties together."—"Pork piggybacks anti-terrorism bill."—"Government's fleet outpaces even Hertz."—"Congressional travel hasn't been stymied."—"Congress raids funds for highway projects." We could go on and on.

In December 2001, Mr. Bush signed a federal transportation bill. The bill was supposed to appropriate money for transportation projects, to be spent as state and local governments saw fit—for example, to rebuild aged and crumbling highways. But it was such a lot of money—a total of $59.6 billion—that Congress couldn't keep its hands off. Lawmakers managed to grab about 11 percent of it to redirect to pet projects, often in the home states of those crafting the bill.[6]

Senator Patty Murray, D-Wash., was co-chairman of the panel that drafted the bill. She grabbed $3 million for Seattle's Odyssey Maritime Museum. Republican Representative Hal Rogers was the other co-chair, and he nailed down $2 million for downtown revitalization in Somerset, Kentucky. House Majority Whip Tom DeLay was able to latch onto $2.9 million for an airport in Sugarland, Texas, by virtue of being on the joint panel that put the final spending blueprint together.[7] California had no representation on the joint panel and it lost about $41.5 million in highway money. Even though it picked up $341 million in pork projects, that still put it near the bottom when measured on a per capita basis.

The Associated Press quoted Representative Tom Petri, R-Wis.: "It's the classic definition of pork." It was also the very first time that Congress had diverted money earmarked for highways that was to have gone to the states with no strings attached. Members of Congress who formulated the bill simply lowered the amount of discretionary highway money and used it to fund "stuff" back in their home states and districts.[8]

It's not just the highway bill that includes myriad pet projects. There are literally thousands of them passed each year, to be paid for by the American taxpayer. Citizens Against Government Waste makes an annual attempt to catalog them. It's a daunting task; not only are lawmakers good at finding money for their projects, they're good at hiding it, too. CAGW ferrets out the waste and holds a news conference; the networks ambush a few big spenders; the red-faced big spenders mumble something about how their project was absolutely necessary for the good of the country; the news cycles once again; and then everything's back to normal.

When it comes to spending in Washington, the more things change, the more they stay the same. CAGW reports for years prior to 9/11 show record pork spending almost each year. Following 9/11, the spending went even higher.

In 2000, CAGW told the story of a four-lane boulevard in Toledo. The thoroughfare linked the northern edge of town to I-280, but Toledo ran out of bucks before the landscaping was done. So Representative Marcy Kaptur, a

Toledo Democrat, came to the rescue by using her position as a senior member of the House Appropriations Committee. She was able to sock away $250,000 so that the street could have two miles of trees, shrubs, and flower beds.[9]

CAGW pointed out that even though Democrats were in the minority in both houses of Congress at the time, they were still able to funnel pork funds to Democratic incumbents who were in tough reelection battles. At the time, with the economy booming and talk of big surpluses, members of both parties went on a major spending spree. Money was flowing freely to such projects in the national interest as sunflower research in North Dakota, reindeer herds in Alaska (the biggest state in both area and per capita pork), and mapping of chicken genes in Michigan.[10]

If Republican Senator Ted Stevens of Alaska is building a solid reputation as a major porker—he was head of the Appropriations Committee—Democratic Senator Robert Byrd of West Virginia is the acknowledged all-time king. CAGW is fond of bestowing the "porker of the month" award on him, as they did in February 2001.[11]

Byrd had been criticizing the G.W. Bush tax cut proposal as "fiscally irresponsible." This seemed somewhat amazing from the acknowledged all-time king of pork. So CAGW reviewed some of the spending schemes that Senator Byrd had been up to after obtaining a seat on the Senate Budget Committee.

This included a recreation area at Lake Sherwood, revitalization of the Strand Theater in Moundsville, building the Kanawha Boulevard Walkway in Charleston, installing fences at the Jackson County Airport, and subsidizing a documentary on the Appalachians.[12]

This might be a good place to point out that pork barrel spending is not all bad to all people. In Senator Byrd's West Virginia, those constituents who enjoy the recreation area at Lake Sherwood will certainly be pleased, as will theater patrons in Moundsville, and all the users of all the other projects that Mr. Byrd was able to fund. Certainly, Mr. Byrd hopes that all these constituents will continue to be pleased right on up to election day.

The problem is simply this: Pork projects use tax dollars, confiscated from taxpayers across the United States, and funnel them into local projects that benefit only a few people. This means that people in Walla Walla are helping to fund those fences at an airport in West Virginia. Why should they be expected to do that? To help Senator Byrd get reelected? (This is one of the reasons that the Campaign Finance Reform Bill of 2002 that was signed by President George W. Bush is sometimes known as "the Incumbent Protection Act." It controls political speech and bans soft money donations, but it fails to address these little schemes that incumbents use to curry favor back in the state or district. This includes the free printing of "newsletters" and free postage known as "franking" that members of Congress use even when an election is near.)

Pork is also a main reason that big spenders like Senator Byrd oppose any and all tax cuts. The less money confiscated by government, the less money they have to funnel into their pet projects. As CAGW reported for the past few years, the amount of waste is staggering. Let's use the 2002 "Pig Book" as the main exhibit.

According to the book, the total amount of wasted spending hidden in the thirteen federal appropriations bills passed in the prior fall came to $20.1 billion, setting a new record for fiscal irresponsibility in Congress. The prior year's figure was $18.5 billion. The Pig Book only goes back to 1991, but in those eleven years, CAGW has documented more than $140 billion dollars in government waste, caused by members of Congress pandering to their local areas.[13]

The CAGW noted that the number of individual pork projects has nearly quadrupled from 2,143 to 8,341 and issued a stern reprimand to congressional porkers: "As the nation pays taxes this month, citizens should look at both parties in Congress with scorn. Here we are, a nation at war, and yet Republicans and Democrats pass record levels of pork. Our representatives and senators should be ashamed, especially the appropriators. Since September 11, we have all hoped our national leaders would exhibit a new sense of seriousness and devotion to defending the nation and rejecting politics as usual."[14]

The 2002 Pig Book list took sixty-one pages to detail all the waste. Here are a few highlights:

- $5,000,000 added by the Senate to provide computer equipment for schools in Armenia.
- $1,000,000 in Vermont, the state of Senate Foreign Operations Appropriations Subcommittee member Patrick Leahy, for the Conflict Transformation Across Cultures (CONTACT) program. CAGW points out that over the past five years, CONTACT has averaged forty participants per year, making the appropriation come to $25,000 per student.
- $52,273,000 for projects in Alaska, home of the Republican pork king, Senator Ted Stevens. This includes $2,500,000 for the Anchorage Museum, $2,000,000 for kilns, and $536,000 for the Ted Stevens International Airport in Anchorage. No wonder it's named after Mr. Stevens.
- $9,200,000 for projects in Illinois, the state of Senate appropriator Dick Durbin, including $8,000,000 for the controversial Abraham Lincoln Library, which was supposed to be a local project.
- $365,000 for the University of South Dakota's old women's gym/ original armory.
- $425,000 for the George Ohr Museum and Cultural Center in

Mississippi. The museum is dedicated to an eccentric nineteenth-century potter.
- $1,500,000 for the Illinois virtual high school.
- $420,000 for Hawthorne Elementary and Junior High School in Nevada to buy each student a laptop computer, and $240,000 for Schurz Elementary to buy each student a laptop computer.
- $750,000 in Idaho, home of Appropriations Subcommittee member Larry Craig, for the University of Idaho to help preserve the history of jazz.
- $50,000 added for the district of House Labor/HHS Appropriations Subcommittee member Nita Lowy (who was going to run for the Senate before Hillary Clinton stepped in) for an after-school music and arts program in Westchester County, an area with a per capita income twice the national average.
- $26,000 added in conference for teacher training, student transportation to Zoo World for a science project, and technology training for a Florida school district.
- $8,000,000 added by the Senate for the Russian Leadership Development Fund. In the past, funds have been used to fly Russian leaders to the U.S. for such activities as a visit to a flea market in Florida and a trip to the Coors Brewery in Colorado.
- $375,000 added in conference for a bicycle commuting project in Austin. Senator Kay Bailey Hutchison is on the Senate Transportation Appropriations Subcommittee.

As we said, there are sixty-one pages of this. And this is not to mention other government waste, such as grant programs (which have local officials adopting the attitude "Hey, if we don't apply for this grant, someone else will"), overspending on routine items such as hammers and commode seats, and foreign aid to countries who turn their backs on us when we need them.

In the wake of 9/11, the appetite for pork did not subside; in fact, the attacks on America provided a new impetus for even more calls for even more spending. Following the attacks, every pork item imaginable was back on the table with some kind of homeland security hook to make it absolutely essential to the continued existence of the United States. Some of the arguments were exceptionally creative and outrageous.

The road-sign lobby began to argue that better traffic-routing devices would help motorists flee cities more efficiently in case of an evacuation. The American Farm Bureau Federation argued that federal subsidies for farmers were essential to national security because of the need for a federal food supply. Ethanol producers came up with the idea that if ethanol were required in gasoline, we could cut our dependence on foreign oil. The superconductor industry argued that rules changes it wanted passed regarding the transmission of electricity would make the nation's power supply more secure.[15]

"You have to get the attention of lawmakers to get something done, and right now, their attention is focused on national security," said Jim Albertine, president of the American League of Lobbyists. "Lobbyists have been very imaginative in their use of the events of 9/11 to advance their particular projects."[16] Mr. Albertine is also a lobbyist for the American Traffic Safety Services Association, a group that, with a straight face, argued that more sophisticated signs could have helped evacuate Washington if a second airplane had come into the city.

And so it came to pass that senators managed to cram nearly $400 million in pork projects into a bill that was designed to shore up the Pentagon and national defense in the wake of 9/11, sparking Senator John McCain to say that the bill "is going to have more Christmas tree goodies on it than the North Pole."[17] Not all the provisions made it through negotiations with the House, but here are some of the measures that senators stuck in:[18]

- $2,000,000 for work on communications software by Coleman Research Corp. in Huntsville, Alabama. (Amendment by Senator Richard Shelby.)
- $4,000,000 for the University of Maine in Orono for research on hand-held computers to be used by soldiers. (Sponsored by Senator Susan Collins.)
- $2,000,000 to buy fleece pullovers for the Marines from Malden Mills Industries, Inc. (Sponsored by Senator Edward Kennedy.)
- $10,000,000 for work done partly by North Dakota State University of a hand-held communications system that could be used by covert operatives. (Amendment by Senator Byron Dorgan.)
- $4,000,000 for work at Tinker Air Force Base in Oklahoma on improving the efficiency of military repair shops. (The handiwork of Senator Don Nickles.)

All this happened in the waning hours of December 8 as the senators added a total of 103 amendments to the bill—with little or no debate.

Senator John McCain, one of the few anti-pork crusaders in Washington, took note of the post-9/11 spending fervor and pleaded for government resources to be spent wisely to fully fund the war. McCain said that wasteful spending was taking away from worthier projects. "Congress has already doled out more than $9 billion for highly dubious and surely less-than-urgent projects never subjected to merit-based review. From killing aquatic weeds, breeding potatoes, and renovating a statue of Vulcan, the Roman god of fire, to lavishing millions of dollars in earmarked grants on well-off universities with multi-billion-dollar endowments, the road to Washington remains, as always, paved with gold."[19]

McCain went on to call the lobbying effort on Capitol Hill "war profiteering" and said that lobbyists were swarming congressional offices to get a piece of the stimulus bill for such "destitute" clients as General Electric and Ford Motor Company. But Senator McCain was, for the most part, a lone voice. Members of Congress were unable or unwilling to even cut back on their own taxpayer-financed (or worse yet, lobby-financed) travel budgets.

After the 9/11 attacks, senators and representatives continued to travel at least as much as they did before, including trips to Hawaii to study airlines, the Breeders' Cup Race in New York to study horses, and the Greenbriar Resort in West Virginia to discuss pesticides.

The Associated Press reviewed 100 post-9/11 trips financed by private interests and found that groups such as the American Israel Public Affairs Committee, the American Banker Association, the American Gas Association, Amtrak, British Airways, and the National Rifle Association were footing the bills.[20] The AP story noted that Congress changed its rules ten years ago to ban payments to lawmakers for speeches, but it continues to be perfectly legal for lobbying groups and companies to pay all their expenses when they're on "fact-finding missions."

"I don't remember canceling anything," said Senator Thad Cochran, R-Miss. "We weren't going to let terrorists shut down our government." Senator Cochran took trips to Gulfport, Mississippi, and New Orleans ten days after the attacks. The trips were paid for by the poultry and crop protection industries.[21]

The AP story details the trips to Greenbriar and the Breeders' Cup. Just two weeks after 9/11, Representative Marion Berry, D-Ark., took a speechmaking trip to the 6,500-acre Greenbriar Resort. (Three championship golf courses, top cuisine, and pure luxury.) The pesticide trade association paid the bill for the trip, which included a three-night stay. A total of four members of Congress attended, some bringing spouses.

In late October, four House members were in New York, where they met with representatives of the American Horse Council and the National Thoroughbred Racing Association. Members who attended were Charles Stenholm, D-Tex.; Ernie Fletcher, R-Ky.; Larry Combest, R-Tex.; and Ken Calvert, R-Calif. The four took time to attend the Breeders' Cup race, with Stenholm commenting, "It was an opportunity for them to lobby me on horse issues."[22]

As bad as it is when lawmakers take worthless junkets on the taxpayer dime, it's even worse when the trips are financed by lobby groups. It's hard to imagine that the nation's business was being conducted by Mr. Berry at the CropLife America meeting at Greenbriar. The trip was financed for Mr. Berry because the industries that sponsored the trip wanted him and his colleagues to do something for them. Lobbying is a fine old political tradition, and in its pure form, there's nothing wrong with it. After all, one of the duties of any lawmaker is to listen to the wishes and desires of the people and businesses in his state or district. It's when the lawmakers accept free gifts—trips, or anything else—that lobbying turns into bribery.

Let's be clear about this. If a member of Congress is traveling on honest government business, then the taxpayers should finance the trip. If a business organization or lobby group finances a trip, no matter what the reason, it is suspect. The taxpayers of the United States should demand that this practice stop.

Unfortunately, most of the American people are wearing blinders. Members of Congress don't publicize these junkets, and most people are blissfully unaware of them. Most people are also unaware that the government has been on a car-buying spree.

The government now owns more cars and trucks than does Hertz, the big car rental company, according to an inventory conducted by the White House. The federal fleet is now at 602,626 vehicles at a cost of $2.29 billion a year. This comes out to one car or truck for every three government employees.[23] The Bush White House was suspicious and wrote a memo asking agencies why there was such a massive build-up during the Clinton years. The memo came from White House Budget Director Mitchell Daniels Jr. "One's first impression . . . is that the numbers seem excessive in many cases and that significant reductions may be in order."[24]

No kidding. The AP story says the Energy Department alone, with 15,600 full-time employees, has 16,351 vehicles. The department offered standard excuses, including that the number may be misleading because some vehicles are used by the 100,000 workers of agency contractors. Did anyone bother to ask if that is an acceptable use?

Hertz, meanwhile, trimmed its fleet after 9/11 to 525,000 vehicles. But as we've seen, not much of anything in government was reduced following the attacks on America.

Bill Clinton and the era of Big Government

During the presidential campaign of 1992, Democratic candidate Bill Clinton promised voters that if they would elect him, he would reduce the budget deficit by soaking the rich with new taxes.[25] Once elected, Mr. Clinton continued down the road of promising changes.

He pledged to save taxpayer money by cutting the White House staff by 25 percent (which he claimed he did, but critics were not so sure), and by cutting the federal workforce by 100,000. Mr. Clinton even assigned Vice President Al Gore to find ways to cut and consolidate government based on Mr. Gore's "re-inventing government" study. But at the same time, the Clinton administration planned a major government takeover of the nation's healthcare system—about 14 percent of the U.S. economy—that would have created massive new bureaucracies.[26]

Mr. Clinton followed through on his plan to tax the rich. On February 17, 1993, he presented Congress with an economic plan calling for huge tax hikes on upper-income people and corporations, which he said would reduce budget deficits by almost $500 billion over five years. Republicans opposed the plan because of the tax increases and additional spending measures. In August, after a lot of partisan wrangling, the bill made it through the House, 218 to 216. The next day, in the Senate, the bill passed 51 to 50 with Al Gore casting the tie-breaking vote.[27]

So now Mr. Clinton had his big tax hikes in place, and, combined with a technology boom, there would soon come burgeoning budget surpluses. (That is, if you don't count the national debt. And, of course, in order to arrive at a surplus, money had to be taken out of Social Security and placed in the general revenue budget. If you take away that accounting trick, there was no surplus.)

To the big spenders in the White House and on Capitol Hill, the word "surplus" was the key to opening the floodgates. Bill Clinton himself could not be restrained. In February 1995, Mr. Clinton proposed a budget that had even the *Washington Post* saying that he was "ducking virtually all of the tough spending cuts needed to bring the budget into balance." In fact, 1995 saw the White House and the Republicans come close to meeting in the middle on several key spending proposals, yet the Democrats worked hard to brand the Republicans as "extremists." The cry went out every time any Republican suggested cutting anything. An editorial in *Investor's Business Daily* charged that the Democrats misquoted the Republican leadership to make it seem as though the GOP wanted to throw seniors off of Medicare. In reality, the GOP plan actually raised per-person coverage by 7 percent a year.[28]

In 1996 Bill Clinton stunned the nation with his declaration "The era of big government is over!" But it was the same Bill Clinton as always, and even in the midst of making this bold statement in his third State of the Union address on January 23, 1996, he also proposed massive new spending. In fact, most of the sixty-one-minute speech talked about "stiff challenges," all needing government attention.

"We cannot go back to a time when our citizens were left to fend for themselves," the president said. He then outlined several new programs (fewer than his usual list), with the most expensive being his education proposal, at $3 billion over seven years.[29]

In February of 1998, President Clinton declared an end to "an era of exploding deficits" and handed Congress the first balanced budget proposal in thirty years. The budget called for a 4 percent increase in overall spending— to $1.73 trillion. Even while claiming a balanced budget, Mr. Clinton had plenty of things he wanted to spend money on: hiring 100,000 new teachers, expanding child care, improving transportation, and cutting greenhouse gasses under the Kyoto Treaty.[30]

With Mr. Clinton's projected spending and revenues, he claimed that this budget would produce a $10 billion surplus. There was a catch. In order to claim the surplus, the president had to lump the $100 billion in surplus funds from Social Security into general revenue. That's the accounting trick mentioned above.

Besides that, something other than Mr. Clinton's tax hikes and budget proposals were driving the economy. One newspaper account put it this way: "The true hero in deficit reduction has been the roaring American economy. Eighty-two months of economic expansion have generated trillions of dollars in new wealth. An economy that kicked out $5.7 trillion worth of goods and services in 1990 produced $8.1 trillion worth last year, a gain of $2.4 trillion."[31]

It later became clear that part of that booming economy was a house of cards that would come tumbling down almost as the Clinton administration was moving out of the White House. But for the moment, high-tech and dot-coms were the darlings of Wall Street and the "surpluses" mounted.

And so the political class continued to spend, packing pork projects into the Highway Bill and continuing to raid trust funds such as Social Security. There was a lot of talk, but not much action, on using the surplus to "fix" entitlements like Social Security and Medicare that faced a so-called train wreck when the baby boomers start retiring.

In 2000, the surpluses were the talk of the town. The ten-year estimate of surpluses had ballooned to $4.2 trillion, with about $2.3 trillion of that coming from Social Security payroll taxes. The *Wall Street Journal* editorialized against the new exuberance: "Whatever else it did, that old devil deficit was at least a restraint on the growth of government. The surplus, we are now discovering, is political grease for the revival and expansion of the entitlement state."[32] The *Journal* mentioned that President Clinton had been blasting candidate Bush's tax cut plan as "irresponsible" because the surplus wasn't large enough.

But with the new estimates, that argument was hard to swallow; after all, a surplus is nothing more than an overpayment of taxes. What could Mr.

Clinton do except propose more spending to avoid having to give any of the money back to the people? He did just that, and that is how the proposed $250 billion pharmaceutical benefit for seniors came about.

The Republicans were in the midst of their own spending spree, with Dennis Hastert in the House and Trent Lott in the Senate proposing their own pharmaceutical plan that was just a bit less costly than Mr. Clinton's. The *Wall Street Journal* editorial criticized the lawmakers for proposing such a plan without reforming the structure of Medicare, saying it would lead to increased demand and runaway costs.[33]

The *Wall Street Journal* worried that the booming economy and the surpluses would provide political cover for an unprecedented expansion of government, with a tax cut being the only way to avoid it. Mr. Bush later got his tax cuts, but as it turned out, there were other ways of avoiding the surplus paradigm.

George W. Bush, tax cuts, and the shrinking surplus

Three things happened early in the George W. Bush administration that caused the surpluses to begin to decline. First, President Bush was able to push through his promised tax cut, which Democrats charged would cut into the surplus. Actually, that was the idea. As we have said, one definition of "budget surplus" is "overpayment of taxes." Mr. Bush believed that the overpayment should be refunded.

Second, the economy began to slow down as the technology boom began to bust. Actually, this started during the final months of the Clinton administration, but the media didn't notice it until George W. Bush was sworn in.

Third, the attacks of 9/11 triggered a War on Terrorism—and wars cost money.

The tax cut was the issue that separated the majority of the Democrats from their more moderate compatriots and almost all of the Republicans. The big spenders in Congress couldn't spend the money if George W. Bush sent it back to the people. What we're going to do now is walk through the tax-cut controversy to show just how hard the Democrats worked to keep all that tax money in Washington—both before and after the events of 9/11.

Mr. Bush sent his outline of the proposed tax cuts to Capitol Hill in early February 2001. It took the Democratic leader of the Senate less than one day to accuse him of favoring the rich. Actually, Mr. Bush's cuts—totaling $1.6 trillion over ten years at the time—were designed to provide bigger dollar amounts in reduced payments for those who earned more and therefore paid more. Mr. Bush did not choose favored groups such as Mr. Clinton did with his "targeted" tax cuts.

Mr. Bush simply wanted to lower taxes for everyone who paid them, and

he wanted to replace the existing five income brackets with four rates: 10 percent, 15 percent, 25 percent, and 33 percent. There were other items included, such as an increase in the child tax credit, marriage penalty relief, and,
down the road, elimination of the inheritance tax known as the "death tax."[34]

In reality, the Democrats didn't want any tax cuts at all; they had other
ideas for the money, but with all the campaign rhetoric about tax cuts, they
had little choice but to join the bandwagon. So they did, proposing to cut
about half of what Mr. Bush was calling for, and—of course—targeted, as
usual. They went to great lengths to paint Mr. Bush's plan as excessive and
favoring the wealthy.

Senate Minority Leader Tom Daschle carried the water for the
Democrats. "Democrats support a major tax cut for all taxpayers this year,"
he said. But with his next breath, he took a sharp left turn and appeared to
disagree with his own statement: "We've already tried what President Bush
is proposing. [A major tax cut for all taxpayers.] The rich got richer. The
poor got poorer. And working families got stuck with the entire bill."[35] It was
a slap at both the Reagan and G.W. Bush administrations. Mr. Daschle made
his comments outside the U.S. Capitol building with a fully loaded Lexus to
illustrate the class warfare that he was waging. A sign in front of the podium
read, "Bush Tax Plan: New Lexus for every millionaire."

Democrats were also charging that the true cost of the Bush tax plan would
be not $1.6 trillion but rather $2.6 trillion. Mr. Daschle and Senator Kent
Conrad, D-N.D., were adding up costs that they said the Bush administration
was not forthright about—things such as $200 billion to make the tax cuts
retroactive; $200 billion to reform the Alternative Minimum Tax; $100 billion
to extend expiring tax provisions; and $500 billion for additional interest the
Treasury will have to pay because of lower payments against the national debt.[36]
It was a stretch, but rank-and-file Democratic members of Congress dutifully
went back to their home districts and told the story to local media.

President Bush took his case to the American public on February 27,
2001, in his first-ever speech to a joint session of Congress. He told lawmakers and the television audience that government had been overcharging
the taxpayers for too long. He placed the surplus at $5.6 trillion over the
next decade and said that would be enough to improve education, bolster
national defense, repay about two-thirds of the national debt, and implement his tax cuts.[37]

Senator Daschle and House Minority Leader Richard Gephardt gave the
Democratic response. Directly targeting the sensibilities of older voters, Mr.
Daschle charged that the Bush tax cuts would "leave the government unable
to meet priorities and repay debt, perhaps threatening Social Security and
Medicare."[38]

It was a calculated response. Older people vote in droves, and they tend to vote against anyone or anything that might threaten those two programs. But Mr. Daschle didn't stop there. "The wealthiest one percent—people who make an average of over $900,000 a year—gets 43 percent of the President's tax cut."

The president edged closer to his goal on March 8, 2001, when the House voted 230–198 to pass the cuts. All of the Republicans voted for the cuts, along with ten Democrats who crossed party lines. Still charging that the cuts were aimed at the rich, Mr. Gephardt declared, "My assessment after a few weeks of this Congress is that bipartisanship is over. President Bush has not changed the climate in Washington." And Senator Daschle declared that the tax cuts would be killed in the Senate.[39]

Just one month later, the Democrats were celebrating a minor victory, having succeeded in trimming the tax cuts by one-quarter—to $1.2 trillion. They had accomplished that by pounding the American people with Chicken Little sound bites that claimed the sky would fall if any spending happened to be cut. Senator John Breaux, D-La., considered a moderate, said this on ABC's *This Week*: "When people see the budget, they're going to say, 'Oh, my God, I wanted a tax cut, but I didn't know what you were going to do to health care and to Medicare, and national defense.'"[40]

Understand that the president's new budget was filled with spending cuts. Those cuts amounted to only a 4 percent increase in the growth of most spending, not counting entitlements like Social Security. (Remember the definition of "cuts" in Washington.) Senator Joe Biden, D-Del., predicted a huge backlash from the American people when they found out about the "cuts." He charged that Mr. Bush's budget would "put in sharp relief what this president is doing in order to be able to get this humongous tax cut."[41]

The Democrats were working as hard as they could to sabotage what was really a very modest tax cut measure coupled with a modest increase in spending for discretionary programs. In a statement that turned out not to be prophetic, Vice President Cheney was threatening that Mr. Bush would wield the veto pen to rein in big spending. The Farm Bill of 2002 would prove him wrong.

In early May, the tax-cut plan came together in its final form—a $1.35 trillion dollar reduction over eleven years. Mr. Bush declared victory. "This is a great day for the American people and the American taxpayer," he said. But Senator Daschle was not moved, saying that he would still oppose the plan. "I'm still concerned, frankly, about what it will mean to our ability to provide the funding necessary for some very important investments in education and health care."[42] In other words, Mr. Daschle was concerned that the cuts might impede Congress's ability to tax and spend.

Texas Senator Phil Gramm was also concerned, but in a different way. He wanted some guarantees that spending would be held in check. The other senator from Texas, Kay Bailey Hutchison, said that she preferred a larger cut but would not "blow up tax cuts because I don't have the number I want."[43]

The Democrats had chipped away at the Bush plan and managed to obtain several significant compromises. The final agreement not only dropped Mr. Bush's tax reduction from the $1.6 trillion that he wanted to $1.35 trillion, it also called for discretionary spending increases of 5 percent, up from the 4 percent that Mr. Bush had called for.[44]

So the Democrats forced a smaller tax cut with higher spending.

On May 24, the Senate voted 62–30 to approve the cuts, with a dozen Democrats crossing party lines to oppose Mr. Daschle and vote with Mr. Bush. Every Republican in the Senate, even Mr. Gramm, voted for the bill.[45]

Democrats who opposed the bill had delayed the vote for almost three days by bringing up dozens of amendments related to the size of the tax cuts and spending measures that they thought might be placed in jeopardy. Strangely enough, the Senate was consumed with the news that Republican Senator Jim Jeffords might defect from the Republican Party. Mr. Jeffords did become an Independent, throwing in with the Democrats, but he waited until after the tax bill was completed, and he voted for the bill.[46] Among the Democrats who ended up voting for the bill were moderates such as John Breaux of Louisiana and Zell Miller of Georgia—and even the liberal Diane Feinstein of California.

On June 7, 2001, President Bush signed the tax cut bill into law, touting rebate checks of up to $600 that were going to be mailed to taxpayers. Mr. Bush was ecstatic. "A year ago, tax relief was said to be a political impossibility. Six months ago, it was supposed to be a political liability. Today, it becomes reality."[47]

The tax-and-spend branch of the Democratic Party did not let the signing ceremony go by without some caustic comments. House Minority Leader Gephardt predicted a middle-class revolt when people saw their benefits cut back. "President Bush and Republicans in Congress have decided to sacrifice [Social Security and Medicare] in order to give massive tax cuts to the wealthiest individuals," he said.[48]

So now the tax cuts were law, but as the calendar moved dangerously closer to 9/11, the budget surpluses were starting to look shaky. On August 23, the *Dallas Morning News* reported that new White House numbers pegged the surplus at just $1 billion for the year after setting aside Social Security. Four months earlier, the estimated surplus had been set at $123 billion. But accounting changes had been implemented, the economy was seeing the effects of the dot-com crash, and there were those tax cuts.[49]

The White House spin was that the government should still manage to take in $3.1 trillion in surpluses over the coming decade, down slightly from the $3.4 trillion estimated in January. "The nation is awash in extra money and it's going to be," said budget director Mitch Daniels.[50] If you added in the extra cash from Social Security, you came up with a surplus of $158 billion, still the second largest ever.

But to Democrats, the sky was still falling, and it was those nasty Bush tax cuts that were to blame. "He has cooked the books," said Senator Kent Conrad, D-N.D., who was chairman of the Senate Budget Committee. And then, referring to a procedure that all presidents have done for decades, he continued, "It is quite remarkable that after only seven months in office, the Bush administration is poised to raid both the Social Security and Medicare trust funds."[51]

Gene Sperling, a Clinton economic advisor, joined in the Bush-bashing. "When you propose a budget that is excessive and does not fit, you have to start sweeping the dirt under the rug."[52] But Mr. Sperling was being disingenuous.

Mr. Bush had acted responsibly, trying to hold down spending growth to 4 percent while trying to restore a devastated military and provide tax relief. Under Mr. Sperling's boss, taxes skyrocketed, spending was out of control (in his last budget request, Mr. Clinton asked for an 8.7 percent rise in discretionary spending.),[53] and military budgets were slashed, and all this was bolstered by a false economy that lasted just long enough for Mr. Clinton to complete his term.

Mr. Bush inherited surpluses, all right, but he also inherited a declining economy and a weakened military. Soon, the government was forced to acknowledge that it would have to take $9 billion out of Social Security to pay other bills. House Majority Leader Dick Armey called for more fiscal restraint, noting that a Democratically controlled Congress had also routinely tapped into the Social Security trust fund.[54]

But Representative Dick Gephardt was busy disseminating the Democrats' standard talking points. "The CBO numbers tell a disturbing story of a tax cut, pushed by the president and congressional Republicans, that was focused on the wealthiest 1 percent and so big it has obliterated record surpluses and jeopardized virtually every other priority of the American people."[55]

To Gephardt, the sky was still falling—at least on everyone except the wealthiest 1 percent. That was his story and the Democrats were sticking to it, except for a select few who agreed with the president's tax cuts.

So—just two weeks away from a devastating event that would change everything—the 2001 surplus was sitting at $158 billion. Even so, as columnist Robert Dodge pointed out, "all but $1 billion of [the surplus] was set aside for Social Security, a reserve that both Democrats and Republicans promised not to touch for other purposes."[56]

Following the events of September 11, the political landscape became very different. The country was embroiled in a new War on Terrorism, and Mr. Bush was perceived to be doing quite well in his prosecution of this war. Because of that, his approval ratings went sky-high, making it difficult for the same old political rhetoric to work for the Democrats. The fact was, with a deficit looming, Mr. Bush could hardly be blamed. The Democrats crafted a plan to have it both ways.

If they came out largely in favor of everything that Mr. Bush did concerning the war, they felt they could still snipe at him about domestic tax-and-spend issues. After all, the source of Mr. Bush's high poll numbers was the war.

So in January of 2002, when Mr. Bush said he might not be able to balance the budget that year because of the war and the recession, the Democrats went right back to the old Daschle-Gephardt language and blamed the tax cuts.[57] Mr. Daschle said that while the Democrats supported Mr. Bush's military leadership, his economic policies were threatening the nation's fiscal health. He said that the tax cuts ended five straight years of budget surpluses produced by the Clinton administration. "It is undeniable that the Republicans turned record surpluses into deficits in the space of just one year," he said. "It is time they explain to the American people what they intend to do about the hole they dug."[58]

Let's be clear about what Mr. Daschle was doing. While saying he supported the president with regard to the war, he was actually doing just the opposite. The Democrats know that in a time of great national catastrophe such as 9/11, followed by an ensuing war, and during an economic slowdown, a balanced budget is not the top priority. But the tax-and-spend Democrats are so opposed to any reduction in taxes that they will use any argument to roll them back.

Mr. Bush fired back at Senator Daschle, saying that any reversal of the tax cuts would amount to a tax increase and that would be a disaster for any economic recovery. He said that tax increases would be approved "over my dead body."[59]

That didn't stop liberal senators like Edward Kennedy, D-Mass., who called for a postponement of $350 billion of the tax cuts. But strangely enough, Mr. Kennedy wasn't calling for more money to spend on the war. He wanted the tax money back to spend on social issues such as schools and health care. Kennedy also pointed out that the tax cut was going to go to the wealthy. Other Democrats had changed their strategy by this time. Senator Daschle preferred to keep the cuts in place and accuse President Bush of creating bigger deficits.[60]

Mr. Daschle was playing politics to the max. He knew better than to actually try to rescind the tax cuts with an election coming up. So he and

Democratic National Committee Chairman Terry McAuliffe simply sat back and griped about Mr. Bush's tax cuts, leaving it to Senator Kennedy to insist that times were different and the cuts were now irresponsible.

No matter what particular strategy they might be employing at the time, the tax cuts had become the Democratic Party's symbol of all that's wrong in America. In early February 2002, when President Bush was laying out his budget request for fiscal 2003, the issue still loomed in the background. Mr. Bush was putting forth a budget in the amount of $2.13 trillion, and this time he wanted to formally assess the performance of government agencies and programs, with an eye toward cutting those that weren't working.[61]

So, on February 4, Mr. Bush sent the budget to Congress, complete with cuts in highway funds, job training, water projects, and the environment. The budget called for an increase of just 2 percent in spending not related to national defense and homeland security. It also called for deficits through 2004. The budget also proposed $591 billion in new tax cuts, but those were pretty much dead on arrival.[62] The big spenders in the Democratic Party were outraged by the budget.

Ignoring the realities of the War on Terrorism, they charged that it exploded deficits and ignored the long-range problems of Social Security. The Democrats made sure that everyone knew the real reason for the new deficits. Not the war; not the economic slowdown; not homeland security issues. The real reason for the end of four years of surpluses was—you guessed it—George W. Bush's $1.35 trillion dollar tax cut.[63]

Ending welfare as we know it

If there's anything that the Congress knows how to do, it's spend money. In order to spend more, it needs to keep bringing in cash, and that's why the big spenders tried to kill the Bush tax cuts. *Investor's Business Daily* put it this way: "For the last three decades, Congress loaded up the pork barrel. It also set up a social spending machine that never stops running. So, in the 80's and 90's, deficits soared—despite growing revenues from a growing economy."[64]

What *IBD* was getting at is this simple fact. In addition to Senator Byrd–style pork, the government has made some big promises to a lot of people, and these promises have been passed into law. Once that happens, the promises have to be kept; only another law could take them back—and that wouldn't be good for reelection. The promises are called "entitlements"— stuff like Social Security, Medicare, and the new pharmaceutical benefit that's now supported by both Democrats and Republicans.

The problem with entitlements is that when you add them to the other things that government has to do—such as fund the military—there isn't much discretionary money left. The choices that Congress has are to spend what's left, indulge in deficit spending, bring in more cash by adding to the tax burden, or actually cut something.

These choices wouldn't be so tough if budget after budget didn't see additional pork and new entitlements.

Go back to 1963. Congress was in a situation where 30 percent of the budget was earmarked for entitlements, so 70 percent was left over for other stuff, including national defense. By 1998, the numbers were tilted the other way. Entitlements controlled well over half of the budget, leaving just 32 percent for other stuff. The General Accounting Office warned that the percentage will shrink even further—to 26 percent by 2008.[65]

It's no coincidence that many entitlements are aimed at senior citizens, a group that can certainly use them, but also a group that votes en masse. The problem with that is that many senior citizens are wealthy or have fat retirements, but since there's no means testing, those seniors who don't need a lot of government help get it anyway.

One group that doesn't vote so much is poor people. So in 1996, Congress decided to reform welfare.

President Clinton had promised to "end welfare as we know it" but was blindsided when the Republicans thought he was serious; they kept sending him reform bills. He vetoed the first two, but after a while, it began to sink in that there would eventually be a welfare reform bill. As all this was coming to a climax, George Melloan wrote in the *Wall Street Journal* that neither party was really interested in ending welfare as we know it. "The authors hope to save some $10 billion a year, mainly by curtailing food stamp fraud and limiting the access of resident aliens to welfare programs, which might persuade some few visitors who didn't come to the U.S. to work to return home," he wrote.[66]

Melloan pointed out that the savings here was mere peanuts in a $1.6 trillion dollar budget, but still, the poverty lobby and socialist-minded Democrats screamed loudly.

University of Texas journalism professor Marvin Olasky called it a "paper blizzard" and asked why, instead of sending out reams of press releases, lobby groups, such as the liberal Children's Defense Fund, didn't cut back on their public affairs staffs and use that money to help the poor.[67]

The massive lobbying effort did not work, and President Clinton (later promising to "fix" the bill) signed it into law. Here are the major aspects of the law:[68]

· It ended a sixty-one-year guarantee of federal aid to poor children in favor of block grants for the state to use to fund their own programs.

- It called for reduced spending of about $55 billion over six years, mainly in the areas of food stamps and aid to legal immigrants.
- It imposed a five-year lifetime limit on welfare benefits, but states could exempt up to 20 percent of their welfare roster for hardship reasons.
- It required recipients to begin working two years after receiving welfare and mandated that 50 percent of single-parent families work 30 hours per week by 2002.
- It called for reduced spending on food stamps by $28 billion over six years and allowed able-bodied people with no children to get food stamps for just three months in any three-year period, unless they're working part time. (They could get another three months' worth if they were laid off.)
- It stopped most federal aid—including Medicaid and cash to future legal immigrants—for five years and barred current immigrants from receiving disability and food stamps during their first five years in the U.S., excepting refugees and immigrants who have generally worked for ten years.
- It made it more difficult for children to receive federal payments due to mental problems.

Just as President Clinton was gritting his teeth and signing this bill, the Census Bureau reported that about 14 percent of all Americans—some 36 million—were on some form of welfare. The report said that nearly one in four children collected some benefit.[69]

There was much gnashing of teeth and pulling of hair, and local social service agencies braced for the coming onslaught. But it never came. In an editorial four years later, the *Wall Street Journal* trumpeted the success of the reforms. "The facts now rolling in reveal that the Republican welfare reform has done more for the poor than the Great Society ever imagined."[70]

By the middle of 1999, there was a 49 percent decrease in welfare rolls nationwide, and more never-married welfare mothers were actually entering the workforce. The *Journal* reminded taxpayers what Democratic Congressman John Lewis of Georgia had said at the time the reforms were passed: "[The bill would] put one million children into poverty. They're coming for the children. They're coming for the poor. They're coming for the sick, the elderly, and the disabled."[71] Whew! That was loud—and wrong, too.

Welfare reform turned out to be one of the country's few successes at turning back a small piece of the entitlement state. Even so, liberals never leave well enough alone. In 2001, they fanned out across Capitol Hill, demanding that Congress restore food stamps and other benefits to legal immigrants. Senator Bob Graham, D-Fla., was among the protestors. "We come together to right a wrong and to restore the right to call ourselves a na-tion of immigrants," he said.[72]

By that time, Congress had already acted to restore some benefits, hand-ing food stamp eligibility back to about a fourth of the one million legal im-migrants that were affected by the 1996 reforms. It had also returned the benefit for Supplemental Security Income and Medicaid benefits to certain other immigrants.[73]

But more than one thousand poverty-based groups around the country were banding together, hoping to get most of the old benefits back. They even wanted to add some things, such as allowing states to extend the new CHIP insurance program to legal immigrant children. Senator Hillary Rodham Clinton supported the groups, saying, "It is important that all our children be treated equally."[74]

The key question in this debate is this: Even though the 1996 welfare re-form bill has been an astounding success, can the Republicans in Congress—in the face of constant pressure from the poverty lobby—prevent a great deal of the progress from being undone? Unfortunately, the answer is probably no.

The Senate Agriculture Committee voted to restore food stamp benefits to thousands of immigrants in late 2001. The only thing that stopped them from going further with the restoration was that they needed the money to fund a corporate welfare scheme for farm subsidies. The committee's action, if approved, would boost food stamp spending some $620 million per year.[75] Not to be outdone, the House, in its farm bill deliberations, took a non-binding vote on April 23, 2002, and voted 244–171 to restore food stamp el-igibility for about 400,000 immigrants.[76] Even the Bush administration has a plan to provide $2.1 billion in extra aid to some 363,000 immigrants who have lived in the country for at least five years.[77]

However, as the reform bill came up for renewal in mid-2002 (it was set to expire on September 30), the House voted to keep some teeth in the leg-islation. On May 16, the House voted 229–197, largely along party lines, to approve a bill that would keep more single mothers working and provide about $300 million in federal funds to promote marriage and sexual absti-nence.[78] The plan also supported Mr. Bush's proposal that welfare not be ex-tended to legal immigrants until they had lived in the United States for at least five years. With the welfare rolls cut by half, Republicans insisted that tough work rules would get even more people off welfare.

But Democrats were not convinced, pointing out that most of the for-mer recipients of welfare were still living in poverty. They contended that in-creased work rules would simply force states to provide "make-work" jobs. Instead, they wanted to spend $11 billion more on child care.[79] They also wanted to open up aid to legal immigrants and get welfare mothers into training programs through the states. That proposal went down 222–198—also along party lines. But even though it failed, the Democrats' alternative proposal made it plain that there is still an ideological split in the country about how to address the issue of poverty.

Some on the Left even used the events of 9/11 to push for more spending on welfare programs. John E. Mogk is a professor of law at Wayne State University in Detroit. In an op-ed piece, he writes that President Bush has raised the total federal aid pledged to rebuild New York City to nearly $21.4 billion. Beyond this, says Mr. Mogk, an additional $5 billion will go to the families of those middle-class families who had their lives shattered. "On the other hand," he asks, "where is the moral fervor for uplifting millions of American children born into single-parent, low-income households with limited opportunities, facing poor education, hunger, poverty and lawlessness?" [80]

While there is certainly an argument to be made that the government set a dangerous precedent by sending so much aid to the victims of 9/11 (as opposed to Oklahoma City bombing victims, who got nothing), Mr. Mogk's emotional contention that we are "neglecting the plight of America's working poor and unemployed families" is nothing more than a liberal tirade. Many of these people brought their problems on themselves and now expect the taxpaying public to bail them out. But as the reforms of 1996 proved, many of these people can and will go to work if the federal spigot is turned off.

CHIP insurance: anatomy of a new government program

Liberal politicians have long used the phrase "for the children" to help push their programs though state legislatures and the Congress. They know how difficult it is for any opposing viewpoint to find a sympathetic ear if children are involved. Usually, when something is proposed "for the children," Republicans just tuck their tails and whimper and it's all over. But in the strange case of CHIP insurance, Republicans enthusiastically signed on.

The Children's Health Insurance Program (CHIP) was created (through the efforts of Senator Orrin Hatch, R-Utah, and Senator Edward M. Kennedy, D-Mass.) as part of the Balanced Budget Act of 1997. Congress set up a program to fund insurance for low-income children through block grants from the federal government and matching dollars at the state level. In Texas, for example, for every 26 cents the states put in, the federal government will send down another 74 cents. [81]

Finally, screamed the liberals and the children's advocates; 10,000,000 uninsured children will now be covered! However, it was, and remains, a made-up crisis that creates lots of busywork for school administrators, social workers, and state and federal bureaucrats, and even creates some money-making opportunities in certain industries. Since CHIP is a combined state/federal program, let's follow the progress in one state to see how it all panned out.

Texas was one of the last states to sign on, and liberals were going nuts because the state might not fully fund the program. Remember that George W. Bush was governor at the time, and Rick Perry was lieutenant governor. It was still early in 1999 when the *Austin American-Statesman* used its editorial page to scold the state legislature for dragging its feet. "An estimated 1.4 million Texas children, about one of every four, lack health insurance. That often means they get little health care, which has far reaching effects in families, schools and communities."[82] The newspaper worried that the state might enact a "limiting" CHIP program that excluded some older children and teens whose family income was in excess of 150 percent of the poverty level.

Some legislators were telling horror stories about put-upon kids struggling in class because they weren't getting any health care, and the *Statesman* was quoting them with great frequency. This quote from state Senator Mike Moncrief, D-Fort Worth, is a beaut: "It's hard to pass the TAAS test if your ear aches or your tooth hurts, or for that matter, if you can't see the blackboard."[83]

How could anyone be so mean as to send kids to school in such a condition? Actually, it's quite doubtful that very many kids were packed off to class each morning with their ears aching and their teeth falling out and their vision fading. But such stories evoked a great deal of emotion among the compassionate advocates for children. Republicans were paying attention.

About two months after the *Statesman's* impassioned plea (and those of other major papers in the state), columnist Dave McNeely was announcing victory. Not only would Governor Bush sign the bill, but it would be a full loaf, covering kids up to the age of eighteen and families up to 200 percent of the poverty level.[84] Governor Bush had considered implementing CHIP only up to 150 percent of the poverty level just in case the federal money dried up. But how could he resist the impassioned pleas of those who cared so deeply about children?

Everyone was writing op-ed pieces urging the passage of the full coverage, and that even included former U.S. Senator Lloyd Bentsen. His column in the *Houston Chronicle*, co-authored by his son, Lan, urged the governor to sign the bill. Lan, by the way, had been a trustee of the national March of Dimes Birth Defects Foundation, one of the groups pushing CHIP. Senator Bentsen had been chairman of the Senate Finance Committee when it originally set up the CHIP program. They pointed out that the federal government would "chip" in $3 for every $1 from the state.[85]

After all, didn't we have big surpluses and lots of free tobacco settlement money? If you can't spend it on social programs now, when can you? And hadn't Mr. Bush promised to "leave no child behind?"

So a leery Governor Bush went along, but many other Texas Republicans were just as happy with CHIP as if it was a perfect match for conservative values. Then-Lieutenant Governor Rick Perry (later to become governor when Mr. Bush went to Washington) wrote an op-ed piece singing the praises of CHIP: "The children's health insurance program is an investment that will pay big dividends down the road. Regular preventive care is the key to a happy and productive life."[86]

Some conservative supporters of the lieutenant governor may have been surprised to hear him essentially say that a government program was the key to happiness. But by this time, most conservatives in the state had been corrupted, and those that actually opposed CHIP were not about to say so.

Mr. Perry went on to say that money from the state's tobacco settlement—$180 million—would fund the program. He then announced the "TexCare Partnership," a new bureaucracy designed to link private- and public-sector resources with families. He even provided a toll-free telephone number and urged everyone to take advantage of this new program being paid for by Big Tobacco.[87]

Mr. Perry's column contained no bad thoughts. There was no mention of families at 200 percent of the poverty level taking tax money from other families to insure their kids. There was no mention of what might happen if and when the tobacco money dried up. There was no mention about what might happen if too many people signed up for the program. To Rick Perry, the lieutenant governor of Texas, CHIP was just a free ride that would ensure that Texas was a "healthier, brighter" state.

You would think that with the "crisis" of uninsured children in the state of Texas, families would be flocking to sign up for CHIP coverage—and many did. Even so, the outreach program to get even more families signed up was massive.

There were CHIP forums held at local churches; the March of Dimes prepared a slick folder jammed with CHIP information with the tag line "Insuring Kids, Reassuring Parents"; and the TexCare Partnership sent out memos through the public school system urging eligible families to sign up.[88] (According to the handout, a family could make pretty decent money and still get cheap coverage. It all depended on the size of your family and how that related to income. A family of two making $16,596 could get into the program for just $15 per year. At the high end of the scale, a family of eight could bring in as much as $55,956 and still be eligible for a premium of just $18 per month per family.)[89]

As the frantic pace to enroll more families continued into April, news accounts were still claiming that 1.4 million Texas kids were without insurance. But curiously, some stories were now placing the national figure at nearly 11 million.[90] No one seemed to question why the numbers of uninsured children were not going down.

An Associated Press story noted that more than fifty groups were working to reach all children and families who might be eligible. At a news conference announcing stepped-up enrollment efforts, Texas Democrats and Republicans alike said all the right things—at least, they said all the politically correct things. State Representative Glen Maxey gushed that he was convinced of the worth of this program, while standing next to a working mother of three. "Just the look of relief on her face—that if my kid gets an illness I will have affordable coverage ... It's a great amount of pride for the Legislature."[91]

The most PC of all was Charles Stuart, a spokesman for the Health and Human Services Commission, who talked about how vital it is to implement outreach programs for CHIP. "It's a big state and a culturally diverse state and we're trying to be culturally sensitive to those parts of the state that have certain needs."[92] It's nice to know that when Mr. Stuart is taking money from taxpayers and the tobacco industry and handing it over to someone else, at least he's being culturally sensitive about it.

As the months went by, there was always some crisis brewing with the CHIP program. In July, the Left was mortified because Texas might not be able to spend all the money that Congress had provided. The states had been given a time limit to get the program going, Texas had a late start, and it was looking as if about $449 million dollars might be left on the table. Texas had begun enrolling kids in May, a year after the legislature created the program, which was three years after Congress had approved $48 billion to send to the states.[93] After all this time, newspaper stories were still saying that about 11 million kids were uninsured.

And after all the outreach, article after article continued to insist that three out of five parents whose children were uninsured didn't have a clue about CHIP. Where were these people—living in caves? No matter; the Left was bound and determined to find them. A study released on August 9 claimed that most parents of eligible children would enroll them—if only they knew![94] It was also revealed that about 2 million children were enrolled in the program in 1999. Still, that did not have the least effect on the set-in-stone numbers which the same AP story still quoted as 11 million uninsured kids.

Some crises just won't be alleviated.

A *Dallas Morning News* article in early 2001 is a perfect illustration of the frenzy inside the social services community in Texas. The article explained that (since not nearly enough kids were being signed up) an aggressive multilingual ad campaign was being launched. Charles Stuart was saying, "We want any family who has children who are uninsured to call our . . . 800 number or fill out an application."[95] State officials were going to run radio and television ads in English and Spanish, put up billboards with the toll-free number, and place ads in community newspapers designed to reach Hispanic, African-American, and Asian prospects. They were even planning to run radio spots in Vietnamese to reach certain areas of Houston.[96]

The article stated that 200,000 children had been enrolled in Texas since the program began, but still, the number of uninsured in Texas was holding at 1.4 million.

All this outreach wasn't enough, and a few days later, President Bill Clinton got into the act by announcing a major national effort to sign up more kids. Mr. Clinton told the nation in his weekly radio address that the government would open a campaign utilizing school lunch programs and child care centers to find another 2 million kids to add to the government dole.[97] This story also revealed that thirty-nine states including Texas had been granted an extension so that all that money that was about to be forfeited was back in play.

A year later, the United Methodist Women were jumping on the CHIP bandwagon to help fend off the latest crisis. We've now reached February of 2002, CHIP has signed up some 500,000 Texas kids, and according to Bill Kidd's "Austin Notebook" column, the program is starting to run short of cash.[98] Who would have thought it could happen? After all, half a million kids is less than half of the 1.4 million that had been pounded into everyone's head. Yet here it was 2002, and the new crisis involved funding—something Lieutenant Governor Perry never warned us about in his op-ed piece.

Kidd wrote that, in a sense, the CHIP program has been "too successful" and the demand for the program had exceeded the resources allowed to it. One supposes that all those foreign-language community newspapers and Vietnamese radio spots must have had the applications rolling in.

Anne Dunkleberg, senior policy analyst for the Center for Public Policy Priorities, said that everyone always thought the program would stop expanding at some point, but "that hasn't materialized yet."[99] But, really—what good government program doesn't expand? Yet so many officials seemed surprised, and remember, if our figures are correct, Texas still had another 900,000 kids remaining to be insured. Who, exactly, created the preliminary budget for this debacle?

So the United Methodist Women (UMW) came to the rescue. To the Methodist women, it was a moral issue, as explained by Barbara Ford Young, a group member from San Antonio: "We can't sit by and watch young children suffer—not as Christians." Thebe Worden of Baytown worried about social service cuts if Texas faced a multibillion-dollar budget shortfall in 2003. "Right now, it appears that the state is out of money, and programs for children and families are especially under threat," she said. "Let every current and would-be lawmaker take note: Texas United Methodist Women will not stand by and watch you steal from poor children so the rich can avoid paying their fair share." [100]

The ladies of the Methodist Church didn't reveal any plans (at least not in this article) to go out and raise money; they simply wanted to warn lawmakers to be ready to fork over tax money if it came to that. These poor, suffering kids in these families making as much as $55,000 were not going to miss out on their government subsidy as long as the UMW was around! And a pox on the rich, too!

In an astounding companion piece to this story, Dr. Nancy Dickey, president for Health Affairs at the Texas A&M University System Health Science Center, wrote an op-ed piece that began, "We live in a country that spends tens of millions of dollars each weekend on the latest movie and hundreds of millions annually on makeup, perfume and personal grooming, yet it leaves 44 million Americans without health insurance." [101]

Dr. Dickey never mentioned that all those leisure items are paid for willingly by free Americans with disposable income. Instead, she proceeded to advocate a socialistic system of government-sponsored health care. She worried that even though CHIP has insured many children, their parents or older siblings might need help in getting insured.

It is a basic principle of the Left that when a major government takeover (such as Hillary Clinton's federal health care proposal) fails, you don't give up; you simply implement the takeover a little at a time. Dr. Dickey's column was treading into this slippery territory.

She informed her readers that a century ago, it was decided that it was worthwhile to have an educated citizenry, so we got public education. "If an educated citizenry is a good thing, so is a healthy citizenry," she reasoned. "Americans already invest their tax dollars in medical research and health care. Let us commit to making sure that none is excluded from the benefits of that investment." [102] Dr. Dickey did not extrapolate what might happen if her public health care ideas became as efficient as today's public education. Nor did she allude to the massive funding problems that were beginning to dog the CHIP program that were outlined in the Bill Kidd column of the same date.

Now-Governor Rick Perry touched on the funding problems in another op-ed piece that ran in March. But the governor, or more likely a ghost-writer, couched the cash shortfall in glowing terms: "CHIP has been more popular and successful than anyone imagined. Last year we increased CHIP funding by $263 million to nearly $1 billion." [103] The governor made sure that the taxpayers realized that they all loved and adored the CHIP program; he used the word "popular" three times when referring to the program. And he actually bragged about the enormous amounts of money being spent.

So the Republican governor, practically all members of the state legislature, most of the state's major newspapers, the social services community, and the United Methodist Women were all singing the praises of CHIP. There were just a few small voices that registered any opposition at all to a program that was "for the children."

One of those voices came from David Hartman writing in the *Lone Star Report,* a newsletter about Texas politics. Hartman referred to members of the state Senate as "thirty-one lost and leaderless sheep" for approving SB 445, the legislation enabling CHIP. He said that states approving the program "have been seduced by copious federal dollars, newly-discovered tobacco money, and good-times surpluses to support Bill Clinton's major breakthrough toward fully socialized medicine."[104]

Hartman also noted that a recent forum on ways to control health care costs had been ignored by every member of the Texas Senate except for the CHIP sponsor. None of the policy people from the governor's office attended, either. If they had been there, they would have heard experts talk about reducing government mandates which could cut the cost of health care up to 30 percent, and the feasibility of a government-sponsored medical risk pool that would be accessible to private insurers.[105]

The DeWeese Report agreed that CHIP was a solution in search of a problem. Columnist Peyton Knight contended that the entire program was based on the statistic that 10 million kids were uninsured—and that simply wasn't true. "The U.S. Census Bureau shows that from 1992 to 1994, 70 percent of children under 18 had health insurance for the entire two year duration, 26 percent had intermittent coverage (usually because they were in between coverage plans), and a mere 4 percent were uninsured for the whole two years. The Department of Health and Human Services reports that only 1.3 million children actually lack health insurance because of its cost."[106]

Knight asked the question: So what happened to the 10 million kids with no medical care? To get to that figure, CHIP had to expand its customer base up to the 200 percent of poverty level, encouraging middle-income families to drop private plans and go government.

World Net Daily reported on a study concerning that very thing. According to the report, the advent of CHIP insurance had forced many kids off of their private insurance plan and had done nothing to lower the number of uninsured kids overall. Research from the Center Studying Health System Change seemed to show that the percentage of low-income kids with public insurance went up, while the percentage covered by private insurance went down.[107] John Goodman, president of a highly respected Dallas think-tank, the National Center for Policy Analysis, said the report pointed out the weakness of government solutions. "What this means is that we're spending a lot of money and not getting a lot in return."[108]

It is true, however, that any government program—no matter how ineffective—can be a windfall for someone. And so it came to pass that Texas officials, still desperate to sign up more and more "poor" kids, decided that there should be "an aggressive increase in advertising funds" to promote CHIP. Initially, $2 million had been set aside for the first two-year cycle of advertising. But this time, the state announced that it would increase the budget by a factor of five—to $10 million over two years—as they kicked off a review for a new advertising agency.[109]

The saga of CHIP turns out to be a story about misguided politicians and a social services community that wanted to feel better about children's health care. But instead of looking for market-based ways to lower the cost of that care and make private-sector insurance more affordable, they simply created a new entitlement. They said that CHIP would be "for the children." It's also "for" the reelection of politicians, expansion of the state bureaucracy, the welfare lobby, the socialists, and the advertising agencies.

But just try to get rid of it.

Corporate welfare: feeding at the trough

Have you ever wondered why big companies like Enron Corp. make huge political donations to politicians of both parties? Have you ever wondered why politicians of both parties pass bills into law that contain giant subsidies for big companies? Have you ever wondered if there's any connection between those two things?

To be sure, big corporations often go to Congress asking for nonmonetary favors, but often, lawmakers bestow cash in the form of grants, subsidies, or low-cost loans—known here as "feeding at the trough."

How much is anybody's guess. The conservative Cato Institute says the figure is about $75 billion per year. Other groups, like the more liberal Native Forest Council and even *Time* magazine, place the figure at $125 billion a year.[110] Any way you look at it, that's a lot of money—taxpayers' money.

Want some examples? Here are some taken from Michael Moore's book *Downsize This!*, pointing out rather graphically that corporate welfare is going to many companies that are well ensconced in the Fortune 500:[111]

· $1.6 million in federal funds to McDonald's to help market Chicken McNuggets in Singapore from 1986 to 1994.
· $278 million in government technology subsidies to Amoco, AT&T, Citicorp, Du Pont, General Electric, General Motors, and IBM from 1990 to 1994.
· $300 million in tax deductions for Exxon for the settlement costs in the Exxon *Valdez* oil spill.

Even the nonmonetary favors turn into profits. According to Mr. Moore and the Cato Institute, the Archer Daniels Midland Company (ADM) has given a lot of money to both parties. The quid pro quo may be something as simple as the government keeping foreign sugar out of U.S. markets. That keeps sugar prices high, and that's a boost for ADM's corn sweetener.[112]

The famed *Crossfire* host and pundit Robert Novak writes that Enron Corp. "gorged itself on corporate welfare." During the Clinton administration, the government came up with more than $650 million in Export-Import Bank loans to companies controlled by Enron.[113] If these loans go into default, the American taxpayer will have to pick up the tab.

And then there's the Farm Bill of 2002—a sterling example of how even conservative politicians can turn their backs on their own core values when an important election is looming. Remember that Jim Jeffords became an Independent but threw his support to the Democrats, making Tom Daschle the Senate majority leader. That event cast a sense of urgency over the elections of November 2002, resulting in a major attitude adjustment on the parts of both Democrats and Republicans.

Back in 1996, the Congress was trying to wean the agriculture industry from government supports and passed legislation called the "Freedom to Farm Act." President Bush, too, had been critical of bloated farm subsidies.[114] But with control of the Senate hanging in the balance, and with the House possibly up for grabs, Mr. Bush changed his mind and threw his support behind the Farm Bill. So did most members of Congress

The Farm Bill was not merely the restoration of some of the subsidies that were lost in the Freedom to Farm Act. Rather, the 2002 bill represented a stunning 70 percent increase in overall subsidies. As passed 280–141 in the House, the bill carried a price tag of $180 billion over the next decade. That's a mere $73.5 billion increase over current programs.[115]

Luther Tweeten, an agriculture economist at Ohio State University, said that the bill was good for farmers but bad for taxpayers. "It certainly gives some security to farmers. It comes at a very high cost to taxpayers and the national economy, however."[116] Humorist Dave Barry tried to look on the bright side, saying the bill was definitely *not* welfare: "Welfare is when the government gives money to people who produce nothing. Whereas the farm money recipients produce something that is critical to our nation: votes."[117] So Barry called the bill something else—bribery.

Let's be clear. The president of the United States and the U.S. House passed a new law, during a wartime economy, in the middle of an economic slowdown, during a bear stock market, at a time of new deficits, knowing that it would be a further drag on the economy and would further slow down a weak recovery—because they couldn't bring themselves to vote against "farmers" with a big election coming up. The bill was also a payback to Senator Jeffords for throwing the Senate to the Democrats; he got his milk subsidies for New England reinstated.

With the bill approved in the House and headed for reconciliation in the Senate, the Republican base was getting somewhat antsy with President Bush. Robert Novak put it this way: "GOP leaders were appalled by this caricature of government excess, but the President sent a contrary signal: He would sign any farm bill passed by Congress." Mr. Novak wrote that the final version of the bill marked an abandonment of efforts to impose market standards on farmers, and there was some hope that the bill might fail.[118]

Fat chance.

Within a couple of days, the Senate had finished its work on the bill, passed it 64–35 in spite of the Republicans who opposed it, and sent it over to the White House. It's interesting to note that Senator Kay Bailey Hutchison, R-Tex., who represents a state with lots of farmers, voted for the bill, as did Tim Hutchinson, R-Ark. But Senator Phil Gramm, R-Tex., who was retiring from the Senate and thus wasn't worried about reelection, voted against it.[119]

The bill as approved by the Senate was packed with government largesse—now to the tune of $190 billion. The bill provided subsidies for grain and cotton farmers; wool and honey; new payments for milk, peanuts, and lentils; and an 80 percent increase in land-conservation programs to benefit livestock farms and fruit and vegetable growers. Senator Tom Harkin, chairman of the Senate Agriculture Committee (by virtue of Jeffords' jump), was thrilled at the new spending. But Senator Fred Thompson worried that the bill would "make farmers increasingly dependent on government subsidies." Thompson said the policies in the bill made no sense and "defy logic and they defy the most basic laws of economics."[120] The final tally had twenty-eight Republicans and seven Democrats voting no.

The fate of the Farm Bill was now in the hands of a nervous George W. Bush. Politically, he knew he had to sign it, even though his conscience and his core values made that very difficult. So the White House staff set up an early-morning signing ceremony—7:45 A.M. EDT—that would be widely seen by early-rising farmers.[121] The president's staff hoped that the rest of the country would sleep through it and never notice.

Too often, these political calculations seem to work in favor of our tax-and-spend politicians. That is to say that even with newspaper columns, talk radio, and talk-TV on cable, many Americans still don't notice. Even with estimates that each of us pays out about $1,383 per year in taxes to benefit big corporations, we still let government get by with it.[122]

We rarely complain about the pork barrel spending—maybe because we like it. We let some politicians convince us that taxes are actually not high enough. We fail to even notice that so many government programs and agencies are full of waste and many have no real mission.

We believe in the arts, so we support the National Endowment for the Arts even when it subsidizes pure smut. We fund a bloated Federal Communications Commission that actually makes laws (isn't Congress supposed to do that?) and has handed out valuable broadcast licenses based on the color of the applicant's skin. We still have the Commerce Department, which is devoted to corporate welfare, and the Education Department, which under the Constitution has no reason for being. And we have the Corporation for Public Broadcasting, which, in today's multichannel cable world, does nothing unique.

It's way past time for the American taxpayer to take notice.

It's time for smaller government

There are certainly things that only the government can do. Only the government can mount armed forces, set up a judicial system, and build a transportation system of highways and airports. And certainly the government can—and should—maintain a safety net for the deserving poor. We will always have Social Security; and there should be smaller programs in place for victims of catastrophic illnesses or events. But we have taken the idea of a compassionate society too far. We have started on the road to socialism.

In today's world, politicians on the national stage occupy a position once reserved for movie stars. Instead of public servants who run for office out of a desire to use their talents for the good of the nation, many of today's politicians are careerists who love the adulation, the attention, and the power afforded by the office. Often, the number-one goal of this new breed is nothing more than their own reelection—holding on to office at any cost. (The most salient recent examples are President Bill Clinton and Congressman Gary Condit.)

People vote for politicians they like. The politicians know that people like stuff. So the trend is to get stuff for the district and hold news conferences for photo-ops and get on the front page of the local paper.

Certain individuals and (nowadays) groups realize that by electing certain people to office, they will get more stuff. The poverty lobby works to elect people who favor CHIP; the farm lobby works hard to get the subsidies restored; the immigration community goes into overdrive to get benefits for aliens; big business contributes to both parties hoping that merger restrictions will be eased. It never stops.

But one of these days, the money will be gone, because the American taxpayer will be fully bled. At that point, there will be only two choices: either we roll back the taxes and government programs, or the government takes over everything—and freedom is no more.

It's way too easy to increase government programs in good economic times when newspaper headlines are screaming about surpluses. But when the bubble bursts—as it always must—the spending programs remain.

Witness some key lines from a newspaper article following new rounds of government expansion, but at a time when events of the day (recession; war) have eaten into the government's money supply: "Costs for Medicaid, the health program for the poor, are soaring. And the bills for doctors, hospitals, and prescription drugs are hitting state coffers at a time when tax revenues have plummeted because of the slow economy." "At the same time, the State Children's Health Insurance Program [CHIP] is also under pressure. Closely aligned with Medicaid, the program's low-income children may be at a greater risk of losing their medical coverage." ". . . the White House and Congress are already struggling to pay their own share of the rising Medicaid bill." "Costs have also risen because states were generous in adding benefits when the bountiful economy of the 1990s filled treasuries with tax revenue. Adding benefits pleased voters." [123]

The fact is that we need a better breed of public servant—one that recognizes that good times don't last forever and that government cannot be all things to all people. At the dawn of the twenty-first century, government is trying to assume the roles that used to be played by church and family. It isn't working.

Making government smaller may be the hardest objective to achieve. It has to be done—one program at a time, one election at a time; we must change the way we think about our current pork-conscious politicians and our entitlement state.

If we continue along the current path, we are only sowing the seeds of our own destruction.

Abolish the Income Tax Code

We must declare that the income tax and the Internal Revenue Service are oppressive to the American people and that they should be replaced with a simple and fair system of taxation.

Simply put, the income tax is government's way of controlling the behavior of businesses and individuals. The income tax is the most complicated, convoluted system of financing a government ever conceived by human beings—and this is precisely where the control comes in. No one fully understands the tax code. You don't, your accountant doesn't, and neither does the person on the other end of the Internal Revenue Service (IRS) information line.

The code is so difficult to understand that a 1987 General Accounting Office survey reported that the IRS was giving out incorrect information to taxpayers a whopping 47 percent of the time!

As long as the American people are in the dark about what the code says and what it means, the government maintains its stranglehold over our paychecks and our lives. Most people threw up their hands years ago and simply pay someone else to fill out their tax returns—and to stand beside them during an audit or in tax court. According to the nonpartisan Tax Foundation, at least 56 percent of taxpayers were going that route in 1999, at a staggering cost of $250 billion per year.[1] That's money that could be used for consumer spending or business expansion, but instead it's going into the pockets of accountants or tax lawyers.

By 2002, an IRS study put the figure at 60 percent. Even taxpayers filing the "simpler" 1040EZ form were using professional preparers—about 21 percent were unable to complete the forms without assistance.[2] But using a professional preparer is often necessary to stay out of trouble with the IRS, which is still the only agency that considers you guilty until proven innocent. IRS agents don't care about the complexity of the code; they simply want your taxes to be paid accurately and on time.

So, how complex is the tax code? It's hard to keep up with all the changes, but recent estimates say it contains about 8 million words—the size of about 150 novels. As recently as 1999, the IRS was publishing 569 tax forms. In 2002, the code filled up 52,310 pages in twenty-five volumes.[3] Of course, the George W. Bush tax cuts have been implemented since then, so that means more words and more forms.

And here's another staggering fact from the Tax Foundation: during the Clinton/Gore administration, the federal tax burden increased 45 percent per person, rising from $4,625 (in 1992) to $6,690.[4] You would expect a tremendous outcry when taxes go up that rapidly, but it didn't happen during the Clinton years. Why not?—because the tax code is so complex that most people have little or no idea what they're paying.

In addition to that, the government extracts its money from taxpayers in so many ways that unless you're an expert, it's hard to keep up. But here are a few things to consider:

Begin by looking at your W-2 form to see what payroll taxes amounted to for your Social Security and Medicare, and add those amounts to your income tax figure. Then add in sales taxes for the year. After you've computed all that, add in the taxes you paid for gasoline, excise taxes on cigarettes and alcohol, automobile taxes, hotel/motel taxes, and taxes on airplane tickets.[5] And don't forget the $1.50 tax each month per telephone line that's supposed to pay for connecting public schools to the Internet. This, of course, is the "cerebral Gore tax" that the former vice president pushed for and that ended up as an FCC levy on phone companies, who simply passed the cost along to consumers.

Wait—there's more. Your employer pays matching money for Social Security and Medicare, plus unemployment taxes and workers' compensation taxes. Many economists consider those taxes part of the tax burden for workers, since the cost to employers tends to hold wages down.[6] "If Americans recognized the high level of taxation, there might well be a second American revolution," according to Bryan Riley of the National Taxpayers Union Foundation.[7] The Tax Foundation attempted to add up all the various types of tax revenue that go to the government and came up with a total of almost $10,000 for every single American—more than the average cost of housing, clothing, and food combined.[8]

But there's more. Columnists Jack Anderson and Jan Moller remind us that there are also indirect taxes such as import duties to consider. When you add everything in, the total tax burden is much greater than most people think, estimated at up to 43 percent of total earnings.[9] So if you really want to know what you're shelling out to the government, you'll have to save your receipts from the gasoline pump, be sure to check the fine print on your telephone and TV cable statements, and look for other items that might not be called a tax but really are. Your license plate fee is a tax, and so is your automobile inspection sticker.

The government even imposes an onerous little policy called "withholding," which takes some of the emotional sting out of paying income taxes. That simply means that employers deduct income and payroll taxes from their employees' paychecks. That has two major effects that ease the pain. First, since most people get paid weekly or every other week, the amount deducted may not seem like a lot. Second, people get used to looking at the net amount on the check because that's what they get to take home. Sometimes, they forget all about the deductions.

Then there's the onerous and complex Alternative Minimum Tax (AMT), which was created to prevent wealthy Americans from avoiding taxes through the use of credits and deductions. But the AMT is being imposed on "millions of taxpayers to whom it was not intended to apply," according to the White House budget released in 2002. The AMT affected about 2.7 million Americans in 2002, as opposed to about a million in 1999.[10]

But what if we switched to another system? Suppose employers were no longer required to be tax collectors? If the American wage-earner had to pull out his or her checkbook and actually write a check to the IRS, the realization of how taxed we are would set in. What if this happened every quarter? Then the amount would be significant enough that the average person would begin to wonder what the government does with all that cash. The IRS does require some companies and individuals to make quarterly payments, but if everyone had to do it that way, some of the complacency might disappear.

Another reason people don't complain about taxes is the constant political spin coming mostly from the Left. To former President Clinton, former Vice President Gore, and Senate Minority Leader Tom Daschle, an across-the-board tax cut would "benefit the wealthiest 1 percent of Americans." It's the old class-envy argument, but many people are jealous of the rich and go along with that type of thinking.

However, the idea that wealthy Americans pay little or no taxes isn't true. The *Wall Street Journal* reports that the top 1 percent of taxpayers coughed up 36.2 percent of total federal personal income taxes in 1999, according to the latest IRS data requested by the Congressional Joint Economic Committee. And that was up from 34.8 percent in 1998.[11]

Besides, if we soak the rich too much, then who's going to build more warehouses, start more ventures, buy more equipment, break more ground, and write more paychecks? Not the poor, and certainly not bureaucrats.

Now take a look at a chart compiled by Citizens for Tax Justice (CTJ) showing percentage of family income for taxes during the second Clinton term:[12]

Income Group	Average Income	Federal Taxes	State and Local Taxes	Total Taxes
Top 1 percent	$659,500	31.9%	10.2%	42.1%
Next 4 percent	$160,560	27.3%	10.6%	37.9%
Next 15 percent	$87,320	26.1%	10.5%	36.6%
Next 20 percent	$56,170	22.9%	10.7%	33.6%
Middle 20 percent	$37,290	20.0%	11.1%	31.1%
Fourth 20 percent	$22,530	15.1%	11.9%	27.0%
Lowest 20 percent	$8,860	5.3%	14.1%	19.4%

Whether you prefer the CTJ numbers or the *WSJ* figures (calculated without including Social Security and Medicare taxes), the conclusion is the same: the rich are paying much more than anyone else—in both actual dollars and in percentage of income. But that doesn't matter. The Democratic Party spin is not about truth; it's about politics. The Left just doesn't want across-the-board tax cuts.

President Clinton's idea of tax cuts was to find someone he thought was deserving (possibly a key voting segment) and bestow upon that favored group a tax cut—essentially taxing some people more to give others a break. That's called "targeted" tax cuts. Al Gore would have continued to use targeted cuts had he been elected. Democrats like to use targeted tax hikes, too, as a way to control behavior. If they want you to conserve gasoline, they raise gasoline taxes. If they don't want you to smoke, they raise tobacco taxes.

Prior to the attacks of 9/11, the government was awash in money. The surplus (which some maintain never existed, due to the national debt) was created by Clinton's massive tax increases, general prosperity, relative peace and cuts in the military budget, and the technological boom of companies known as "dotcoms." The dot-com collapse came too late to affect policy during the Clinton years, and so we had a big national debate on what to do with the surplus.

By the way, a lot of the surplus was in the Social Security Trust Fund, that pyramid scheme that requires each generation to fund the government retirement of the prior generation. For years, there had been a bipartisan raiding of the fund. Since the Johnson administration, the fund had been just part of the budget anyway, so politicians of both parties grabbed the money when they could. After all, spending back in the district is good for business—and reelection.

But now that surpluses were in the billions, Democrats began to talk about a "Social Security lockbox" to keep the trust fund from being raided. Never mind that the Democrats had done as much or more raiding than anyone else; now they were attempting to make it appear that they were being responsible. Of course, that would not bode well for tax cuts. After all, how can we put Social Security money in a lockbox *and* cut taxes? We have roads to build and social programs to fund and jogging trails to build back in the district.

So the few cries in the wilderness, usually from publisher Steve Forbes and U.S. Representative Dick Armey, R-Tex., to revamp or abolish the IRS went unheard. Good ideas were floating around. There was talk of a flat tax or a national sales tax, but no one seemed to believe seriously that either of these ideas would take hold.

Liberals certainly didn't. They saw the surplus as a unique opportunity to spend more. With a surplus, who cared about cutting back on anything? Who cared about political pork or wasteful spending or entitlement fraud? The boom was in full swing, taxes were at their highest level in history, and the government was raking in the money. The economy was good enough that there was no hue and cry from an overtaxed people who had no idea of how much they were forking over. Some politicians called for even higher taxes to fund more educational programs, more child care, more everything.

The sad truth is that the more we tax, the more we spend, the more government does for the people, the less the people do for themselves, the more dependent we become, and the less freedom we have.

How we got an income tax

Whenever an income tax rears its ugly head, it's usually due to some crisis. In the case of the United States, the crisis was the War Between the States (the Civil War). The Union needed cash to pay for the war, so in 1862, the tax was adopted, and it stayed in effect for ten years.

By that time, the damage was done. Washington had had a taste of the easy way to get money, and the Civil War taxes had been ruled constitutional, so there were renewed efforts to get a permanent tax installed. In 1894, Congress passed another income tax law and based it on the Civil War tax. The new law taxed businesses and individuals at a rate of 2 percent. This time, the courts didn't buy into it and declared it unconstitutional in 1895.

The unconstitutionality of the income tax was not due to the high-mindedness of the justices, but rather due to a technicality in the Constitution. There was a section that required that any tax levied directly on individuals must be proportional to the state's population. This was a problem for the Congress, but one that could be fixed.

In a test case in 1909, Congress passed a sort of corporate income tax that withstood court challenges. But not desiring to go to court every time a new tax was added, tax backers decided that an amendment to the Constitution was necessary.

Mark down this date in infamy: February 3, 1913.

On that day, the Sixteenth Amendment to the Constitution was ratified, removing the requirement about taxes being levied in proportion to state population. Here is the exact text of the amendment:

"The Congress shall have power to lay and collect taxes on incomes, from whatever source derived, without apportionment among the several States, and without regard to any census or enumeration."

Congress was now able to levy income taxes with impunity, and it wasted no time. That same year, on October 3, the Underwood Tariff Act was passed into law, and it included income taxes—fixed at 1 percent. There was nowhere to go but up!

By the way, that same tariff act got us off to a good start on soaking the rich. That 1 percent assessment was for individuals with annual incomes over $3,000 and married people making more than $4,000. But for those who were doing well in 1913—over $20,000 in annual income—Congress added a surtax ranging from 1 percent to 6 percent.

Congress had found its cash cow, selling it to the American people on the basis of low rates and progressivism. But newspapers of the day didn't buy in as so many do today. University of Texas journalism professor Marvin Olasky pointed out that the major editorial pages were livid about the new taxes—both in 1894 and in 1909, when the Sixteenth Amendment was sent up for ratification.[13]

The *New York Times* called the 1894 law "a vicious, inequitable, unpopular, impolitic and Socialistic scheme . . . the most unreasoning and most un-American movement in the politics of the last quarter century." The *Washington Post* griped that the income tax would force employers to catalog employees as though they were beasts of burden.

The *New York Times* was at it again in 1909: "When men get the habit of helping themselves to the property of others, they are not easily cured of it." But Olasky says that the *Washington Post* was changing its tune, saying an income tax was needed to "wipe out the deficit [$89 million] without impairment of the public service or calling a halt upon needed public improvements."

The *Post* went on to say that the income tax would hold down congressional appropriations because more spending would cause the president to have to increase the tax, and he would place the blame on Congress. The *Dallas Morning News* actually wondered if the Congress would use this new power to levy taxes.

Of course, we know the answer to that question. The Congress became addicted to spending and implemented new ways to lessen the pain to taxpayers by keeping taxes complex and hidden. In 1943, we got the pay-as-you-go system. In 1944, simplified returns and standard deductions came into use. In 1948, new laws allowed exemptions for blindness and old age, and joint returns for married people. By 1954, the tax code had amassed almost 200,000 words.

In modern times, two presidents are known for their policies on income taxes: Ronald Reagan for cutting taxes and Bill Clinton for raising them. Critics have scorned the Reagan cuts, saying that the national debt quadrupled after they were enacted. Is that true? An editorial in the *Investor's Business Daily* says no.

In fiscal year 1989, Mr. Reagan's last budget, revenue from individual taxes rose to $446 billion. In fiscal year 1981, the year that Mr. Reagan began to cut personal rates, the revenue figure was only $286 billion. As *IBD* points out, that's a 56 percent gain.

So if tax receipts were growing this fast under the Reagan tax cuts, how'd we get such a massive rise in the national debt? Easy: the spending side was growing much faster. In 1981, spending was just $678 billion. In 1989, Congress was writing much bigger checks—$1.143 trillion. As *IBD* points out, that's a 69 percent gain.[14] Simply put, while Mr. Reagan was cutting taxes and actually increasing the amount of money coming into the treasury, Congress was on a spending spree that wiped out all the gains.

Mr. Clinton, on the other hand, who presided over a sustained period of economic growth, used the tie-breaking vote of Vice President Al Gore to pass huge tax increases. Fortunately for Mr. Clinton's hopes for a legacy, there was a gigantic mitigating factor that prevented his new taxes from sinking the economy. The technology boom, especially investors' exuberance over the new dot-com companies, pulled more revenue into the economy than Mr. Clinton's taxes took out. When the dot-coms began to fail, the economy began to slide. The technology boom lasted just long enough for Bill Clinton to wrap up his presidency and leave George W. Bush stuck with its aftermath.

What should replace the income tax?

On June 7, 2001, President George W. Bush signed into law the first major tax cut since 1981. The bill was designed to reduce taxes by $1.35 trillion dollars over ten years before the tax cuts expire on December 31, 2010. While the bill did provide a modest tax cut, it also added to the complexity of the tax code.

Among other things, the Bush tax cuts tampered with the estate tax, tax credits for children, and rates for married couples. However, it did not lower the number of pages in the code, or cut back on the number of forms, or make it easier to fill out a Form 1040. It did not do away with, or even weaken, the IRS. So far, President George W. Bush has shown no interest in doing any of these things.

In addition, the Bush tax cuts are backloaded. Many of the cuts don't take effect until just before the expiration date in 2010. Of course, the Left screamed that most of the benefits go to the wealthiest 1 percent of taxpayers.

So is it possible to have a system of revenue for the federal government that brings in enough money to run the country and yet eliminates the complexity, the cost of compliance, and the political squabbling? Actually, there are a couple of ways to do it—the flat tax, which makes filing your taxes much easier, and the national sales tax, which eliminates the income tax code and the IRS altogether.

The flat tax—alternative to "abomination"?

President George W. Bush has never called for elimination of the code and IRS, but he has promised to work for simplification. The president made the commitment on March 19, 2002, to a group of female small-business owners meeting in Washington.

At that same conference, Treasury Secretary Paul O'Neill told the group, "You all know this, but I'm really happy to reinforce it in your mind: our tax code is an abomination. There is not a single person in the IRS who can be proud of the fact that they give wrong advice, that they are slow to respond."

Presumably, if Mr. O'Neill believes that the tax code is an "abomination," then the president believes it, too. The question then becomes, what are they going to do about it? So far, other than tax-cutting measures that actually increase the complexity of the code, no simplification proposals have been offered.

One thing the president might consider is the ultimate simplification method known as "the flat tax."

Like its companion proposal, the national sales tax, the flat tax would succeed only if it meets a few basic goals. First, it must be revenue neutral, meaning that it would bring in roughly the same amount of money to run the government that the current tax code does. Second, it must be perceived as fair. Third, it must be simple. If these goals are met, then two things should follow: compliance with the code would increase tremendously, and billions of dollars would be saved in tax preparation fees.

Where's the downside? There isn't one for the taxpaying public—only for those in Congress and government bureaucracies who use the tax code to control the people.

The flat tax is sometimes known as a "single rate system," replacing the tax brackets with just one rate for everyone. Champions of the flat tax, such as publisher Steve Forbes and former U.S. representative Dick Armey, differ slightly on the details but agree that it's the best way to replace the outmoded, antigrowth code that seems to have such a grip on government.

Mr. Forbes explained why the flat tax is better in an op-ed piece in the *Wall Street Journal:* "This crushing tax burden is fueled in part by the 1993 tax increase—the largest tax increase in American history—and in part by the 'progressivity' of the tax code, which ensures that no matter how fast a worker's income is growing, his federal income taxes will grow even faster." [15]

In the same article, Forbes noted that payroll taxes are another major problem with the current system: in the past fifty years, the Social Security payroll tax rate has increased from 2 percent to 12.4 percent. In addition, the amount of income subject to Social Security and Medicare payroll taxes has grown from the first $7,800 of income in 1972 to the first $72,400. Forbes' position is that this makes it almost impossible for many working families to have a savings account.

The Forbes plan, with its 17 percent flat rate, would carry with it an income tax cut, as well as simplification. Mr. Forbes would take about 20 million working Americans off the tax rolls altogether. He would institute personal exemptions of $13,000 for each adult and $5,000 for each child, so that a family of four earning $36,000 would pay no income taxes at all. Forbes would give single parents an exemption of $17,000. There would be no taxes on personal savings, pensions, Social Security benefits, or capital gains, and no "death taxes." [16]

Following a transition period, Mr. Forbes' plan would also establish the 17 percent rate for businesses on their net profits after operating expenses and capital investments. But to the chagrin of some in the homebuilding and real-estate field, Mr. Forbes' plan carries with it no deduction for home mortgage interest.

As Baylor economics professor Dr. John Pisciotta points out, the revenue neutrality of the flat tax proposals is often due to how the tax base might be expanded. So if there are no more deductions for mortgage interest, charitable contributions, and such, then more money will enter federal coffers, even with a lower rate. [17]

The Dick Armey plan, outlined in his 1995 book *The Freedom Revolution,* called for a 20 percent rate, even though some of his literature on the issue used the 17 percent figure. As Pisciotta points out, the Armey plan coincides with Forbes in not allowing deductions for mortgage interest and charitable deductions, but it would tax some income that now is not taxed. For example, Mr. Armey would tax the value of employer-paid health insurance and some retirement pensions. Like Forbes, Mr. Armey would not tax unearned income such as interest, dividends, and capital gains.

Several other prominent Republicans have also come up with flat tax proposals. Another Texan, Senator Phil Gramm, once an economics professor at Texas A&M, proposed a 16 percent flat rate. During the 1996 campaign, Mr. Gramm said he preferred to keep the deductions intact for mortgage interest and charitable contributions. Unlike the Forbes/Armey proposals, Mr. Gramm would continue to tax interest income and capital gains. The *Los Angeles Times* quoted Mr. Gramm: "I do not believe it is defensible to say that if someone earns their income by laboring, that that income should be subjected to a tax, but if they earn their income by investing capital that income should not be subjected to a tax."

That, of course, was the bugaboo that Democrats and liberal think tanks used to oppose the flat tax. Pisciotta's article used this example: Say a person inherits a lot of wealth and invests it, receiving $200,000 of interest and dividend income each year. This person has no tax liability under the Forbes/Armey plan.

The defense, at least for dividends, is that this income has already been taxed in the corporation income tax.

Even some Republicans were skeptical. Bob Dole, running for president in 1996, said that he could not support any measure that would increase the federal budget deficit or shift the tax burden toward the middle class and away from the wealthy. Quoted in the same article, Clinton's treasury secretary, Robert Rubin, couldn't wait to agree: "Every Republican flat tax we have seen either explodes the deficit or raises income taxes on middle-income families."[18]

Of course, Mr. Dole and Mr. Rubin never mentioned the government's insatiable appetite for spending. Any serious income tax reform should carry with it meaningful spending cuts. Mr. Gramm's proposal made spending cuts a centerpiece. He wanted to reduce the government to its smallest share of the economy since the Korean War. But, while Mr. Gramm was handily reelected, his flat tax idea coupled with spending cuts never made it to first base.

The ideas that a flat tax would "cost" government or business and that it is "untested" have been floated by those who prefer the current system. Robert Eisner, professor emeritus at Northwestern University, insists that the lower rate, combined with the loss of major deductions, would explode business taxes by some $200 billion. In an opinion piece in the *Wall Street Journal,* he said: "Taxes are onerous; but despite all the complaints, we have probably the best system in the world for collecting them."[19] Really, professor? The best system in the world? Let's check that out, along with the "untested" claim, by looking at a couple of places where other ideas have been tried.

The *Wall Street Journal* ran an editorial in which it discussed the system of taxation in Hong Kong and found it similar to some of our flat tax proposals. While explaining that the system there is not exactly flat—it has four levels of taxation, from 2 percent to 20 percent, the *Journal* opined that it nevertheless is most likely the reason that Hong Kong has the world record for economic expansion. And it's been expanding for more than three decades.[20]

No one in Hong Kong has to pay more than 15 percent of his or her income to the government. About half the citizens pay no incomes taxes at all; the rest pay about 7 percent of their income. There is no tax on capital gains or interest. The tax form is four pages long—including sections in English and Chinese. Oh, yes—the *Journal* points out that almost 75 percent of Hong Kong's tax revenue comes from the wealthiest 10 percent of the population. (This was before Hong Kong became part of China in 1997.)

Even in Russia, the flat tax idea is taking hold. Columnist Deroy Murdock has written about the new Russian tax system that took effect on January 1, 2001. It's a 13 percent flat rate, with no tax brackets. It's still early, but Murdock reports that the new system has exceeded the expectations of the government. There are no forms to fill out, compliance is up, and revenue has increased by about 28 percent.[21]

But here in the land of the free, we still have plenty of forms to fill out, and brackets, and noncompliance, and there is no end in sight. In May of 1995, Senate Majority Leader Bob Dole and House Speaker Newt Gingrich appointed a special commission to look at the income tax code. "The National Commission on Economic Growth and Tax Reform," headed up by former Housing Secretary Jack Kemp, ended up recommending the flat tax.[22] The Kemp Commission, however, did not recommend a rate, and it did not address who might pay more or less under the new system, or how it might affect the budget deficit. The commission didn't even have an opinion on whether the "Big Two" deductions should be kept intact.

In other words, the Kemp Commission was so afraid to speak out in favor of anything specific that if it had been a motion, it would have died for lack of a second. Without anything specific to recommend, the commission went out of business, and the idea of a flat tax pretty well died along with it.

The national sales tax: so long, IRS!

Have you ever heard of the Schaefer-Tauzin National Retail Sales Act of 1996? You probably haven't, but here is what the bill was designed to do: eliminate the income tax, institute a 15 percent national sales tax, provide a tax credit against payroll taxes for the poor on expenditures up to the poverty level, and provide refunds to Social Security and welfare recipients.[23]

The bill would also require a two-thirds supermajority to enact any increases in the rate of taxation. The big spenders in Congress shouldn't worry just yet; few people even know about the sales tax, and the talking heads on television ignore it most of the time. It has few champions in Congress, with Bill Archer, former chairman of the House Ways and Means Committee, a notable exception.

Here is what the national sales tax would do: It would fundamentally change the way we collect revenues to run the government, by eliminating income taxes and the IRS altogether and replacing the current system with a simple tax on the things we buy.

More recently, the Linder-Peterson Bill (H.R. 2525) has been introduced, which calls for a national sales tax with a rate of around 23 percent.[24] Twenty-three percent?—sounds like a lot of money to be shelling out every time you purchase something. But here's the difference: Every time you get a paycheck, you'd be getting every dime you earned. Nothing would be deducted for taxes, Social Security, or Medicare. Since the national sales tax is calculated to replace all federal taxes, you wouldn't have to deal with corporate, self-employment, capital gains, gift, or inheritance taxes, either.

The only deductions from your paycheck would be programs that you voluntarily sign up for, such as 401(k) plans. And April 15 would be just another day.

The national sales tax is a consumption tax. That means that your taxes become almost voluntary. The more you purchase, the more taxes you pay. The more you save, the less taxes you pay. Some experts on the Left believe this makes the tax regressive, because smaller portions of income are used for domestic consumption. Others see it this way: the wealthy buy the largest homes, the biggest cars, and the fanciest clothes. When a wealthy person purchases a $200,000 yacht or a $2 million home, the sales tax becomes quite progressive. The wealthy person is plunking down a much larger amount than the middle-class person who buys a $150,000 home.

And don't forget that the poor people do quite well under most national sales tax proposals. The plan supported by the organization Americans for Fair Taxation[25] calls for the poor to pay no taxes at all. That's because every household would receive a rebate equal to the taxes paid on essentials such as food and medicine. Before you ask, yes, the "Fair Tax" plan gives millionaires the rebates, too. But let's look at an example provided by AFT.

Suppose a rich person spends $10 million. Under the Fair Tax plan, his sales tax bill would amount to $2.3 million. If he's married with no children, his rebate would be only $2,440, an effective tax rate of 22.98 percent. Meanwhile, a middle-income earner, married with no kids, spending $30,000 would pay $4,460 in taxes after getting the same rebate of $2,440. That equals an effective rate of 14.9 percent. There's no question that the sales tax is progressive, although in a fairer manner.[26]

The argument about mortgage interest deductibility goes away under the sales tax, because there's no longer an income tax to deduct it from. Charitable contributions are another matter. Of course, there'd be no deduction, but since contributions would come from pre-tax dollars, it would actually be less costly to give money to your favorite charity. This is one of those truth-versus-perception matters that charities would have to work at to make people understand.

There are many other advantages to the national sales tax. Tax evasion would be more difficult and less desirable, since the tax is obvious and easy to pay. It would be easy for retail businesses to collect the tax; most already collect state sales taxes anyway. The income tax imposed on investment income and pension benefits—even IRA withdrawals—would be gone, and that would benefit seniors. People who sell their homes and realize large capital gains would pay no taxes.

And this may be the biggest advantage of all: goods and services that we buy all cost more due to IRS rules and regulations and the cost of compliance. With those costs gone, consumer prices could go down. Of course, about $250 billion per year in the cost of income tax preparation fees could go back into the economy or into savings.

It sounds so wonderful that one is hard pressed to imagine why there's no national clamor for the consumption tax. There must be a downside. Professor Eisner, calling both the flat tax and the sales tax "fads," warns that the tax might discourage consumption. He worries that this might lead people to—gasp!—save. Well, of course, if there's too much saving going on, no one is consuming and no taxes are being paid.

So would that drive home builders and automobile dealerships into bankruptcy? Unlikely. Remember, people will actually have more disposable income under the new system, and they'll be paying nothing for tax preparation. There will be billions of new dollars unleashed into the American economy. There would likely be a sharp upswing in savings accounts at first, but then realization would set in. Besides, there are some things people will buy no matter what.

Even so, the normally logical Marilyn vos Savant, in her *Parade* magazine column, says, "a switch to a national sales tax is so fundamental that the risk would be enormous. I, for one, would not take that risk."[27]

What about you? Would you be willing to take such a fundamental step, which might even require repeal of the Sixteenth Amendment? Imagine no income tax code, no IRS, no record keeping, no forms to fill out, and no need to hire a CPA.

Let's abolish the IRS now

During the Clinton administration, people began to suspect that the president of the United States was using a government agency to harass his political opponents. Such periodicals and organizations as *National Review,* the *American Spectator,* Oliver North's Freedom Alliance, the Heritage Foundation, Citizens Against Government Waste, and the National Rifle Association stepped forward to voice their suspicions.

These magazines and groups had one thing in common: they were all conservative. No liberal publications or think tanks came forward to complain.

The government agency in question was, of course, the Internal Revenue Service, and the harassment was in the form of audits, presumably ordered at the highest levels to hammer those with opposing viewpoints. If Mr. Clinton was indeed guilty of such tactics, then he, at least, derived some benefit from the IRS. It takes a liberal to love this agency.

Outside of Washington and except for some members of the tax-preparation industry, few people have any use for the IRS. Let's be clear. The IRS is vile, costly, oppressive, and evil. It can be used for contemptible purposes. It should be abolished. It is immoral to force the American taxpayer to shell out $250 billion in annual compliance costs. The income tax code should be abolished.

Either the flat tax or the national sales tax would be a major improvement, taking power away from government and placing it with the people, where it belongs. Of the two, the national sales tax seems fairer—and it would rid us once and for all of the income tax code and the IRS.

CHAPTER 4

Restore the American Family

We must declare that the traditional nuclear family, built around a husband and a wife acting as parents to their own children, is indispensable to the American way of life.

Liberals are playing havoc with the word "family." That's "family" in the traditional sense—a nuclear family—with a husband and a wife and children. There's a new meaning of the word, and it's much more permissive. If Heather has two mommies, that's a family. If Heather has a mommy, but Daddy has skipped town, that's a family, too. There's no such thing as a "broken home" anymore. The Left has redefined the concept of family to mean any group of people cohabitating under the same roof. So if a young woman should get pregnant and then tell her man to get lost, she doesn't really want a husband. She just wants a family.

The front-page headline in the *Dallas Morning News* makes it sound like a simple lifestyle choice: "Growing number of moms choosing to remain single." The story begins with the saga of an eighteen-year-old who got pregnant and wanted her baby. But she didn't want her guy. "I've seen too many marriages fail," the teenager said. "I just can't picture myself married."[1]

This type of situation is far from unusual in modern America. A 1999 study released by the U.S. Census Bureau made the trend lines perfectly clear: more and more females—from young girls to older women—are making a conscious decision to get pregnant and have babies, with no intention of staying with the father. Take a look at the numbers:[2]

Percent of never-married women who are mothers:

· Women who are white: 1982—6.7%; 1994—12.9%
· College graduates or higher: 1982—2.7%; 1994—6%
· Managers and professionals: 1982—3.1%; 1994—8.6%

Unmarried mothers by age group, 1994:

· Ages 15 to 19: 29%·
· Ages 20 to 24: 38%
· Ages 25 to 29: 16%
· Ages 30 to 44: 17%

Things have changed since the 1960s, when three out of five single women got hitched if they became pregnant. But when the bureau studied the period from 1990 to 1994, it found that less than one in four single pregnant women went on to marry the child's father. The statistics beg for answers to two very important questions: Why are these women deciding to forego marriage? And since many of them are poor, how do they manage to get by?

Both questions are answered by Amara Bachu, the Census Bureau demographer who authored the study. She said that parents simply don't force their daughters into marriage anymore. "The idea of shotgun weddings is gone," she said. "These women are often better off alone."[3] The fact that parents are often correct when they suspect the worst about the men who impregnated their daughters points to a very large part of the problem: America needs to raise the moral standards of its young men. Guys who want to engage in consequence-free sexual relations with girls have always been with us—but not in these numbers. Conversely, the moral standards of girls who freely give them what they want are also at an all-time low.

As to the second question—how do they make ends meet?—it is families, government programs, and private-sector social service agencies that make it all possible.

In the case of the eighteen-year-old in Dallas, there's an aunt and a cousin who help baby-sit, and a state pilot program for single moms called "Second Chance" to help pay for day care while the young mother attends classes at her high school. Ms. Bachu says, "The society is making provisions for them."[4] The *Dallas Morning News* story confirms it. It reports that while states are pushing to curtail welfare rolls, community organizations are popping up to make raising a baby in a single-parent home more viable.

In Dallas, for example, Parkland Hospital provides free transportation for pregnant women and young mothers in the "Mom Mobile"—seven vans that shuttle mostly single mothers to their clinics. Practically every city of any size in the nation has similar programs that provide women with transportation, maternity clothing, and even free prenatal care.

Let's be clear about what this means. While many segments of our society decry the rise in out-of-wedlock births, it is society itself that has become the enabling force. The more tolerant society so coveted by the Left has taken the stigma out of what used to be called "illegitimate births." Misplaced compassion has dictated that government programs must be implemented to take the place of the missing parent, usually the father. Beyond that, private groups spring up to fill in the blanks for any needs that young single mothers may have. Like it or not, society's message to young girls is clear: It's all right to get pregnant, and you don't need a husband and father.

Part of the problem stems from the times in which we live; part stems from the radical feminist agenda, which holds that men are unnecessary and that women should be masculinized—at least to some degree. The *Dallas Morning News* ran an editorial about *Time* magazine's cover story entitled "Who Needs a Husband?", concluding that women simply have more choices these days—"to work, marry or mother in any order."[5] But that attitude actually turns out to be mild.

The radicals seem to want to be rid of males, or at least to wipe away anything that points to a difference between males and females. They complain that vocational schools are biased, sending boys out to be automobile mechanics and girls to be cosmetologists. A group called the National Women's Law Center even petitioned the Education Department to see if such schools are in violation of Title IX.[6] The group is upset that 96 percent of the students who study cosmetology are girls whereas boys account for 92 percent of the students learning about car repair and 93 percent of the welding class. The Education Department agreed to "vigorously investigate." But whatever happened to logic? Doesn't it make sense that most of the kids learning about makeup would be girls, since almost 100 percent of the people who wear makeup (apart from movie and television performers) are women? Wouldn't most women prefer a man to crawl under a car to repair a transmission or to spend the day in a sweaty shop brandishing a welding torch? That's true, of course, but radical feminists are bound and determined to change those attitudes.

For attitude changing, there's no better venue than the public school system, where for decades boys and girls have been addressed as "boys and girls." To the radical feminists who have infiltrated the teaching profession, that's part of the problem. Rebecca Bigler is a University of Texas psychologist who studies "gender bias" in children. The idea behind her research was to determine if society's tradition of using gender as a group is contributing to gender stereotyping.[7] Just in case you're not following this, Professor Bigler was trying to prove that by calling boys "boys" and girls "girls," cosmetology classes across the nation are doomed to be stuffed with females.

One experiment called for control groups in which classrooms were set up to test her theory. In one classroom, the kids were addressed as "boys and girls." In another, the class was divided into "red and green" groups, and in the third, no descriptive term was used at all. After four weeks, the boys and girls (sorry about that) were given questionnaires and asked to rate certain occupations. Naturally, the kids who were gender-neutral were less likely to think that some jobs were "only" for men or women.[8]

One wonders exactly what Professor Bigler and her followers thought would happen in such an experiment. These kids were in the six-to-eleven age group—very impressionable—and suddenly, many of them had one of their self-identifiers, their gender, removed. This was a serious mind game that the professor was playing with the kids—a form of brainwashing. Imagine if such language as "Good morning, boys and girls" was banned from schoolrooms across America and all gender-specific terminology and roles were forbidden. By the time these kids reached high school, they would be totally confused and questioning their own sexuality.

Of course, by that time, the radicals would also have changed gender-specific pronouns such as "he," "him," "his," "she," and "her" so that only neutral pronouns could be used. Since those pronouns do not exist, someone would have to create them, changing the language and rendering millions of printed books obsolete. To the radicals, it would be worth it to achieve their blended unisex world in which men are just as likely to be a hairdresser as a test pilot.

While all this is going on—more women "deciding" to have babies on their own, and radical feminists attempting to do away with gender and males in general—what is the government doing to promote the American family? Not much.

Child care: government taking over the role of parents

"No government program can ever replace the love, warmth and support of a family. But as a society, we can make it a whole lot easier for families to be strong." An excellent quote that sounds very family-friendly. Unfortunately, the person who made that statement was, at the very same time, proposing a major government intrusion into the area of child care.

The comment, made by Vice President Al Gore during the latter stages of the 2000 presidential campaign, was part of an overall program in which the vice president was promising a ten-year, $8 billion program designed to get the states to improve their supervision of child care facilities. The other part of his program was $30 billion in tax incentives to working parents who needed day care services.[9]

Gore appeared alongside talk show host and single lesbian mother Rosie O'Donnell to promote the plan, which stipulated much federal government oversight, such as background checks, mandatory trailing, and surprise inspections of day care centers. In short, Mr. Gore's plan was a $38 billion federal government takeover of the child care industry.

You might think that Governor George W. Bush fired back with some lofty rhetoric about how the government shouldn't try to take the place of parents or meddle in what should be a private child care industry. He didn't. He answered through his spokesman, Ari Fleischer, that he has worked in Texas to double low-income child care funding.[10]

Most politicians these days seem to fall right in line with Mr. Gore and Mr. Bush. They are willing to talk about "the love and warmth" of a family as Mr. Gore did—but in their unbridled support of child care programs, they are encouraging young parents to let someone else, often the government, raise their kids. Children who spend eight to ten hours a day in the care of a third party will almost certainly develop differently than if they are raised in a more traditional manner with a mother staying home to take care of them. But is that really a bad thing for children?

Common sense tells us that a biological mother who has carried her child for nine months, given birth, and in many cases even breast-fed him should be the person who takes care of him during the formative years. In order for that to happen, a traditional nuclear family has to be in place. For a new mom to stay home with her baby, she needs a husband who goes to work and brings home enough money to pay the rent and put food on the table.

The problem is that in today's economy, two paychecks are required for most young couples to survive. But that's only one of the forces at work. The other force is political correctness—radical feminists and other liberals who tell a young mother that she doesn't really need a husband or a father for her baby. She ought to put her own happiness first. If the feminists are correct— if the only thing that matters is a young woman's happiness—then by all means, day care is a wonderful thing. But for just a moment, let's put the interests of the baby first and take a look at a few facts.

According to one of the country's most respected researchers in the area of child care, the first three years of a baby's life are all-important. Burton L. White, Ph.D, has spent more than four decades studying how infants develop. He started the Missouri New Parents as Teachers Program, directed the Center for Parent Education in Newton, Massachusetts, and wrote two books on the art of parenting. Among his findings:[11]

- During a child's first three years, he *must* find at least one older person to make a solid commitment to him in order to survive.
- For bonding, a baby needs a couple of years of solid interaction with at least one person.
- Without that interaction, a baby will *not* become a normal adult.

Dr. White believes that children from weak families start to fall back while children from strong families move ahead of the national average—and that by the third birthday, the gap cannot be closed.

"If you're going to have a baby and you want him or her to have the best start in life, somebody has to put in the time," says Dr. White. "And if you feel you can't put much time into the life of a baby, you shouldn't have a baby."[12] Dr. White is "totally convinced"—after decades of study—that no one can do the job of raising a child like a family can.

A more recent study from a team of researchers at Columbia University has produced similar results.[13] The Columbia study shows that the children of mothers who take full-time jobs before their babies are nine months old have poorer mental and verbal development at age three than those kids whose moms stay home to raise them.[14] This research—like that of Dr. White—found that the age of three is key. When they measured the congnitive and verbal development of kids at various ages, the scores were lower for three-year-olds whose moms worked thirty hours per week or more before the child was nine months old.

The study didn't find any significant problem with children whose moms worked less than thirty hours, and it found that having a very "sensitive mother" who's responsive to the child also lessened the effects. But mitigating factors aside, the study showed once again that it's best for mothers to stay home with the babies. That seemed to disturb one of the authors of the study, Jeanne Brooks-Gunn, who was quick to come to the defense of working mothers: "There are effects, but they are not huge effects," she said. "Your child's life will not be ruined."[15]

Like Vice President Gore, Brooks-Gunn sees a solution in government intervention: "Western European countries have much more generous family-leave policies, reflecting people's concerns about the well-being of children," she said. "We can do better in this country by taking results such as ours and not using them to say women shouldn't be working and instead ask what can work best for families in America so that mothers can work fewer hours when their children are younger."[16]

Something is dreadfully wrong with this picture. Both logic and empirical studies tell us that our country would be far better off if young mothers stayed home with their babies at least until the age of three. And yet political leaders and academics who constantly seek more government intervention never seem to understand that government is a big part of the problem.

The marriage penalty: a government incentive to shack up

Diane Ollis, a bride-to-be and op-ed writer for the *Austin American-Statesman,* had some great lines in a column she wrote after becoming engaged. "Nowhere in the extant catalog of advice to brides do they tell you that when it comes to 'taking' a spouse, the IRS is right there in the receiving line," she wrote. And then, "The bottom line: The wages of (living in) sin are taxed at a lower rate." [17]

Ms. Ollis was right on the money. Her lament was even the subject of a much earlier episode of the old ABC-TV series *Love, American Style,* in which a retired couple decided to "live in sin" rather than get married, because it would cost them too much in taxes to actually tie the knot.

It's all because of a little quirk in the income tax code known as the "marriage penalty"—perhaps the number-one government incentive for people not to get married. The marriage penalty occurs because of our progressive tax system. A man and a woman who each have an income often fall into lower tax brackets individually than they would if all their earnings were lumped together into a single filing. Therein lies the problem: if a couple in this situation gets married, it will cost them a lot of money in extra taxes. So why not just live together? Millions of people are going the "shack up" route.

There really isn't a way to smooth out our current system of taxation so that everything is fair between married couples and singles, even though government has been tampering with the situation for years. Look at the way things were prior to 1948, when only individuals were taxed. In those days, a husband and wife who each earned $30,000 per year would pay considerably less taxes than a married couple in which the husband made $60,000 and the wife stayed home. [18] In addition to that, couples could lower taxes by assigning all the investment income to the lower-earning spouse. The government didn't like that at all, so in 1948, the Congress passed a law calling for joint returns in which a married couple would pay twice as much tax as a single person would pay on half the income. [19]

But this benefited wealthier married couples, because it meant that they were paying at a lower rate. For example, that married couple where the man makes $60,000 and his wife isn't working would pay double the tax of a single earner making $30,000. But a single person making $60,000 would be in a higher bracket and so would pay more. Confusing, huh?

The public was not happy and demanded changes, which came about in 1969. That's when the tax code was changed and the marriage penalty was born. Ever since then, the arguments have been going strong on whether to end it, how to end it, and whom it hurts or helps the most.

Columnist Joan Beck of the *Chicago Tribune* writes that more than 20 million married couples are hit by the penalty and it costs them about $1,400 in additional taxes over what they would have paid if they'd just shacked up. Because of that, she says, the government should get out of the business of taxing marriage: "It is immoral. It is unfair. It is stupid. It is bad social policy. And the direct hit on their paychecks keeps reminding millions of couples just how inept and unfair Congress and the IRS are."[20]

There have been many attempts to abolish the marriage penalty. In 2000, as Al Gore and George W. Bush were battling for the White House, the Republicans in Congress put together a plan that would have amounted to an end to the penalty and a big tax cut for married people. President Bill Clinton issued a written statement saying he'd veto the bill because it was "one part of a costly, poorly targeted and regressive tax plan promoted by Republicans" that ignored more pressing financial priorities and other tax cuts aimed at the middle class.[21]

Senator Edward M. Kennedy agreed with the president that the whole idea of cutting taxes and promoting marriage was just another costly Republican scheme: "Once again, our Republican friends are using an attractive label like the marriage penalty as a cover for unjustified tax breaks for the wealthy, and at the expense of urgently needed priorities like prescription drug coverage for our senior citizens."[22]

Just so you'll know what President Clinton and Senator Kennedy were against, here's what the Republican bill would have accomplished:[23]

- Tax brackets: The bill would have expanded the lowest 15 percent income tax bracket for married couples until it equaled twice the current corresponding bracket for single taxpayers. If it had been in effect in 2000, it would have expanded the 15 percent bracket for married couples from $43,850 to $52,500, meaning that less of their money would have been taxed at the next-highest, 28 percent level.
- Standard deduction: For married couples who did not itemize, the standard tax deduction would have risen to be equal to that of two single people. That would have increased the standard deduction from $7,350 to $8,800.
- Earned income tax credit: The bill would have raised by $2,000 the income limit for low-income families who claimed the earned income tax credit. Under existing law, the credit phases out completely for families earning above $30,850.
- Alternative minimum tax: The bill would have extended through

2004 a current exemption from the complex alternative minimum tax for married couples who claimed personal credits, such as the $500 per child tax credit and education credits.

The legislation reached Bill Clinton's desk in August, and he vetoed it.

In his weekly radio address, Mr. Clinton accused the Republicans of "advancing a series of tax giveaways." In a letter to Congress, the president charged that the marriage penalty bill, along with some other tax-cutting items that were coming out of the House Ways and Means Committee, would "provide about as much benefit to the top 1 percent of Americans as to the bottom 80 percent combined."[24]

In truth, marriage penalty relief is popular, and so the Democrats were being as careful as they could, proposing some alternative legislation so that they could say they supported a marriage penalty relief bill, and sticking hard to their tried-and-true mantra decrying tax breaks for "the wealthiest 1 percent."

The argument over the penalty is not likely to go away anytime soon, according to the Concord Coalition. "Politically, the marriage penalty is an attractive issue because it unites cultural conservatives with the anti-tax caucus," the organization states on its web site. "While the latter appreciate the appeal of a tax cut, cultural conservatives relish the opportunity to advance a 'family values' agenda by defending the institution of marriage."[25]

No matter how popular the idea of eliminating the penalty may be, and no matter how family-friendly it may be, getting it done is another matter. The government doesn't want to give up the estimated $30 billion[26] that is brought in under the current system each year. About 25 million couples actually get a marriage "bonus" of about $1,300 per couple.[27] And last but not least, there is no perfect way to fix it under the current tax code.

The National Center for Policy Analysis (NCPA) points out that just about any solution is likely to increase complexity and raise many questions about cost and fairness.[28] While it's not necessary to remove the family as the basic unit of taxation to eliminate the penalty, the NCPA says Congress would have to allow couples the option of filing as singles or jointly. And that would mean passing new rules about dividing joint income such as interest and dividends, and allocation of itemized deductions such as dependents and mortgage interest.[29]

Reaching the obvious conclusion, the NCPA's Bruce Bartlett writes: "A better solution to further tinkering with the tax code would be a flat tax or a national retail sales tax. By eliminating progressivity, they get at the root of the marriage penalty."[30]

But no one in Congress is suggesting that approach. Instead, one high-profile proposal is that of Representative Gerald "Jerry" Weller, R-Ill., and Representative David McIntosh, R-Ind. Weller's "The Marriage Tax Penalty

Elimination Act" would use the same band-aid approach that was vetoed by Bill Clinton: increasing the size of joint filer tax brackets and the standard deduction for joint filers. The Joint Committee on Taxation estimates that the Weller proposal would cost about $32 billion per year.[31] In June 2002, Republicans actually pushed through a bill that would allow couples who do not itemize to receive the same deduction as two single people. The bill passed 271–142, with some Democrats crossing party lines in an election year, but Senate Majority Leader Tom Daschle showed no inclination to bring it to the Senate floor.[32]

Marriage penalty relief remains unlikely. The government won't give up the income that the marriage penalty provides, Democrats will continue to play the class-envy card, and those who are serious about changing the tax code will find that their tinkering is making things more complex than ever.

Until we actually implement a simple flat tax or a national sales tax, those blushing new brides will continue to calculate the high cost of marriage and may consider the age-old remedy that government can't provide. They'll simply shack up.

Let's do something to promote traditional families

It's no wonder that the traditional American family is in trouble. Women are deciding to have kids without a husband and father; governmental and private-sector programs enable and even encourage single parenthood; child care programs take away the parental relationship that very young children should have; and the government can't even figure out a way to tax couples without encouraging them to live together out of wedlock.

What a mess.

And yet, when government steps in to save the day, it almost always makes things worse. In 1999, with Bill Clinton still in the White House, the House of Representatives passed a bill known as the "Fathers Count Act"— a name that literally pointed out the fact that traditional families are crumbling. But in spite of the obvious good intent of the bill, there was much hand-wringing and fighting over the contents of the legislation.

The intent of the bill was to promote fatherhood in low-income areas by providing more job training and job opportunities to help men meet their responsibilities to their wives and children. But before the vote was taken, members of the House argued vehemently about (of all things) separation of church and state.[33]

One of the bill's co-sponsors, Representative Nancy Johnson, R-Conn., said that nearly 20 million children live without fathers, increasing their chances of school failure, drug addiction, delinquency, and crime. But that wasn't as important to those who opposed the bill as the idea that money might be funneled through a house of worship. Representative Chet Edwards, D-Tex., one of 93 House members to vote against the bill, said it "obliterates" the constitutional wall between church and state. Edwards' amendment would have allowed money to go to church-affiliated groups, but not directly to what he called "pervasively sectarian" groups. The amendment failed 238–184.[34]

Of course, the National Organization for Women (NOW) chimed in, complaining that money for noncustodial parents (usually men) would undermine support for custodial parents (usually women). What really got the NOW people upset was that the legislation intended to promote the institution of marriage in all its programs. Patricia Ireland was irate: "Pressuring a poor woman to marry the father of her children—without regard to his character—could do great harm," she said. "Congress is telling women that the way to get out of poverty is to find a husband."[35]

Edwards' amendment and Ireland's tantrum point out that even when Congress tries to do something right to promote families, there will always be those distracters who will find the monkey wrench and throw it in.

The same thing happened when President Bush tried to support marriage and families. Mr. Bush asked Congress to set aside $100 million for some programs designed to see if single mothers on welfare could be persuaded to marry. After all, if single moms married their kids' dads, or even some other man, the government and taxpayers would stand to save a lot of welfare money and the kids would have the benefit of a father. The Left went berserk.

"The news reports of the President's plan note how some officials are uncomfortable about 'putting government that deeply into people's lives.' I am, too," wrote Dr. Sheron C. Patterson, senior pastor of St. Paul United Methodist Church in downtown Dallas. She pointed out that middle-class single moms who could take care of their children weren't targeted, nor were celebrity single moms. She said, "Mr. Bush's plan to encourage the poor to marry must not become an experiment that our government launches to prove a theory. We are humans, not experimental animals."[36]

She made some good points. If marriage and parenthood are good for poor people, why not for everyone? But the president's point was well taken, too. Those middle-class moms and celebrities are not such a drag on the welfare system as the poor women are, so if marriage is to be promoted, that would be the logical place to start.

Again, though, we find that when government makes an attempt to do something positive to promote marriage and family, it almost always arouses the ire of those who think government's butting in is worse than kids growing up with no father. So is there something the government should do? How about this: instead of promoting marriage and fatherhood, what if the child's rights were put at the forefront? What if there were severe penalties for creating a human being and then abandoning it?

As a matter of fact, there are laws in place against deadbeats—mostly fathers—who don't lift a finger to help raise the children they created. But the problem with those laws is that smart operators can always stay a step ahead of the courts. Deadbeats who know how to work the system move from state to state, keeping their whereabouts as secret as possible, and can avoid paying child support indefinitely. In one recent case, a court said "enough" and made a long-overdue ruling. As you might expect, the Left—and some of the Right—was not impressed.

The case is that of David Oakley of Manitowoc, Wisconsin, a hardcore deadbeat father. In 2001, at the age of thirty-four, Oakley already had fathered nine children with four women and had racked up $25,000 in back child support that, for whatever reason, he wasn't paying. Two years earlier, Judge Fred Hazlewood read the riot act to Oakley: five years probation, on the condition that he not create any more kids during the probation period. If he did, he would have to show the court that he had the financial wherewithal to take care of all the kids he had created—or he would go to prison.

Oakley filed an appeal to Wisconsin's top court—and he lost. Of the seven justices on the Wisconsin Supreme Court, the four men supported Judge Hazlewood's ruling, while the three women opposed it. Justice Ann Walsh Bradley wrote in her dissent that the right to have children is so basic that it should apply even to people on probation.

Columnist Leonard Pitts of the *Miami Herald* wrote about the case, saying that "irresponsible" doesn't begin to describe Oakley—but he agreed with Justice Bradley: "To procreate or not is one of the most fundamentally intimate questions that human beings face. And while it might be tempting to look the other way as that decision is taken out of the hands of a cavalier deadbeat, we ought to worry about what comes next."[37] Of course, the American Civil Liberties Union called the decision "unconstitutional."

But why would it be unconstitutional? Why did Mr. Pitts believe that the state of Wisconsin was heading down the "proverbial slippery slope"? It's because of the view on the Left that the rights of people who have been around for a few years, or even for a few months, take precedence over the rights of those people who are not yet born or just barely born. How else could you explain it?

The Constitution doesn't specifically spell out a right to create children, just as it doesn't spell out a lot of rights that we all assume we have. And yet, there are many precedents that we have put into place that create limits—or place parameters—on those rights. For example, the Constitution doesn't specifically mention our "right to fish," yet most of us would say that we have that right. However, many states require a fishing license, and if you fish without one, you could face a fine or jail time. The same thing is true for hunting, driving, cutting hair, and owning a dog. All of these things are legal, and yet they all require a license and in some cases they require training.

How much more profound is creating a human life? And what does society require for that to take place? Nothing. Nothing at all. Yet it seems that, with all this freedom to procreate, should come some modicum of responsibility.

Let's be perfectly clear. It would be difficult—and almost certainly unconstitutional—to attempt to require a license for making babies. But once that child is born, it also has rights, and that's why we, as a society, do not have to let deadbeat parents get away with taking no responsibility for the well-being of that child.

Let's pass laws that require any pregnant woman or single mother who wants government assistance to name the father. Today's DNA technology gives us assurance beyond a reasonable doubt that the wrong man will not be fingered. Following DNA testing, the government should put the squeeze on any David Oakleys who try to get out of supporting their own children until the kids are at least eighteen.

If the deadbeat dad (or mom; we don't discriminate here) is able-bodied but can't or won't support his own kids, he goes to prison and the mother gets the welfare. But any woman who won't name the scoundrel who impregnated her doesn't deserve taxpayer support. She doesn't deserve help from the private sector, either, but in such a case, charitable organizations would certainly be there to help the child.

The simple fact is that under these conditions, women who are in desperate need of government assistance would almost certainly provide the name of the father and swear out a complaint. The father would then be forced to provide financial aid or go to jail. After a while, the word would be out: make a baby and you're making a big problem for yourself for at least eighteen years. This might cause a small surge in the abortion rate, but more likely, it would result in more contraception being used, meaning fewer out-of-wedlock births.

It might even result in more traditional families. Imagine a United States in which deadbeat dads are caught and forced to support their own kids. Think about a system in which welfare incentives for women to get pregnant with no husband have been removed. Consider the implications of a family-friendly, simple tax system that contains no financial penalty for being married. Our government has the ability to implement all these things.

Other than that, there is very little that government can do. The rest is up to us, as a society, to turn the situation around. It's the people, not the government, who can return the stigma to out-of-wedlock births. Only the people can stop the glorification of celebrities who lead decadent lives both on and off the screen. Only parents can use their own example to teach their kids how to become parents.

The traditional American family is slowly but surely fading away. Certain forces, including radical feminism, the radical homosexual agenda, the tolerance movement, our corrupt popular culture, and an enabling welfare state have been working for years to bring it down. If we believe the family is still essential, and if we want to preserve it, there is much work to be done. But the time to do it is now, for the hour is late.

CHAPTER 5

Foster an American Culture

We must declare that America is one nation, united, arising from a "melting pot" with a culture uniquely its own.

On June 10, 2002, a police lieutenant in Corpus Christi, Texas, used a power saw to slice apart the handgun that was used to murder the young singer Selena. Once the gun was cut up into more than a dozen pieces, it was dumped into Corpus Christi Bay, about a half-mile from shore. Some scholars felt that a cultural artifact had been destroyed. "You have literally the smoking gun," said Manuel Pena, an ethnomusicologist at Fresno State, "the weapon that killed the symbol of Tejano pride."[1]

Far more interesting than the basic story about disposing of the gun is the tangential mention of Selena not as a person or an entertainer of note but as a symbol of a certain culture. It's hard to imagine a singer such as Tammy Wynette or Willie Nelson being singled out as "the symbol of Anglo pride." In fact, if that were to be done, it would be decried as racist. But in today's multicultural society, cultural hooks are very important. Go back a couple of decades and see if you can find the term "ethnomusicologist."

Even major corporations are getting into the act. A recent Food Marketing Institute workshop, held in Chicago, focused on multicultural marketing in supermarkets. The workshop was based on a study by the Coca-Cola Retailing Research Council of North America that predicts a major shift in demographics by the year 2040. The study indicates that by that time, the nation's minority population—including Hispanics, blacks, and Asians—will have grown from 32 percent to 50 percent of the population.[2]

The supermarket people were told that the changing demographics must be accompanied by changes in their grocery stores. Terry Soto, a marketing executive from Burbank who helped conduct the study, told the group to think like their ethnic customers in order to connect with them. "The language in which you choose to communicate will determine whether or not you make that connection," said Soto. "Accept that you are creating the foundation for a whole generation of ethnic supermarket professionals."[3]

Accept for the moment that the United States is creating a whole new foundation. What exactly are we creating? When our nation was established, it was based on the idea of a "melting pot"—a salad bowl approach that mixed and mingled a lot of different people, cultures, and languages but always resulted in a sum that was greater than its parts. The Founding Fathers believed so strongly in the melting pot that the concept was digested into the Latin phrase "*e pluribus unum*," meaning "out of many, one." To this day, the phrase—now all but meaningless—still appears on our coinage.

The fact is that we are headed in the direction of an enclave society where the various "peoples" of the United States migrate to areas that speak their particular language and practice their particular culture. Even that isn't enough. Immigrants who come from various parts of the world now expect the areas where they settle in America to adapt to their languages and customs, just as the supermarket people were instructed to do.

Assimilation—the opposite of multiculturalism—is no longer the goal. Multiculturalists now inhabit the halls of government from council chambers to the statehouse to the highest levels of all three branches of our federal system. Multiculturalism permeates our schools from kindergarten through high school to college and graduate school. It has become a self-sustaining force; the more it succeeds in grabbing a foothold, the more its power multiplies.

The power of multiculturalism is derived from the principles of political correctness. Some years ago, multiculturalism was deemed "PC" as part of the "diversity" and "tolerance" movement—mostly emanating from elite college campuses. Once it became "racist" to oppose the multicultural movement, anyone who dared to speak out against it could be demonized, usually by references to Hitler or Nazi Germany. And so multiculturalism is now fully embraced by educators and reluctantly accepted by many politicians and individuals who wish to avoid the wrath of the PC elitists.

Is the concept merely an agent for change? Or is it dangerous?

Author Paul Craig Roberts is blunt about it. He says it's very dangerous: "Countries have armies in order to prevent their being overrun by foreigners who would displace their language, destroy their cultural and communal integrity, and economically exploit the overrun population."[4] Dr. Roberts says that immigration policy has, for all practical purposes, defeated United States defense policy. He points out that liberal politicians have gone so far as to create incentives for immigrants not to assimilate.

We'll take Dr. Roberts' statement a step further. It's not just the Left that encourages cultural separation these days. Now that anyone who isn't on the multicultural bandwagon is branded a racist, and now that the failure of immigration policy has come home to roost, even conservative politicians are ready and willing to capitulate.

Many, if not most, of our elected officials seem to believe that the multicultural train has left the station. In their minds, it's a matter of getting on board that train (and being reelected) or standing on the tracks and getting steamrolled.

But Dr. Roberts, mentioning that Americans of European descent will be in the minority no later than 2050 and will have lost control of their own political destiny, asks a chilling question: "How does this differ from being overrun by the Chinese army?"[5]

Glenn Spencer, the president of a California-based nonprofit group called "Voices of Citizens Together," was quoted in an internet column saying he believes that Mexican and U.S. policies are leading to an eventual breakup of the United States. Spencer says the aim is to create a new state that would combine the southwestern United States with northern Mexico for eventual reunification with Mexico. The same article quotes Armando Navarro, a professor at the University of California at Riverside, who believes it's possible—if current demographic and social trends continue.[6]

And what about Muslims? Right now, there are about 15 million Muslims living in Europe; in fact, Muslims make up almost 10 percent of the Dutch population. British journalist Roger Scruton asks the question—will they assimilate? Not likely. Mr. Scruton writes about "a clash of civilizations" that's becoming a reality in many European nations, including Britain, Germany, the Netherlands, and especially France, where Muslim immigration was seen as the enabling factor in the rise of the far-Right politician Jean-Marie Le Pen.[7] Le Pen lost to Chirac in France, but he and other politicians like Pim Fortuyn in the Netherlands have at least given the issue a high profile, which isn't an easy thing to do in some countries.

Part of the problem in Europe is that social censorship is, if anything, worse than it is in the United States. The European Union (EU) is even considering making racism and xenophobia outright crimes, which would shut down all discussion on the matter.[8] Le Pen was branded a racist and faced massive demonstrations, and Fortuyn was assassinated for his beliefs.

There is a Muslim population in the United States as well, and even here, it's hard to imagine any type of wholesale assimilation. Since the Muslim culture is not just ethnic but is largely religious in nature, Muslims normally view American culture as sinful in the eyes of Allah. How, then, could they possibly assimilate? It may simply be impossible for Islam, with its views on women's rights and anything modern, to mix with Western culture at all. To many in the Islamic word—including those who attacked the United States on 9/11—we are the "infidels." Yet ask yourself if any American politician is willing to close our borders to Muslim immigration, even during the War on Terrorism.

There aren't many who will risk being called "intolerant" or "racist."

What is multiculturalism?

As with so many good words, the term "multiculturalism" has been co-opted by the Left, which seeks to define it this way: "Multiculturalism is an acceptance of and an appreciation for other cultures and other ways of life." That's how school administrators will defend it when they're saturating every classroom from algebra to zoology with it.

However, the education and diversity communities are using words to disguise the true meaning of the term. We have a different reading of what multiculturalism has become: "Multiculturalism is the irrational acceptance of all other cultures as equal to or superior to our own."

Understand that there is a difference between multiculturalism and natural diversity. When not corrupted for political purposes, diversity is a normal thing that occurs naturally in any growing society. Diversity, tossed into the melting pot, creates a unified society, but like oil and water, multiculturalism will not allow for mixing. Under this type of system, various cultures emerge from the pot still separate and no assimilation takes place.

But with multiculturalists, the concept goes even beyond cultural separatism. They see it as a way to bring up a litany of complaints against Western civilization and get those complaints into a classroom setting so that they can be taught to generations of American students. William E. Simon, president of the John M. Olin Foundation, puts it bluntly: "Multiculturalism . . . is thus more concerned with promoting domestic grievances than in studying the languages, history and institutions of other civilizations—which is why I suggested that such courses are largely worthless from a genuine academic standpoint." [9]

Any careful analysis of the concept, as practiced in public schools, colleges, governments, and even some companies across the United States, reveals few if any redeeming features. Multiculturalism teaches our children that anything is all right if it's part of a culture. Any culture, that is, except Western civilization.

Former Vice President Dan Quayle discussed this very thing in a speech to the Des Moines (Iowa) Christian School. The vice president told his audience that some people would have our children believe that the American story is not based on heroism and achievement, but rather on racism, sexism, imperialism, and oppression.[10]

Mr. Quayle went into detail on three concerns that he called "dangers" of multiculturalism:[11]

· It threatens to destroy our national memory through distortion and revision.
· [It promotes] the denigration of Western culture, which is the source of the ideas behind America's founding.
· It seeks to turn America into a nation of groups instead of a nation of individuals.

Toward the end of his speech, the former vice president quoted Professor Thomas Sowell, who noted several places around the globe where multiculturalism had already been tried: Yugoslavia, Lebanon, Sri Lanka, Northern Ireland, Azerbaijan—or wherever group identity has been promoted.[12] All of those places have seen constant unrest, if not out-and-out hostilities.

The United States is headed in that direction. The term "American" has largely been replaced by a multitude of hyphenations: African-American, Native-American, Mexican-American, Chinese-American, and so on. If these modifiers are ever to be discarded, major changes will have to take place in our schools, and government regulations that encourage separatism will have to be repealed.

The many faces of multiculturalism

The United States saw an unprecedented surge in patriotism following the tragic events of 9/11, but that didn't mean that the multiculturalists were out of business. When the New York Fire Department made plans to commission a memorial based on a famous photo taken by Tom Franklin of *The Record* of Hackensack, it decided to tamper with history.

The photo showed three firemen—all white—raising a United States flag. Unfortunately, in today's society, a statue of three white men would not be PC, and so the department changed the ethnicities of two of the men so that one would be black and one Hispanic.[13] The department felt that such a change would more accurately reflect the composition of the NYFD, which is 2.7 percent black and 3.2 percent Hispanic. Conservative pundits had a field day.

Columnist Kathleen Parker retracted her earlier statement that political correctness had died after the attack on America. Symbolism over substance, she wrote, was back in style: "I'm all for symbolism. But I love truth more. And the problem with changing the races of the men who were photographed raising the flag is that it's not true. It's not factual. It didn't happen that way."[14]

And from Ann Coulter: "We should probably be relieved it's not going to be a statue of three Muslims raising the flag."[15]

The two columnists made their points well. In these days when Christopher Columbus, George Washington, and James Madison are considered villains by multiculturalists, truth was not about to get in the way of building a monument that "looks like America"—or in this case, the New York Fire Department.

In a similar manner, multiculturalists enjoy trashing the great traditions of Western civilization and replacing them with the traditions of some other culture. A few years ago, at Thanksgiving time, the *Wall Street Journal* noted on its editorial page that the web site of the nation's largest teachers' union, the National Education Association (NEA), was promoting a holiday. But instead of commemorating Thanksgiving, the NEA was touting "Human Rights Day," saying that the nation will note human rights transgressions with various events across the country.[16] "In this mindset," the *Journal* said, "one meditates about sweatshop horror stories ... and Thanksgiving is merely a prelude to the coming Indian genocide."[17]

If it seems somewhat out of the mainstream for the Left to replace Thanksgiving with Human Rights Day, consider the strange case of Kwanzaa—multiculturalists' answer to Christmas.

Kwanzaa, meaning something like "fresh fruits of harvest" in Swahili, is not a long-standing holiday that's based on traditions that have built up over the centuries; Kwanzaa was simply invented in 1966 by a black radical named Ronald Everett. Since then, many people have embraced the new "holiday." Check out any appointment calendar and you'll find it duly noted on December 26 that "Kwanzaa begins." Stroll through your local card and party store and you'll find Kwanzaa items on the shelves.

You can even look it up in the *World Book Encyclopedia,* where you'll find an article written by "a black cultural leader" that explains all about Kwanzaa. Those who celebrate the holiday will often explain that it's not just for African-Americans. They're not telling the whole story; in fact, it's doubtful that everyone who celebrates Kwanzaa really knows its origins. Most stories about Ronald McKinley Everett refer to him as Dr. Maulana Karenga and rarely examine his past. But in recent years, much of the Everett/Karenga story has been told in a few print exposés and in op-ed columns.

Forget the notion that Kwanzaa is a holiday for all people. Dr. Karenga states that he created it at the height of the black liberation movement as part of a "re-Africanization Process—a going back to black."[18] Dr. Karenga, still just "Ron Everett" at the time, was heavily involved in the black power movement. He started an organization called US—"United Slaves"—as a violent rival to the Black Panthers. Everett and his organization became dupes of the FBI, which wanted to use radical groups such as the United Slaves to split and discredit the Left.

He dropped the "Everett" name and adopted the Swahili one, which means "master teacher," shaved his head, and began wearing traditional African clothing. US members, similarly attired, and often encouraged by the FBI, clashed with the Panthers over which group would control the new Afro-American Studies Center at UCLA.[19] There were incidents involving beatings and shootings, including one in 1969 in which two US members shot and killed two Black Panthers.[20]

Dr. Karenga had other run-ins with the law, including charges that he abused women. In 1971, he was convicted of assaulting two female members of US, and he served time in prison. A *Los Angeles Times* snippet describes the torture of the women as involving a hot soldering iron placed in the mouth of one, while the other's toe was mashed in a vise.[21]

For his part, Dr. Karenga insists that he is the victim in all this; he was quoted in the *Dallas Morning News:* "All the negative charges are in fact disinformation and frame-ups by the FBI and local and national police."[22] Members of the multicultural community either believe his denials, or they don't care. But they have to face the fact that they are accepting the teachings of a man whose organization—and who personally—committed heinous crimes against members of his own race.

So what happened to Dr. Maulana Karenga after he served his time in prison? Some nine years after Kwanzaa was invented, he decided to moderate his views and become a Marxist.[23] In 1979, he was hired to run the Black Studies Department at Cal State Long Beach, in all likelihood the first ex-con to hold such a position. His biography, appearing on a web site called "Profiles in Black," says that he is also chair of "the President's [Clinton] Task Force on Multicultural Education and Campus Diversity" at Cal State Long Beach and director of the "Kawaida Institute of Pan-African Studies." It also lists him as chairman of "Operation Us" (sound familiar?), which the site says means "black people"—so named to stress the communitarian focus of his philosophy, Kawaida, which is an ongoing synthesis of the best of African thought and practice.[24]

The extensive bio made it apparent that Dr. Karenga is enamored with all things African—though it never once mentions anything about United Slaves, or shootings, or the torture of women, or prison time. The militant past of the creator is now ignored in favor of the so-called seven principles of Nguza Saba, principles such as unity, family, and self-determination that could have come from Bill Bennett's *Book of Virtues,* although Bennett would not likely approve of the collectivist tone of the principles.

Dr. Karenga does his part to promote the holiday and blur his personal history. In December, he goes on an annual "Kwanzaa circuit" of speeches and appearances. And he writes. Among his writings are many articles and ten books, mostly concerning black studies, and his commentaries on ancient Egyptian texts. And remember that little article in the *World Book Encyclopedia* that legitimized Dr. Karenga as a "black cultural leader"? You guessed it—he wrote the article himself.

Toward the end of his presidency, Bill Clinton issued a formal proclamation in support of Kwanzaa. Ann Coulter described the announcement as beginning with "some claptrap about preserving 'what we value of our past' and Kwanzaa being a 'wonderful example' with its 'focus on the values that have sustained African-Americans through the centuries.'"[25] Either the president of the United States had not done his homework, or he really believed in what Coulter called "a lunatic blend of schmaltzy sixties rhetoric, black racism, and Marxism."[26]

More likely than that, President Clinton simply believed in multiculturalism, which, to many politicians, simply means embracing other cultures in return for votes.

Multiculturalism goes to school

Many of the true believers in the multiculturalism movement are connected in one way or the other with our education system. The debate on campuses ranges from the ridiculous (discontinuing the use of certain names for sports mascots) to the deadly serious (changing the curriculum to reflect a whole new set of values).

Names such as Indians, Braves, Chiefs, and Seminoles have been used for decades, ostensibly because sports teams want names that reflect power and determination. Of all the American Indian names that come to mind, only one—"Redskins"—carries much of a derogatory connotation. And yet one of the principles of multiculturalism—sensitivity to other cultures—is being violated through the use of such names.

And so, in 2000, the United States Commission on Civil Rights recommended that all non-Indian schools and colleges abandon Indian team mascots so that no one would be offended.[27] Richard Allen, a policy analyst with the Oklahoma-based Cherokee Nation, complained that no human being should be portrayed as a mascot, and he pointed out that it's okay to use the name "Cowboys" because that's an occupation.[28]

Some schools and colleges, such as Stanford, have already made the change, with Stanford dropping the nickname "Indians" in favor of "Cardinal." In February 2002, students at the University of Northern Colorado decided to make the point by calling their intramural basketball team the "Fighting Whites,"[29] but that produced only brief publicity and little if any reaction from the white community.

But what about the real dangers of multiculturalism—the movement to revise history, change reading lists, and make multicultural classes a requirement for graduation? On the campuses themselves, the debate has been raging for years, but the multiculturalists are winning, with well over half the nation's colleges now having such requirements.

A long article in the *Dallas Morning News* made it quite apparent that the drive toward a multicultural curriculum has nothing to do with showcasing the superiority of Western culture and everything to do with changing the attitudes of students. Those who enter a class believing that America is a wonderful place to live—even for minorities—may leave the class with a new "understanding" that racism is still rampant in our society.

At Temple University, Dr. Molefi Asanta, chairman of the school's African-American Studies Department, called for more specific courses on the origins of racism: "My sense is that most universities do not want to make white American students uncomfortable, so they don't want to really deal with the issue of racism."[30] Other professors quoted in the article had similar views. Dr. Lisa Garza was teaching a class at Texas Women's University entitled "Culture, Inequality, and Self." She explained that a lot of white Americans have to be forced to think about racism. Dr. Paul Parrish, an English professor at Texas A&M, said that students who take an African-American literature course or a course on contemporary Russia might come out of the class "never looking at the world the same again." And at the University of Texas, journalism professor Dr. Wayne Danielson led a committee that created a multicultural proposal, saying that it would make the country "a more tolerant and accepting place."[31]

In the entire article, only one professor—Dr. Richard Stadelmann of Texas A&M—and one student, a member of the Young Conservatives organization, were quoted on the other side of the issue, with Dr. Stadelmann expressing concern that such courses simply increase "the tension between ethnic and racial groups" because of their "extraordinarily strong bias."[32]

The debate also rages in the public schools, where it often becomes a battle over what young students are assigned to read. An editorial in *Investor's Business Daily* discussed the reading-list controversy in San Francisco, pointing to the fact that books are often chosen because of the color of the author's skin. A proposal in the California city called for four books out of ten to be written by "authors of color." The *IBD* editorial quoted the proposal's authors—Keith Jackson and Steven Phillips, both black—who offered the theory that black children "learn differently" because of "an en-

vironmental impact from where they come from."[33] That may be psychobabble, but as *IBD* stated, if a white had said such a thing, he would have been
run out of town.

Why is it so important to the leftists within the education community in
San Francisco that the reading list come from authors who "look like
America"? The stated reason sounds innocent enough; it's just a simple matter of demographics: Only 13 percent of the student body is white. The district is mostly Asian, black, and Hispanic.

But let's be clear. In a school district where Western culture is "underrepresented" and might not be fully appreciated, shouldn't we take extra
pains to teach these kids about the virtues of American history? It's just
nutty to take a class of predominately minority students and teach them
about other cultures at the expense of our own. It's no wonder that race relations remain strained in the United States.

Unfortunately, you will find few school districts that subscribe to the melting pot theory—not even in affluent suburban districts such as Round Rock,
Texas, which reaches into the city of Austin. In the mid-1990s, a controversy
erupted there that the local news media portrayed as a battle between educators and the "Religious Right." It wasn't. It was a battle over a multicultural
agenda that insisted on having the kids at Westwood High School read books
by diverse authors even if those books were completely inappropriate.

Two of the books that were being assigned in ninth-grade English classes
were *Bless Me, Ultima* by Rudolfo Anaya and *I Know Why the Caged Bird
Sings* by Hillary Clinton's friend Maya Angelou. The former book was promoted by the publisher as "showcasing the richness of his culture," referring
to Anaya. That was enough for the multiculturalists at the school to place
the book on the reading list.

The problem with the book has nothing to do with its cultural background. The problem is that the book is chock full of profanity and pagan
images of characters vomiting green bile and hairballs that wriggle like live
snakes, and characters "pi....." against the church wall. In fact, you'll find
just about every profane word you can think of, including the F-word, scat-
tered all through the pages of *Bless Me, Ultima*.

The Maya Angelou book moves away from the paganism of the Anaya
book and goes more into straight pornography. Promoted as "the autobiog-
raphy of a talented black woman," the book may very well recount true experiences. But the question here is: Are these vivid descriptions of rape, incest, and homosexuality appropriate for ninth-graders?

Indeed, Angelou is a fine writer, weaving tantalizing images of her youth.
Unfortunately her youth included such experiences as her being raped by a man
who might have been her "real father"; her discovery of homosexuality and "the

mysterious world of the pervert"; her comparisons of another young woman's ample breasts to her own; her concern about a growth on her vagina; and her seduction of a young neighborhood boy and her subsequent pregnancy.

These are not books without redeeming social value; they might even be fit for some mature college classes. But in the Round Rock School District, not one official would even comment on the content of this material; they would only say that multiculturalism is promoted heavily by the boards that select the reading material.

This unrelenting drive toward multiculturalism in the public schools and on into college is placing our American culture—one we've been working for more than two hundred years to establish—in great danger. When a high-ranking school official cannot look you in the eye and say that some of this reading material is inappropriate for high school children, something is dreadfully wrong.

When the leftists within the education community use the word "multiculturalism" to conjure up soft and fuzzy images of students simply learning about other cultures, they are lying. If that's what they really intended to do, why not choose from the hundreds of excellent books authored by people from diverse backgrounds that *should* be included in the curricula of our schools? Why not showcase books written by immigrants who came to this country to escape the horrible conditions in their native lands? It is fitting and proper to teach our children about other cultures—in light of being an American. But that's not what the multiculturalists have in mind.

Years of multicultural indoctrination in our education system have taken a toll. Former Education Secretary William Bennett's web site "Americans for Victory over Terrorism" carried results of a poll of 634 college students conducted nationwide May 2–12, 2002. When presented with a statement that American values are superior to other cultures, only 5 percent "strongly" agreed, while another 20 percent "somewhat" agreed. On the other side, 71 percent disagreed and another 34 percent "strongly" disagreed. When asked if American culture is superior to Arab culture, 16 percent said "yes" and 79 percent said "no." Only 3 percent were willing to say that they "strongly" agree that Western culture is superior, and 4 percent went so far as to say they "strongly" disagree.[34]

The anti-American attitudes of college students should come as no surprise. That's precisely what the multicultural agenda has been teaching them for years.

Immigration—the new political battleground

The United States—often called "a nation of immigrants"—passed its first law to restrict immigration in 1882. Up until then, the practice had been totally open, and people in other countries were increasingly anxious to take advantage of the benefits of the New World. Reacting to the demand of citizens, the Congress decided to bar convicts, insane or severely retarded people, and those who would need public care. That same year, Congress banned immigration from China. Later laws would go so far as to restrict the number of immigrants that could come to the United States each year.

In modern times, there are still laws about who can come in and who can't. There are still limits, and there are certain preferences for those who are relatives of U.S. citizens, refugees, or people with specific kinds of training. But more and more, immigration policy and the granting of citizenship has become a purely political matter.

It is well documented that the Clinton administration worked hard to naturalize 1 million immigrants in time for the 1996 elections because it was believed that they would vote for Democrats. In his book *Sell Out*, David Schippers—the chief counsel to the House Judiciary Committee during the Clinton impeachment trial—explains that Vice President Al Gore was put in charge of pressuring the Immigration and Naturalization Service (INS) through the Citizenship USA (CUSA) program to rush the backlog through by the deadline of September 1, 1996. The administration targeted the big states like California, Texas, Illinois, New York, New Jersey, and Florida.[35]

But the administration didn't have much time to get the job done. There were little matters of rules and regulations that stipulated that the applicants should have criminal background checks, have usable fingerprints on file, and pass a civics test. Mr. Gore was able to work around all those pesky little rules, and the administration got its 1 million new potential voters in time to affect the 1996 elections. Unfortunately, that meant the United States got thousands of citizens with no classifiable fingerprints, who passed the civics test through questionable means, and who may have criminal backgrounds.[36]

You may be asking why there was no outcry about an administration that was willing to circumvent all the rules and laws in order to naturalize thousands (at the very least) of unqualified immigrants in order to get votes. Indeed, why has this story been told only in a handful of conservative books and columns and on talk radio? The reason is simple: multiculturalists have made it politically incorrect to oppose immigration, lest those who do so be branded as "anti-immigrant." Political commentator and former presidential candidate Pat Buchanan has dared to speak and write openly about his views on immigration and the loss of traditional American culture—and he has been identified as an "extremist" by the Left.

President George W. Bush and southern governors like Rick Perry of Texas do not want to be lumped in with Mr. Buchanan. And so, Governor Perry is taking Spanish lessons, while President Bush tries to decide what to do about immigration policy, especially in the wake of 9/11.

The new census figures show about 8.7 million "undocumented immigrants" in the United States.[37] "Undocumented immigrants" is the new politically correct term that multiculturalists and the mainstream media use in place of the less tolerant but more accurate term "illegal aliens." It is this new, softer approach to dealing with immigration that makes life tough for President Bush.

The president's quandary is this: If he stands tough in the face of his critics and deports all the illegals, he will be slammed by the Left and by the mainstream media as being intolerant and uncaring. He also risks losing the support of minority groups—especially Hispanics—who tend to have the most to gain from open immigration policies.

On the other hand, he is being pushed by some on the Right to tighten the borders both for cultural and security reasons. When the 2000 Census Bureau report showed that about 115,000 illegal aliens from the Middle East were living in the United States, columnist Cal Thomas made a suggestion: "If we are going to be hit again by our enemies, let's make sure we've done everything possible to protect ourselves, beginning with the deportation of everyone from nations who breed terrorists, followed quickly by those from other nations who are not entitled to be here."[38]

Thomas and many other pundits picked up a pointed quote from Steven A. Camarota, director of research at the Center for Immigration Studies, a Washington-based advocacy group: "While the vast majority of illegals from the Middle East are not terrorists, the fact that tens of thousands of people from that region and millions more from the rest of the world can settle in the United States illegally means that terrorists who wish to do so face few obstacles. We can't protect ourselves without dealing with illegal immigration."[39]

As if to make Camarota's point, it soon became known that the INS had made a major blunder by issuing visa approval notifications to Mohamed Atta and Marwan Al-Shehhi—six months *after* they piloted airliners into the World Trade Center towers. The INS said the original visa approvals came months before the attacks, when neither man was on any terrorist list, and that the backlog of paperwork made the approvals late in getting to the flight schools. The incident made big headlines and drew a heated response from President Bush: "I was stunned and not happy," he told reporters. "Let me put it another way: I was plenty hot."[40]

The incident served to point out how porous American borders really are. But while the statistics on Middle Eastern illegals were arousing passion from a security standpoint, the numbers on other ethnicities were drawing attention to multiculturalism. For example, nearly half of the illegal aliens were from Mexico, prompting advocacy groups to charge unfairness in the wake of 9/11. Cecilia Muñoz, vice president for policy of the National Council of La Raza, said those who want less immigration should not use 9/11 as their justification: "It is unreasonable to use this as an opportunity to stir up fear and division," she said.[41]

President Bush and most other politicians were listening. In fact, they had been listening for some time. Just prior to the events of 9/11, U.S. and Mexican officials had been discussing amnesty for the Mexican illegals in the United States. But, since words are so powerful, that very same National Council of La Raza had suggested that the word "amnesty" not be used at all. Instead, La Raza preferred softer words that would be easier to sell to the American people: "regularization" and "legalization."[42] The fact that these aren't even real words seemed to matter to no one.

It was much like the case of the out-of-favor term "illegal alien," which, by definition, implies wrongdoing. "Amnesty—there's an implication that somehow you did something wrong and you need to be forgiven," said Representative Luis Gutierrez, D-Ill., chairman of the Hispanic Caucus's Immigration Task Force.[43] In Mr. Gutierrez's world, breaking U.S. laws to come and live in this country illegally did not rise to the level of being illegal.

And so the two parties found themselves in competition to woo the hearts (and votes) of Hispanics. In early August, just over a month away from the terrorists' attacks, the Democrats announced their amnesty plan, which involved "earned" legalization, family reunification, border safety, and a guest-worker program. The plan was formally endorsed by Senate Majority Leader Tom Daschle and House Minority Leader Richard Gephardt.[44] Just twenty days away from the attacks, Hispanic groups were converging on the White House with dire warnings about the political implications should the president not support "legalization." The groups—members of the National Hispanic Leadership Agenda—met with White House aides to demand that legalization be extended to all people who have lived here at least three years and are productive.[45]

Three weeks later, everything changed. As of this writing, there still is no amnesty or "legalization" plan for illegal aliens and there is no consensus. Some in Congress, such as Representative Tom Tancredo, R-Col., are opposed to amnesty, while others support any measure that will curry favor with immigrant voting blocks. Bill O'Reilly of Fox News Channel's *The O'Reilly Factor*, constantly urges use of the military to secure our borders.

One thing is certain. The Left has changed the language and the Right has let them get away with it. It will be difficult, if not impossible, to win the war against radical multiculturalism as long as such terms as "illegal alien" and "amnesty" are swept away by political correctness and "multiculturalism" itself is a plan for teaching our kids about the evils of Western civilization.

"Multi-heritage-ism"—the dehyphenating of America

There never has been a culture such as ours. It has created a political and economic climate in which every citizen—no matter how rich or how poor—can achieve his goals through individual effort. It has stressed what has become known as "the American Dream"—the ability to own land, a home, and even a business. Most of all, our culture is based on precious freedoms that allow us to congregate, to dissent without fear, and to effect change at the ballot box.

For most of our existence, we Americans have been held together with the glue of unity, even though we've always been a diverse society. Our plan to stay unified was a brilliant one; we called it "assimilation." The plan is falling apart.

No one policy or thought process is to blame. It is simply a convergence of several missteps, combined with the political correctness movement on campuses, that has gotten us into this mess. Rapid immigration has made it harder for assimilation to occur. Our failure to control our own borders has resulted in millions of illegals who now want to attain citizenship. Many of them wish to continue speaking their native languages, and our tolerant society will not require them to learn English.

All of which brings us back to the emerging enclave society—a recurring theme in James Dale Davidson's and Lord William Rees-Mogg's landmark book *The Great Reckoning* that warns of "a return to tribalization and tribal thinking." The authors note that in any newspaper, many of the headlines are concerned with ethnic groups pitted against other ethnic groups: "Like vandals chipping away loose bricks from an old house, small groups and fractions of groups reassert their own special interests against the cosmopolitan interests that all people share."[46]

More evidence of the enclave society comes from a seminal column written by Georgie Anne Geyer. The column concerns a meeting convened by Senator Joseph Lieberman in which he gathered a group of academics who were concerned that Americans—especially young Americans—are losing our sense of history. At the meeting, Gordon Wood, a history professor at Brown, stated the problem: "Without some such sense of history, the citizens of the United States scarcely can exist long as a united people."[47]

"One of the worst areas of all is to be found in what euphemistically is called 'citizenship testing,'" wrote Geyer. "It is particularly dangerous that new immigrants, whose natural rooting and bonding is after all in other cultures, receive almost no serious citizenship training anymore."[48] This could lead, she wrote, to a country with no unifying cultural sense in which various groups will be interested only in their own narrow, selfish goals.

Another columnist, Roger Hernandez, disagrees. In an op-ed piece trashing Buchanan's *The Death of the West,* he disputes the author's central theme that the West is committing suicide: "Change isn't a sign that something is drastically wrong in American culture. It's a sign that the culture is dynamic, always correcting itself or at least trying to. Yet Mr. Buchanan persists in his fear of change. And much of that fear comes from that old Buchanan bogeyman, Hispanic immigrants."[49]

But Mr. Hernandez has not read Mr. Buchanan with an open mind. The problem never has been who the immigrants are or where they are from. The problem is lack of assimilation.

And the problem with lack of assimilation is lack of leadership. A conscienceless Bill Clinton was ready to naturalize the backlog immediately for the sake of a few votes, and it mattered not a whit to him or Al Gore what that might mean to America. But as the Geyer column points out, we don't ask much of our new citizens anymore, even with Mr. Clinton out of office and no longer trolling for votes.

Ask yourself: How would the United States of America be different if we took steps to actually foster an American culture? What if we took just a few significant steps to secure our borders, deport those who enter illegally, require a working knowledge of American history and English for new citizens, and remove the multicultural agenda from our schools?

Will President Bush provide the necessary leadership to fight such a tough battle? Already, he's delivered his Saturday-morning radio address in Spanish, celebrated another country's holiday (Cinco de Mayo) on the South Lawn, and marked yet another country's holiday (Cuban Independence Day) in the East Room.[50] Like Mr. Clinton, Mr. Bush seems to be thinking more about the next election than the next generation.

Of course, President Bush is right to expect all Americans to be proud of their heritage. That's why we should create a new word to replace "multiculturalism." The new term should reflect the pride that we all have in our various cultures, while recognizing that all those diverse ideas have come together to create something entirely new. It should restore the concept of "*e pluribus unum.*"

The new word is "multi-heritage-ism"—the process whereby many cultures merge into a distinct American culture and each new immigrant group brings its own nuances without seeking to effect radical change.

At the end of the path we are now taking lies great danger. After all, if we devolve into a true multicultural society, then we hyphenated Americans will one day be living in tribes and looking out for our own tribal interests. If we can find the national will, and statesmen who put their country ahead of their own political futures, we can return to a multi-heritaged society that will lead us down the path of unity. Only then can we become one people and one America.

CHAPTER 6

Establish English as
Our National Language

We must declare that a common tongue is vital to national unity and, as the language of our founders, English should be the official language of the United States government.

At a large lumberyard in a southwestern state, the customer who was next in the checkout line couldn't speak a word of English. Not to worry! The store—quite familiar with such occurrences—simply called for a Spanish-speaking associate. The man was able to do his business with only the faintest hint of inconvenience.

In states like California, Arizona, New Mexico, and Texas, it is no longer necessary to know the English language. In fact, there are so many Spanish-speaking people in those states that politicians have given up any thought of controlling the border and instead are competing for what they see as a major voting bloc. The story of how this came to be is not particularly complicated. These states are just across the "Big River" from Mexico. Things are really crummy for a lot of people to the south of that border; but to the north lie greener pastures—the famous American way of life.

So they come. Legally if they can, but if they have to swim the river, they do that, too. Once they make it across, various forces conspire to keep them here. Sometimes, it's companies looking for cheap labor, hiring them with no questions asked. Other times, it's nothing more than modern-day political correctness that says it's "insensitive" to send them back to Mexico. Sometimes, it's self-serving politicians such as Bill Clinton and Al Gore, who bend and break all the immigration laws just to get a few extra votes.

Once they're here—especially if they have children—we compassionate Americans have no stomach for turning them down for anything. We open up our schools, our hospitals, our welfare system, our government. Since they can't speak English, we install bilingual education programs in our schools—and sometimes even dual-language programs. We hire Spanish-speaking caseworkers to make sure social services are provided in a timely manner. And by all means, we make it a point to provide funding to print every single government form in both English and Spanish.

As Buddy Holly used to sing, "It's so easy; so doggoned easy." Spanish is everywhere. It's all over cable TV and on AM and FM radio stations; it's on ATM machines; and the front of the phone directory explains "como comunicarse con Southwestern Bell." If you have a question about your electric bill, just press "2" for Spanish.

On the political front, the League of Women Voters of Texas has announced that, for the first time, it will issue a guide to statewide candidates written entirely in Spanish. The league had been printing parts of its guide in Spanish for years and told the AP that this seemed like the "logical next step."[1]

In some parts of the country, the same situation is occurring involving other foreign languages. What, then, is the point of learning English?

It may be somewhat more difficult to get around in the Southwest and some other parts of the United States without a working knowledge of English, but it's far from impossible. And it's getting easier all the time. It's no wonder that so many people from many foreign countries are looking to the U.S. with great anticipation.

All this is not to take anything away from those immigrants who have entered our country through legal means and have learned English. It's just that language is one of those things that unite a nation and help form its culture. Recognizing that, we used to ask people—at the very least—to know some English and to study our history and traditions if they wished to stay here.

But these days, we don't ask very much of immigrants, and so we get thousands of them—often ending up in low-end jobs—who speak English quite poorly. At the aforementioned lumberyard, it was the customer who was having communications problems, but USA Today discovered that most of the time, it happens the other way around. The newspaper cited a USA Today/CNN/Gallup Poll showing that nearly one of four consumers had encountered some type of language difficulty within the past year while trying to conduct business.[2] The paper called it "verbal gridlock" and reported problems across the nation ranging from sheer frustration to safety and medical concerns.

An example from the USA Today story: Timmy, a young boy in Long Beach, got a shaved head because the barber misunderstood his request for a trim. His mom, Suzanne Schirmer, was furious: "Everywhere I go—the doctor's office, the eyeglass shop, fast-food restaurants—I'm getting more frustrated," she said. "It's hard to buy anything when you can't communicate with people who aren't from here."[3]

But frustrated kids and moms are just the tip of the iceberg. According to studies made by Ohio University economist Dr. Lowell Gallaway, the language gap is costing businesses about $175 billion annually in lost productivity, wages, tax revenue, and unemployment compensation. "I'm not an immigrant basher," says Gallaway, "but I strongly favor doing whatever we can to increase language capabilities of immigrants."[4]

The USA Today report went on to cite additional problems, including language-based discrimination lawsuits and the likelihood that medical malpractice claims will rise along with the ballooning number of foreign-born doctors who speak poor English.

The language barrier also makes for uncomfortable workplace situations when enclaves of immigrant workers address one another in their native tongue and those who speak English get intimidated. So, in Houston, the head of the police department's janitorial and maintenance crews, William Shelton, wrote a brief memo in an attempt to unify the department by language:

"It has been brought to my attention that individuals are speaking Spanish during duty hours in the presence of their non-Spanish-speaking coworkers. Effective today, August 25, 2000, only English is to be spoken during working hours by the employees of the facilities operations and maintenance division."[5]

As you might suspect, Hispanic leaders in Houston blew their stacks and the order was quickly overturned. Johnny Mata, a spokesman for the League of United Latin American Citizens (LULAC), said, "This is highly insulting to us. It leaves you to wonder exactly what kind of managerial training these people have."[6] Mata said he would push for sensitivity training. And City Councilman John Castillo told the Houston Chronicle that he was amazed when he heard about the memo, that "in this age of sensitivity and diversity that we would have somebody that would think that way."[7] But Mr. Mata and Councilman Castillo were not concerned about sensitivity toward those English-speaking workers who had to go through their day wondering what was being said in their presence that they couldn't understand.

And then there's the public school system, which has been turned upside down by an influx of immigrant students who come to class without the ability to speak the language of the land where they now reside. So what do we do about it—tell immigrant parents to learn English and teach it to their kids before they send them to school? Of course not; that would be insensitive. And so we have embraced the idea of teaching kids in their native languages until they learn English.

Dr. Mike Moses, superintendent of the Dallas Independent School District, uses as an example the case of a ten-year-old student from Bosnia who comes here to escape the war and can't keep up with his classmates. This student suddenly finds himself in a foreign country that speaks a foreign language, and, according to Dr. Moses, he needs three to five years to get up to speed in English. Dr. Moses says that while the challenges that schools face are compounded by what he calls "the critical nationwide shortage of bilingual educators in Spanish," there is also the problem of "the virtual nonexistence of teachers who speak and translate other languages and the fact that there are no plans to produce the TAAS [standardized tests] in other languages."[8]

Dr. Moses' attitudes are typical of those generally found in the academic community. In fact, over the years, the educational establishment's near-total dedication to bilingual education has taken on a religious fervor not unlike that associated with radical environmentalism and "a woman's right to choose." In their eyes, if you oppose bilingual education, no matter what your reasoning is, you are anti-immigrant and intolerant. The fact that bilingual education doesn't seem to work doesn't seem to matter.

California: the bilingual battleground

Bilingual education in our public schools can be traced as far back as the 1840s in northern cities like New York and Cincinnati. But bilingual education as we know it today got started much later, arising out of the civil rights—or Chicano rights—movement of the 1960s. The concept was passed into law with the Bilingual Education Act of 1968, sponsored by ultra-liberal Texas Senator Ralph Yarborough. It got a boost in 1974 when the Supreme Court ruled that public schools are required to provide special programs for students who are not proficient in English.

Based on emotion rather than sound teaching principles, bilingual education grew into a monster alongside images of pathetic little children—such as Dr. Moses' hypothetical student from Bosnia—sitting in classrooms, trembling with fear, unable to grasp what the teacher was saying. Columnist Joan Beck of the *Chicago Tribune* wrote that the impulse is strong to speak to that student—and teach him—in his own language.

According to Beck, that's exactly how bilingual education became what it is today: "Back that inclination with civil rights consciousness and a spate of laws and court decisions guaranteeing every child schooling in his native language. Allow a bilingual bureaucracy to grow entrenched. Add the politics of race and ethnicity. Answer every criticism with accusations of racism and bigotry."[9]

Beck's column refers to a book by Rosalie Pedalino Porter entitled *Forked Tongue: The Politics of Bilingual Education,* in which the author explains that she was once one of those little lost kids in an English-speaking classroom. But Porter, having been immersed in English, went on to do well in school and college and eventually became the director of bilingual and English-as-a-second-language programs in Newton, Massachusetts. Porter soon became convinced that bilingual programs were doing more harm than good.[10] For one thing, some Hispanic kids who spoke pretty good English were stuck in bilingual classes anyway—possibly to keep the numbers high so that special funding would keep coming. For another thing, the bilingual classes emphasized native cultures instead of moving the kids into the mainstream of American life.

Ms. Porter was not the only one who had a taste of bilingual education and found it lacking. In the battleground state of California, a search-firm executive named Hal Netkin had an occasion to sit in on a second-grade bilingual classroom in Van Nuys.

In a column in the *Wall Street Journal,* he explained how the class worked: "A group of Anglo, Asian, Armenian and other children labeled 'English proficient' sat on the left side of the class, while an all-Latino group of 'native-Spanish-speaking' children sat on the right. An English-speaking teacher stood in front of the group on the left, which read from books in English; a Spanish-speaking teaching assistant stood in front of the group on the right, which read from books in Spanish."[11] It was really more of what he called a "primary language" classroom with part of the class learning in English and the other part in Spanish.

Netkin was outraged, questioning why all the little kids from Armenia, China, Haiti, and other children whose native language was not English don't get instruction in their native tongues. He saw a clear implication that Latino children were considered to be inferior to other ethnic groups. Netkin was right—even though Joan Beck's column pointed out that bilingual education is practiced in 145 languages around the country, it most often targets Spanish-speaking kids.

Latino parents were starting to get enough. A poll conducted by the *Los Angeles Times* found that 83 percent of Latino parents would prefer that their kids be taught in English.[12] California teachers paid no attention to those numbers, possibly, as Netkin wrote, due to the fact that bilingual education had become a $500 million-a-year industry. But change was in the wind as a grassroots initiative known as "English for the Children" gained momentum.

Some trace the movement to a little protest against bilingual education that took place at the Ninth Street School in downtown Los Angeles in early 1996. More than seventy parents were there to march and implement a boycott. They came armed with pamphlets that carried their message to educators:

"If our children can't read and write English at their grade level, they will never be able to attend university or become doctors, lawyers and teachers."[13]

The parents, many of whom were workers in the garment industry, were Hispanics. They said they would pull their kids out of the school until their demands were met. One of the parents, an immigrant from Mexico City, explained that she came to the United States so that her son could get an education in English. She said that the bilingual program was a failure in two languages. Educators may have turned a deaf ear to these parents, but someone else was paying attention.

Ron Unz was a former candidate for governor on the Republican ticket who also happened to be a millionaire in the software industry. He took up the cause and founded the "English for the Children" movement. Unz called bilingual education a "bizarre government program that costs hundreds of millions of dollars and doesn't succeed in teaching children English."[14] Unz's goal was to get the initiative on the California ballot and let the voters decide.

Joining Unz in the fight was a prominent California civic leader who was not only an Hispanic but also a staunch Democrat who had worked in the 1992 Clinton-Gore campaign. If that wasn't enough, he was also a key figure in creating California's bilingual program. Now Fernando Vega was saying that the program was a failure. "There is no shame in admitting that you once supported a program which you now see doesn't work in practice," he said. "What is shameful is that so many politicians and other officials continue to support such a program year after year, even after they see that it has failed to work and that it is harmful to the future of the young children who are in it."[15]

With the heat turned up against bilingual classrooms—and much of that heat coming from the Hispanic community—a school district south of Los Angeles decided to return to all-English classes and see what would happen. What happened was a lawsuit.

School officials in the 29,000-student Orange Unified School District, including Hispanic areas of Garden Grove and Santa Ana, said the program was a failure. But Deborah Escobedo, representing the "Multicultural Education Training and Advocacy Institute" (META), maintained that the district's program was "outstanding." Her San Francisco–based organization sued to keep the program intact.[16] The suit was filed on behalf of four parents along with several organizations, including Los Amigos of Orange County (a parents' group), the Association of Mexican American Educators, the California Latino Civil Rights Network, and the California Association of Bilingual Educators (CABE).

CABE was looking out for the interests of California's bilingual teachers, who in some cases made as much as $5,000 more than English-only teachers. A CABE spokeswoman, Silvina Rubinstein, blamed the failure of bilingual programs on inadequate funding.[17] Officials in the Orange district countered that they had put up plenty of money for twenty years and students were not learning English as they should have. Neil McKinnon, an assistant superintendent, said that after as many as six years in bilingual programs, many students still had poor English skills. In fact, one sixth-grade teacher had gone back to teaching entirely in Spanish.[18]

The push continued to get the initiative on the June ballot, and polls were boding well. Eighty-five percent of the voters surveyed in the Orange Unified School District said they supported the district's decision to scrap the program. Statewide, a *Los Angeles Times* survey produced similar results, showing that 80 percent of whites and 84 percent of Hispanics were backing English for the Children.[19] The main opposition seemed to be coming from liberal Latino groups and teachers' organizations.

In June 1998, English for the Children made it to the ballot as Proposition 227 and passed with 61 percent of the vote. And so, with some exceptions, educators in the Golden State would teach entirely in English, right? Not exactly.

As an editorial in *Investor's Business Daily* pointed out six months after the voting, "never underestimate an educrat when his interests are threatened." The new law was simple—classes would be conducted in English—but schools all across the state were finding ways to get around it.[20]

The day after the balloting, several school districts, joined with the ACLU and the Mexican American Legal Defense and Education Fund, sued in an attempt to halt the new law. In early December, the state teachers' union filed another lawsuit. In San Francisco, the school superintendent openly refused to comply. Other districts went to the state capital of Sacramento to seek waivers. And still other districts complied somewhat with the law—such as the Riverside District, which decided to teach 60 percent in English and 40 percent in a student's native language.[21]

There was only one school district that made an attempt at full compliance—the Oceanside School District just outside of San Diego. Officials there carefully implemented the law, immersing young Spanish-speaking kids in English. A nearby school district, Vista, California, took a different path. The superintendent there granted waivers to about half of the limited-English kids so that they could continue their studies in both Spanish and English.

Not quite a year into implementation of the new law, published reports described the results in Oceanside as "dramatic." On the SAT-9 standardized tests, reading scores zoomed up 56 percent for third-graders and rose a staggering 475 percent for seventh-graders.[22] The Oceanside schools had returned to a back-to-the-basics curriculum, but officials attributed the high test scores to Prop 227.

One of those most shocked by the "Oceanside Effect" was a former bilingual instructor—now school superintendent—Kenneth Noonan, who originally thought Prop 227 was too extreme. "The results speak for themselves," he said. "This is not news the bilingual industry is interested in hearing."[23] Noonan, who had founded the California Association of Bilingual Educators thirty years ago, was right on the mark.

Those with a vested interest in keeping bilingual education alive found all the reasons in the world to be unimpressed with the scores. First of all, the gains for limited-English students were still below the fiftieth percentile on the standardized tests.

And if that wasn't enough, Elena Soto-Chapa, the statewide education director of the California chapter of the Mexican American Legal Defense and Educational Fund, complained that the tests were "designed to assess English speakers on content areas." According to Soto-Chapa, the return to English in classrooms had little to do with the dramatic improvements. "The state has put an emphasis on test-taking skills, the state has allocated money for class-size reduction, and Oceanside has had a back-to-basics approach," she said.[24]

Ms. Soto-Chapa might not have been convinced, but school district officials were. They said that Prop 227 was working even better for limited-English kids than for other students. Because of that, opponents of bilingual education, such as Jim Boulet Jr., executive director of a Washington-based organization called "English First," had their eyes on Oceanside, hoping for a trend.

After two years had gone by, the kids in Oceanside were storming through the second grade. The average reading score of students there was up nineteen percentage points over the two-year period, according to figures released by the state. In second-grade classes all over California, the story was much the same. The average score in reading for limited-English students was up nine percentage points—to the twenty-eighth percentile, up from the nineteenth in national rankings. It wasn't just in reading, either. In math, the increase for the same students was fourteen points, moving from the twenty-seventh percentile to the forty-first.[25] It was only in the upper grades—the tenth and eleventh, where Spanish-speaking kids had not been immersed in English—that test score improvements were not as sharp, but even those scores were up almost four percentage points.

Superintendent Noonan was still beaming about the results. "I thought it would hurt kids," he said. "But the exact reverse occurred, totally unexpected by me. The kids began to learn—not pick up, but learn—formal English, oral and written, far more quickly than I ever thought they would."[26]

And what about Vista, California, where waivers were granted so that about half the kids could keep on learning in bilingual classes? The news there was not so good. Unlike its neighbor Oceanside, Vista saw only limited improvement in scores—about half of what Oceanside experienced. And this was true in nearly every grade.

With his mission accomplished in California—along with a similar success in Arizona—Ron Unz moved on to Colorado and Massachusetts, states that can effect change through the initiative process.

In Colorado, he found an ally in a former Denver school board member named Rita Montero, who had changed her mind about bilingual education when her English-speaking son got trapped in a bilingual classroom. Ms. Montero had reached the conclusion that supporters of bilingual education were clinging to a failed dream: "It's like giving up a piece of something they fought for during the seventies, and by God, whether it's good or bad, it's something they advocated for, and damn it, the white folks aren't going to take it away from them." [27]

Unz's movement became "Amendment 31" in Colorado and made it to the ballot in the elections of November 2002, when it went down to defeat. However, it took an expensive advertising campaign—about $3.2 million—to bring it down. Most of the cash came from billionaire heiress Pat Stryker. The pro-Amendment 31 forces had no such benefactor and could only come up with about a tenth of that amount.[28] At the same time, voters in the more liberal state of Massachusetts passed the "Question 2" English immersion amendment by a two-to-one margin. The Massachusetts measure was helped along by strong support from Republican gubernatorial candidate Mitt Romney, who succeeded in his bid for the governor's mansion. By contrast, the incumbent governor of Colorado, Republican Bill Owens, opposed English immersion.[29]

Meanwhile, in Texas, bilingual educators continued to ply their trade with little fear of Mr. Unz. That's because Texas, with its Hispanic population of 6.7 million, has no initiative and referendum. Because of that, Mr. Unz would have to find some way to convince the state legislature to pass a bill to send to the governor for his signature. Mr. Unz was finding it much easier to deal with ordinary parents and taxpayers than politicians, who were often fearful of the teachers' unions.

Besides that, newspapers in the Lone Star State were giving big play to poll results that showed that Texans—unlike Californians and Arizonans—supported their bilingual programs. In a story published a month after the California initiative was passed, the *Austin American-Statesman* ran the poll results along with quotes from several supporters of bilingual education. There were no quotes from the other side.

The Texas poll asked three questions, and each time, the respondents seemed to favor bilingual education. Seventy-one percent said that bilingual programs for students with limited English proficiency were important. Forty-six percent felt that bilingual programs were effective, as opposed to just 30 percent who didn't. In the final question, only 24 percent of those polled would opt for English-only classes, while 38 percent said that students should be assisted in their native languages for a brief time, and 36 percent felt that classes should be taught in both English and a student's native language.[30]

Rodolfo de la Garza, a University of Texas government professor, put his own spin on the results of the poll versus the results in California. "In California, because there are so many immigrants, bilingual education is seen as a program that only benefits immigrants," he said. "In Texas, there is broader recognition that Mexicans have been here a long time and that Spanish is important to the vitality of the state."[31]

The Republican chairman of the State Board of Education, Jack Christie, said he was absolutely certain that Texas' bilingual programs were superior to the English immersion that had just passed in the Golden State. As proof, he offered a story about when he was a volunteer at a Houston middle school, working with a Hispanic student named José. "I started explaining to José the electron configuration and how elements form molecules, how for example, sodium attached to make salt," he explained. "José gave me a blank stare. A student tapped me on the back and said, '*José no comprende ingles*.' José didn't have a clue about what was going on in the classroom," Christie said, adding that José was sure to be a dropout unless he was taught in his native language.[32]

Even the governor of Texas—himself a Republican—wasn't about to jump off the bilingual bandwagon and alienate all those Hispanic voters. Speaking to the national convention of the League of United Latin American Citizens, Governor Bush left no doubt as to where he stood on the issue. "Remember, the goal is to teach children how to read and write and add and subtract in English. And here is my position loud and clear. We are going to measure it, and if the bilingual program serves to teach our children English, then we ought to say thank you very much and leave it in place."[33]

Mr. Bush got standing ovations before and after the speech and loud applause when he said that he wanted all students to be proficient in English and Spanish. "In this state, we understand that English is the gateway to freedom, so what I've promoted is not English-only but English-plus."[34] Strangely enough, Governor Bush was coming out against his own state party platform, which stated that bilingual education was a failure. He shrugged off the issue, saying that leadership often puts you "at odds with all kinds of people."

If Governor Bush—now President Bush—wants Texans to speak both languages, he's getting his way in some school districts; English-speaking students are now being immersed in Spanish! At Bedford High School, six-year-old first-graders at a magnet school are being taught the core curriculum—language arts, math, and science—in Spanish. Even when they ask a question in English, the answer comes back in Spanish.

Check out this exchange between first-grader Alex Martino and his teacher, Ana Levario, as reported in the *Dallas Morning News:*

Alex: "May I go get a drink of water?"

Levario: "*Si, puedes ir a tomar agua.*"

Alex: "Huh?"[35]

Imagine being a young English-speaking child subjected to this in math class. On the other hand, programs such as this are a godsend for bilingual teachers, who usually earn more than teachers do in a regular English-only classroom. Maybe that's why the teacher pictured in the *News* article has a big smile on her face while the child looks perfectly miserable.

Sanchez y Morales: the great debate

While California became the bilingual battleground over how children should be taught in public schools, in Texas, the nation's second-largest state, the issue was being framed in a different manner. With more miles of shared border with Mexico than any other state, and major metro areas with high concentrations of Spanish-speaking people, the issue in Texas was becoming more centered on matters of convenience—and votes.

In Texas, the goal seemed to be a total bilingual state with no real necessity for anyone to learn English, because all important information would be presented to the public in both languages. Democrats certainly subscribed to this methodology, and Republicans were jumping on board because to do otherwise might alienate large groups of Spanish-speaking voters who presumably would look with disfavor on any candidate who favored English over Spanish.

And so Democrats went out and recruited a Hispanic candidate for governor, a wealthy oilman and banker named Tony Sanchez, who was also bilingual. When a former Texas attorney general—Dan Morales, also Hispanic—jumped into the race at the last minute, the stage was set for a political first: a debate between state gubernatorial candidates conducted in Spanish.

Even in Texas, the debate had a California connection. The Los Angeles–based "Southwest Voter Registration Education Project" negotiated the details, after Victor Landa, news director for the Telemundo station in San Antonio, called both camps and suggested it. "This will be a debate about Latino issues," said Landa. He added, "What people are going to find out is that our issues are not that different from anybody else's."[36]

And so it came to pass on March 1, 2002; the two candidates in the Democratic primary met in a televised debate in Dallas. Sanchez and Morales debated for an hour in English, then returned to the stage for a second hour entirely in Spanish. What the two men discussed is unimportant for our purposes here—except for the debate over the debate.

Morales, who from time to time had shown some conservative leanings (especially in his rulings on affirmative action while attorney general), seemed to be uncomfortable with the idea of an all-Spanish debate. The Sanchez camp accused Mr. Morales of violating the rules of the debate by promising to translate his Spanish-speaking answers into English. Some supporters of Mr. Sanchez charged that Mr. Morales was making an attempt to appeal to conservative white voters.[37]

Tony Sanchez went a step further with his accusations, suggesting that Mr. Morales was not being true to his own ethnicity: "I think he is ashamed and embarrassed to be Hispanic," said Mr. Sanchez. "He has never shown the pride we show to be Hispanics, and that hurts me a lot."[38]

But Mr. Morales insisted that if he didn't translate, a majority of Texans would not be able to understand the Spanish debate at all. "I'm proud of my ethnic background," he said. "I'm proud to be Hispanic." But he went on to say that English is the key to success in Texas and that Mr. Sanchez was trying to create racial divisions by not debating more in the English language.[39]

So what about the pluses and minuses of such a debate?

From the left, Edward Rincon, a research psychologist specializing in ethnic-related research, says simply that people who speak Spanish prefer it to English. "Our experience in conducting public opinion polls of Latinos confirms that seven in ten prefer to communicate in Spanish when given the choice. Eighty percent of the Latino TV viewing audience tunes into Spanish-language television for newscasts."[40] Mr. Rincon listed "key realities" about the Latino vote, including his finding that Latinos are more likely to support a Latino candidate, especially a Democrat with the right (liberal) message.

From the right, columnist William Murchison wrote that the Morales-Sanchez debate was setting "an awful precedent." Stipulating that Spanish is "one of the great Romance languages" and that knowing a foreign language is desirable, he insisted that those things skirt the central issue. "The point is that the language of governance in the United States (like our public language in general) is English. That monopoly not only is sensible, but also vital to civic engagement and unity."[41] According to Mr. Murchison, the Spanish-only debate was an invitation for Hispanics to opt out of the mainstream—to "huddle apart from Anglos or gringos or whatever (who cares?). Listening to Spanish radio, dreaming Spanish dreams, and laying Spanish plans."[42] The more foreign people we take in, he said, the more we need one language.

The debate, and the debate over the debate, came and was gone; Tony Sanchez handily defeated Dan Morales and went on to challenge (and eventually lose to) Republican Governor Rick Perry, who was busy taking Spanish lessons.

Ebonics: legitimizing illiteracy

Disagreements over bilingual education and foreign-language political debates are one thing. But what happens when educators decide to accept language that really isn't language at all but rather is simply bad grammar? This is what took place in Oakland, California, in December of 1996.

The Oakland School Board combined two words—"ebony" and "phonics"—and proclaimed "Ebonics" to be a distinctive language spoken by American blacks, including most of the 28,000 black kids in the Oakland School District. The board was saying that what was once called "black English" was not just a dialect of standard English or, worse yet, a largely ungrammatical system of verbal communication, but rather that it was an actual language.

Sherri Willis, speaking for the district, explained it this way: "The goal is to give African American students the ability to have standard English proficiency in reading, writing, and speaking. To do that, we are recognizing that many students bring to the classroom a different language, Ebonics."[43]

The resolution passed the school board in a unanimous vote and carried with it some interesting implications. For example, if Ebonics was a language, then teachers could receive merit pay for studying it and teaching Oakland's black students "in their native language." Not only that, but if Ebonics was a language, then shouldn't Title 7 funds that go toward bilingual programs be available for black students as well?

In his *New York Times* article, Peter Applebome wrote that the Oakland schools were not planning to actually teach in Ebonics: "Unlike standard bilingual programs, courses would not be taught in black English."[44]

Not true, countered Nicholas Stix in a major "exposé" of Ebonics in the Libertarian magazine *Liberty*. Criticizing Applebome's article as going out of its way to "conceal the nature of the Oakland scheme," he pointed out that the first resolution in Oakland clearly states that black American kids speak an "African language," rather than English, and that they should receive instruction in both.[45]

Stix's five-page article charged that the Ebonics movement is just "one division of the movement for 'bilingual education,' in which we see the partnership of the welfare state and racism in making the world safe for illiteracy."[46] Stix cited a study of the "Bridge Program" (a reading curriculum designed to use black English) to prove that teaching in Ebonics is a failure.[47] Even though the study was used by its authors in support of Ebonics, some of the results were not favorable at all. In using "dialect readers," students seemed to score worse on comprehension tests (46.3 percent correct) than did the kids who read the stories in standard English (and who scored 90 percent correct).[48]

Even though there didn't seem to be any valid research that would recommend Ebonics, the idea was not without its proponents. Barbara Boudreaux, the only black member of the Los Angeles School Board, was ready to jump in: "I applaud Oakland for what they've done," she said. "Every African American . . . has some kind of dialectical pattern that is laughed at by others. So I am willing to recognize Ebonics as a language."[49]

Robert L. Steinback, a columnist for the *Miami Herald,* was also willing to give it a try. He noted that for some black kids, standard English is nothing more than "talking white," while inner-city language is, culturally, "talking black." Under the Ebonics system, he said, "The presumption that speakers of black English are intellectually deficient would be replaced by a presumption that they are normal students who, like immigrants, simply need help mastering an unfamiliar language."[50]

But of course, black students in the United States are not immigrants, and English is not an unfamiliar language. Steinback's fellow writer on the *Herald,* Leonard Pitts, understood that. "Your humble correspondent has exhausted his thesaurus looking for the word that best describes what he thinks of this. Absurd, asinine, imbecilic, and moronic all come to mind. Most of all, though, this is insulting," he wrote.[51] Pitts went on to say that if these kids must be taught English as a second language, then we have to consider the places they come from—South Central Los Angeles, Harlem, and the like—to be foreign countries. Check your map, he wrote.

These columns were written near the end of December—just days after the resolutions were passed in Oakland. And although paired columns such as these gave viewpoints from both sides of the issue to provide all-important "balance" on op-ed pages, support for Ebonics had already begun to erode after some all-important black voices started speaking out.

On NBC's *Meet the Press,* the Reverend Jesse Jackson engaged in some pointed name-calling. He said the Oakland School Board was "both foolish and insulting" to black students throughout the nation. "I understand the attempt to reach out to these children," he said. "But this is an unacceptable surrender, borderlining on disgrace."[52] Jackson went so far as to call the Oakland School Board "a national laughing stock" and said their actions were an attempt to win extra federal funding under bilingual programs.

Reverend Jackson's voice was joined by that of a major icon in the black community, writer and poet Maya Angelou, who called the decision a mistake: "I'm incensed," she said in an interview with the *Wichita Eagle.* "The very idea that African American language is a language separate and apart is very threatening, because it can encourage young men and women not to learn standard English."[53]

It's hard to imagine that any program involving the black community could succeed with the Reverend Jackson and Ms. Angelou adamantly opposed. But the last straw may have been an op-ed in the *Wall Street Journal*, written by a famous black entertainer much beloved by all communities. As you might expect, Bill Cosby peppered his column with humor, but he pulled no punches.

"I remember one day fifteen years ago, a friend of mine told me a racist joke," wrote Cosby. "Question: Do you know what 'Toys "R" Us' is called in Harlem? Answer: We Be Toys."[54]

Cosby conjured up example after example of what might happen if Ebonics were practiced in schools across the land. Imagine an Oakland teenager speaking Ebonics to a policeman. The teen, needing information on why he was being pulled over, might say, "Lemme ax you ... ," at which point the policeman might fear that he is about to be hacked to death. Notices would have to be posted in cars with warnings that "this driver speaks Ebonics only," wrote Mr. Cosby. And he axed ... er ... asked about what might happen if an Ebonics-speaking youth from California ventured into Pennsylvania? The Ebonics there would be quite different—and Tennessee Ebonics would be impossible to decipher![55]

But, having made his point with humor, Mr. Cosby turned serious at the end of his column, writing: "Legitimizing the street in the classroom is backwards. We should be working hard to legitimize the classroom—and English—in the street."[56]

After all was said and done and Ebonics had been thoroughly trashed by so many of the major voices of the African-American community, a Harvard professor expressed his opinion on what the whole thing was about from the get-go. It wasn't really about teaching standard English to black kids, said Tom Loveless, assistant professor of public policy at Harvard's John F. Kennedy School of Government. It was simply a way for teachers to avoid telling kids that they were speaking incorrectly, "because, heaven forbid, students would feel 'devalued' and suffer irreparable harm."[57]

Ebonics was not some weird, out-of-the-mainstream idea that just popped up in Oakland, California, according to Mr. Loveless. "This is where Ebonics is solidly in the mainstream of modern educational thought. It shares with constructivism [the idea that learners construct their own knowledge, such as in 'whole language' programs] the same relativism, the same reluctance to let students know when they are wrong."[58]

Ebonics, it turns out, may be about nothing more than self-esteem.

It's time for a national language of government

No one wants to abridge anyone's personal freedom to speak any language that he or she pleases. What we are advocating is that the United

States government—including the public school system—speak in a single, united voice—the voice of English. We should make it official.

It has been attempted. On August 1, 1996, the U.S. House of Representatives had a rousing discussion about citizenship and the melting pot and eventually voted—259 to 169—to establish English as the official language of these United States. The bill would have required most official government documents to be printed in English and would have allowed (but not required) states to stop using bilingual ballots.[59]

To its credit, the bill contained logical exceptions for such items as public safety warnings and to ensure that criminals could be informed of charges against them in their native languages. The federal law wouldn't have even overridden state and local laws about how governments could use languages. Still, many Democrats screamed bloody murder, saying the GOP-backed legislation was an election-year "wedge" issue. Then-Texas Governor George W. Bush came out against the measure. And Rep. Patrick Kennedy, D-R.I., talked about the "seeds of hate" as he lectured Republicans: "If you don't like the way they look, if you don't like the way they sound, they're not American."[60]

That drew the ire of the bill's chief sponsor, California Republican Randy Cunningham, a decorated Vietnam War pilot. Cunningham responded to Kennedy by asking if he had ever "volunteered" to serve his country and then said his goal was not to build a wall: "We're tearing down a wall. If I were mean-spirited, I would say, 'stay where you are. Don't learn the English language.'"[61] Cunningham also pointed out how much money could be saved if agencies such as the IRS didn't have to print forms in multiple languages.

Naturally, such organizations as the National Council of La Raza and the American Civil Liberties Union opposed the bill, with the former noting that the U.S. 9th Circuit Court of Appeals had already ruled that a similar law in Arizona is unconstitutional. The groups actually had little to worry about. Congress adjourned before the Senate acted, and that was that.

The Arizona English-only case ended up in the U.S. Supreme Court, where it was thrown out on a technicality, settling nothing. Judge Ruth Bader Ginsburg wrote the text of the ruling, which dealt with errors in legal procedures in the case of Maria-Kelly Yniguez, an employee of the state who sued over her right to freedom of speech at work. But she had resigned from her job seven years earlier, and so the case was deemed moot.[62]

But English as the official language of government should transcend partisan bickering and legal technicalities. Look at the mess in the 2000 elections in Florida, created at least partly because many voters couldn't understand the ballot. And yet, every message sent by today's society seems to encourage immigrants not to learn English.

In an amazing op-ed written more than four years before the election debacle in Florida, John Silber, president of Boston University, said it was high time for one language at the ballot box. Mr. Silber began his column by mentioning that our nation was established by English speakers, its founding documents are in English, its laws are in English, and its legislatures conduct business in English. "Citizens who are not proficient in English cannot, in most cases, follow a political campaign, talk with candidates, or petition their representatives," he wrote. "They are citizens in name only and are unable to exercise their rights." [63] Mr. Silber wrote that the federal mandate for bilingual ballots represents a "dangerous experiment in deconstructing our American identity."

As a nation, we have not listened to Mr. Silber. We have made a mess of at least one election, we have seen a major political debate conducted in a foreign language, and we continue to teach our students in other languages—even to the extent of making up Ebonics-style excuses for them when programs fail.

Dr. Paul Craig Roberts writes that so many legal-aid agencies are suing government social service agencies over language issues that governments are forced to discriminate against the English-speaking native-born. In Santa Ana, he writes, the police department will hire only bilingual people. [64]

Phyllis Schlafly, president of Eagle Forum, has called on President George W. Bush and the Congress to take action against federal bureaucracies that want the United States to be a bilingual nation. Ms. Schlafly says it was Bill Clinton's Executive Order 13166 that directed all federal agencies to offer all government services in foreign languages. [65]

Even though the Supreme Court neutered the Clinton EO with a ruling in *Alexander v. Sandoval* in April 2001, she says that the Bush administration should have immediately rescinded Clinton's order. (Martha Sandoval had demanded that the state of Alabama administer a driver's license test in Spanish even though she had lived in the United States for ten years without learning English.) But instead, Ms. Schlafly says that the administration stayed the course with Clinton's policies—even issuing new language regulations. [66]

Calling on President Bush to help sort out the nation's language mess probably isn't going to do much good. As conservative as Mr. Bush is on some issues, he has never shown the slightest inclination—either as president or as governor of Texas—to move toward an English-only policy.

Perhaps the president could be convinced if he would take a long, hard look at the bilingual program in the schools, which, according to Nicholas Stix, "operates a political patronage machine that churns out illiterates at a cost from ten to forty percent higher than conventional methods." [67]

Or perhaps the president's head would be turned if he paid more attention to language battles in foreign countries—and not just in remote regions of the world. Canada was almost torn apart in 1995 when voters in the province of Quebec narrowly decided against secession. About 60 percent of French-speaking Quebecers voted to create a sovereign, French-speaking state. Some Hispanic groups in the Southwest have declared that secession and possible reunification with Mexico is their goal. It would be a mistake not to take these groups seriously.

The two forces that must be overcome if we are going to reunite the nation under a common language are political correctness and politicians' never-ending quest for votes. On the one hand, it's difficult to even discuss such issues in the current political climate; on the other hand, when the issues are discussed, politicians run for shelter, calling the issue "divisive."

It's just the opposite.

If we wish to maintain a truly "united" United States of America—a country in which people understand one another and can work alongside one another—and if *e pluribus unum* is still an American goal, then let's at least make English the official language of government. That would mean that everyone would have to know at least some English; and that would do more to unite us than any other single thing.

CHAPTER 7

End Racial Preferences

We must declare that all Americans are equal under the law and that no one shall be discriminated against or receive special treatment on the basis of race or ethnicity.

In a nation where freedom was a founding principle, some people had been left out. In a nation newly freed from oppressive British rule, some people still owned other people. In a nation instrumental in crushing the Nazi threat, some people still had to ride at the back of the bus. There is no question about it; through the 1950s and into the '60s, the United States of America had a problem with that particular part of freedom known as "equality." It needed to be fixed.

In Montgomery, Alabama, in 1955, a black woman named Rosa Lee Parks had no intention of riding at the back of the bus. When she refused to give up her seat to a white passenger, she became a powerful symbol for a new movement. Less than a decade passed before the movement and a new awareness produced a law that would literally change the face of America.

By that time, a case was being made for a remedy designed to make up for all the years of inequality. This new way of thinking held that passing a law wasn't nearly enough, because much of the country was still closed to blacks. Things were still unfair.

Separate water fountains went away, but "discrimination," as it came to be called, remained. The remedy was dubbed "affirmative action," so named in 1965 by President Lyndon B. Johnson. In the beginning, it was designed to offset the effects of discrimination against black people, particularly relating to jobs. Affirmative action, while well meaning, was a government program. Unfortunately, government programs often get out of control.

In today's society, affirmative action has morphed into something quite different. Affirmative action now means that certain set-asides are available for people who are members of any protected group to ensure that such practices as hiring, the awarding of business contracts, and even college admissions produce results that are racially proportionate.

Remember, this all originated with the residual effects of slavery—a practice that, admittedly, held back an entire race of people for generations. How, then, did other groups get in on the action? Women, for example, draw median wages that are 77 percent of what men make.[1] But could there be extenuating circumstances at play? Some women choose to stay home and raise a family; some choose not to pursue advanced degrees. More men become engineers, and more women go into teaching.

When all the facts are taken into consideration, should women be a protected class? What about people of Hispanic origin, whose ancestors were never enslaved in this country? What about immigrants?

Without a doubt, affirmative action has been a tool to help erase the effects of past discrimination. But like so many government programs, it became bloated and self-perpetuating, with no end in sight. Should it continue forever? When do we say when?

As we examine the ramifications of racial politics in the United States, keep this in mind: Even the United States Supreme Court has trouble deciding when discrimination has taken place.

Was there discrimination against Allan Bakke in the 1970s when he tried to enroll in the University of California, Davis, Medical School? How about the case of Cheryl Hopwood in the '90s, when she was denied admission to the University of Texas Law School? Both were refused admission even though their test scores were higher than those of others who were admitted. And yet, those who were accepted over Bakke and Hopwood were members of a class of people who had once been denied on the basis of race.

The key piece of legislation in cases such as these is the Civil Rights Act of 1964, proposed by President John F. Kennedy and passed during the Johnson administration after a seventy-five-day filibuster. The law said there can be no discrimination based on race, color, creed, national origin, religion, or sex. The law established the Equal Employment Opportunity Commission (EEOC) as a venue for complaints to be filed. The act specifically forbade discrimination by any entity that receives money from the government, and it helped foster the concept of affirmative action.

Affirmative action plans require that companies such as banks and radio stations that are licensed by the government, schools that receive government funding, and any company that desires to do business with the government must actively move to correct deficiencies in their workforce. These deficiencies occur when there are positions in which a smaller percentage of minorities (and women) are employed than the overall percentage of those groups in the labor market.

However, laws are subject to the Constitution, and the "Equal Protection Clause" in the Fourteenth Amendment mandates that no state shall "deny to any person within its jurisdiction the equal protection of the laws." The clause would seem to forbid such practices as affirmative action and government set-asides based on race, but in reality, it hasn't worked out like that.

Today's society is more race conscious than ever. "Diversity" is the new watchword in every setting across America, from the courtroom to the boardroom, in companies large and small, in all areas of government—and especially in schools.

John Leo writes in *US News & World Report* about an updated version of the old high school history text Todd and Curti's *The American Nation* (Holt, Rinehart & Winston). The book literally bends over backward to be "inclusive." It teaches that "rural residents, African-Americans, Hispanic-Americans, and Native Americans continued to endure poverty and prejudice" in the '50s. It says that American independence "failed to benefit" women, blacks, and American Indians. Study questions are a hodge-podge of hyphenation, asking such things as: "How were African-Americans and Mexican-Americans affected differently by the Depression? How did the New Deal affect African-Americans and American Indians? What gains did African-Americans and Mexican-Americans make during the war?"[2]

Leo writes that efforts to make the text more diverse sometimes produce a comic effect, and he wonders what's next: "'Describe the impact of the Los Angeles earthquake on Polish-Americans'? Or 'Explain how the people of Minneapolis feel about Rodney King'?"[3] The textbook makes sure that just about everything it covers is viewed through a racial lens. (Don't laugh. Headlines with similar slants pose as news all the time. The *Dallas Morning News* carried a story about how the 2002 recession will affect Latinos according to research from the Pew Hispanic Center. The headline blared, "Recession may hurt Hispanics the most.")[4]

In the classroom, the old concept of the nation as a melting pot is just that—old, and out of date. Using concepts of multiculturalism as justification, the Austin Independent School District initiated a diversity training program for the district's 9,000 employees, with everyone from the custodians to the administrators required to participate. "The melting pot theory hasn't worked," said Brenda Banks, a middle school counselor. "We're not all alike. It's okay for our differences to be valued and appreciated."[5]

A closer reading of the new policy indicated that while ethnicity never could be blamed for any of the problems that students have, parents almost always could. School officials explained that students who arrived in class with no supplies weren't lazy—they might simply be homeless. Students who failed to do their homework might just be staying in a shelter to avoid domestic violence at home. Students who were late to class—well, they might have a unique set of problems at home.

Other school districts created committees to study diversity issues. Most of them have also thrown out the concept of the melting pot and have recommended sweeping measures aimed at changing the mission of the schools. They suggest such things as sensitivity training, cultural awareness programs, identifying the "struggles" of minority students, assuring nondiscrimination compliance, and providing bilingual materials to non-English-speaking parents and guardians. Sometimes these committees will talk about a "challenging curriculum" and "bringing test scores up," but forget it. That's just edu-speak, and it means nothing when there's always a ready-made excuse for any student who has a problem. More often than not, that excuse involves diversity.

In college, diversity is more than just an excuse; it's a way of life, and, to most college administrators, learning simply cannot take place without it. Lee Bollinger, who has been president of both the University of Michigan and Columbia, is a leading advocate. He says, "It's a question really of educational policy, not a matter of redressing past social injustices. People learn better in an environment where they are part of a mix of people . . . not like themselves."[6]

Really? Being in a class with people of varied skin color helps students learn geometry? Not according to the most intense study, a UCLA database covering 10 million students at 1,700 institutions. Surveying data on "attitudes, values, behavior, learning, achievement, career development, and satisfaction," the study pooh-poohs the notion that skin-color differences advance education. "No effect on learning or anything else," said the study.[7] But the closed minds of academia have already decided. To them, nothing is quite as important as diversity.

If public schools and colleges are the nation's bastions of diversity, then how long can it be before the outside world catches up? It had better not be too long—especially for big business—or the diversity police will come knocking at your door. Take the case of the four big television networks.

For some time, the National Association for the Advancement of Colored People (NAACP) had been calling on ABC, CBS, Fox, and NBC to employ more blacks, both in front of and behind the cameras. In late 1999, the civil rights organization got representatives from all the networks to show up at a meeting in Los Angeles to explain what they intended to do.

CBS's Leslie Moonves made a passionate talk on his network's new commitment to diversity, but lower-level executives from the other networks had their presentations put off until a later session. They walked out. An angry NAACP President Kweisi Mfume said, "These are not drive-by hearings. See us now, or see us later. Sooner or later, you're going to see us." The NAACP had set a deadline for the networks to have their diversity goals ready or face demonstrations and a boycott.[8]

It was a bizarre situation that amounted to fighting over the shape of the table. Moonves had promised the moon and more, and presumably, the other networks had come prepared to give, as well. Besides, the NAACP's threat of a Jesse Jackson–style boycott was risky. Some of these boycotts were successful, and some weren't, and this time, the threat was against organizations that had plenty of pull with the media; they *were* the media.

The fact is, though, that no company—not even a TV network—wants to be branded racist. The NAACP knows that, and also knows that the threat of a boycott is more potent than the actual thing. Some companies just see the handwriting on the wall and fall in line.

An amazing op-ed piece, written by the chairman and chief executive officer of American Airlines, Donald Carty, was carried in the *Dallas Morning News*. American Airlines is diverse, and Mr. Carty wanted to trumpet that fact from the highest mountaintop. "At American, we have seen what many other large companies also have witnessed: small pockets of resistance from a very few people for whom a diverse workplace apparently is unacceptable," he stated. "Simply put, some people 'just don't get it'—and I suspect some never will."[9]

There was no question that Carty "got it." Either he was a complete devotee to the concept of diversity, or he had seen what the TV networks and other companies had been forced to endure and he wanted no part of it. His column was full of details about "the richness in tapping the divergent views of people of all races, genders, national origins and lifestyles" and American's new "zero tolerance plan" to fire people for hate-related behavior. But Carty failed to explain how a diverse workforce would contribute to airline safety or to having his airplanes arrive at their destinations on time. He never quite got around to actually telling his readers how "the richness of divergent views" would get luggage checked more efficiently.

Let's be clear: People who write passionately about diversity in the workplace or in the classroom are engaging in the most politically correct sort of psychobabble. Lee Bollinger and Donald Carty can sing the praises of diversity until the cows come home, but neither of them can give you one single good reason to promote something that simply doesn't need to be promoted.

What is diversity?

There are two kinds of diversity. Let's call the first kind "natural diversity." This simply means that diversity—of ethnicity, gender, and sexual orientation—has always been with us and it always will. Diversity is a normal, usual thing. If the concept of natural diversity were to take hold, then schools and companies could simply grade or hire people on how well they perform. Of course, this would assume that logical differences in the sexes and the races would be taken into account (the physical differences between men and women, or the fact that a black actor would be needed to play the role of Malcolm X), but other than that, little attention would be paid to diversity at all.

Natural diversity holds that about half of the population will be women. There will be continued immigration as people from other countries come into the United States to attend school and seek employment. U.S. service-men abroad will marry foreign women and bring them home to live and start families. At this point in our history, some people aren't even sure what their dominant ethnicity is.

Natural diversity is a fact of life. It is not always a good thing, nor is it always a bad thing. However, it cannot be stopped, and it does not need to be promoted.

The other type of diversity could be referred to as "adversary diversity," or AD. The definition is: "Using ethnicity to one's own advantage at the expense of others."

When the NAACP threatened to boycott the networks, they were utilizing adversary diversity. All the Jesse Jackson corporate shakedowns are based on adversary diversity.

Race-based college admissions policies are a form of AD. Affirmative action in all its forms—quotas, set-asides, racial preferences of any kind—are based on AD.

Under this theory, now considered fact at all major universities and by government in general, diversity is an end unto itself. That makes it all right to take something away from a member of one group (mostly white males) and give it to a member of an approved group. In other words, adversary diversity requires someone to give something up so that someone else can obtain it.

Adversary diversity always looks for the racial hook and can find it almost anywhere.

Adversary diversity in (affirmative) action

On August 28, 1997, the California Civil Rights Initiative, a.k.a. Proposition 209, went into effect in California. It was a new law, voted in by a 54 percent margin, that banned preferences for minorities when applying to state colleges and universities, applying for jobs with the state, or for minority-owned companies that wanted state contracts. The law didn't quite end all affirmative action, because programs at public schools and many other agencies were covered by federal laws.

Proposition 209 was proof positive of a major principle of set-aside programs: once a protected group obtains preferences, it never wants to give them up.

Lisa Campbell, the owner of an environmental cleaning business, claimed that her safety net had been pulled out from under her. Ms. Campbell said that she was getting as many as forty calls and faxes each day from companies that wanted to use her as a subcontractor in order to meet government goals for the use of minority-owned companies. But after Prop 209 passed, the calls dwindled. "What I'm hearing now is: 'We don't need your bid.'" she said. "The big boys don't just want a bigger piece of the pie; they want the whole pie." [10]

Think about it. Wouldn't you want programs in place that practically forced other companies to subcontract with your company? And if you saw those programs falling by the wayside, would you be unhappy? Probably so, because there'd be no more sitting by the telephone taking orders; you'd have to actually work to make your business grow.

And so there were court challenges and charges of racism that acted as a magnet to draw the Reverend Jesse Jackson to California. Jackson organized a protest that brought thousands of Prop 209 opponents to the Golden Gate Bridge, where they chanted, "We shall overcome." [11]

News stories reported that it wasn't even clear whether the new law would have any immediate impact, because some officials—such as San Francisco City Attorney Louise Renne—were saying that local affirmative action programs would be continued. But Reverend Jackson, always anxious to keep victimhood alive, ranted on: "In this country, there are those who are dreamers and those who are dream-busters. The dreamers need to outlast the dream-busters." [12]

The protesters on the Golden Gate Bridge were fired up, but their anger was driven by emotion rather than logic. It is simply not logical to assume that every white-owned company in California that had been subcontracting with minority businesses would suddenly drop them like hot potatoes if relationships had been established and the minority companies were doing a good job. Business just doesn't work like that. Besides, there is every indication that many companies desire to do business with minority-owned firms because they think it's the right thing to do. Some even take diversity to ridiculous extremes, such as American Airlines' Donald Carty.

But the screaming in California continued anyway, with some officials likening Prop 209 to Jim Crow laws.

Jim Crow himself was a black character in an old song and became the symbol for segregation—the separation of the races. Segregation, in the form of "separate but equal" public schools, was dismantled in the 1954 case *Brown v. Board of Education of Topeka.* When Oliver Brown, a black railroad worker, filed suit against the Topeka School Board for not allowing his daughter to attend an all-white school near her home, the decision of the Supreme Court in favor of Mr. Brown was unanimous.

But this was not adversary diversity. No one else had to give anything up in order for Mr. Brown's daughter to attend the white school. Somehow, though, in the days since the *Brown* decision and the Civil Rights Act of 1964, things have changed.

Even segregation is back in vogue—if it's practiced by a protected group. You can have an NAACP or a Congressional Black Caucus, as long as there is no white counterpart. In the Millwood Public Schools in Oklahoma City, kids are treated to something called "The Black Pledge of Allegiance," which is posted on the school's web site:[13]

"We pledge allegiance of the red, black and green, our flag, the symbol of our eternal struggle, and to the land we must obtain. One nation of Black people, with one God for us all, totally united in the struggle for Black Love, Black Freedom, and Black determination."

The school superintendent, Dr. Gloria Griffin, insisted that the black pledge was not about racism or separatism, and she wondered if those who opposed it "want to incite some kind of division within the United States."[14] Dr. Griffin received many e-mails both for and against the pledge. But can you imagine the national outrage if some district had posted a "white pledge"?

Mark this down as another principle of adversary diversity: Organizations, events, and publications may be established in the name of protected groups only. But of all the effects of adversary diversity, the displacement of whites in favor of members of protected groups is the most frequent and the most disturbing.

This is a major concern of author Paul Craig Roberts. He contends that discrimination has become anything that doesn't produce racially proportionate results and that quotas have become the only way to avoid debilitating lawsuits. "The imposition of proportional outcomes requires legal discrimination," says Roberts. "Discrimination against white males is required by federal agencies."[15] For instance, a female assistant secretary of education in the Clinton administration made a ruling that axed 350 men's college sports teams. The ruling made the men's and women's programs more equal—by downsizing sports for men.[16]

Dr. Roberts wrote a book with Lawrence M. Stratton, called *The New Color Line,* that explored the affect of quotas on democracy.[17] Some examples: Chevy Chase Savings Bank near Washington, D.C., was forced to open up unneeded branches in minority areas and provide blacks with below-market loans. The Daniel Lamp Company in Chicago had a workforce that was 100 percent minority, but the government sued because the ratio of blacks to Hispanics was wrong.

Dr. Roberts flatly states that there are two classes of citizens in America—those who are protected by civil rights laws, and white males, who are not.

In a story about the construction of the new arena for the Dallas Mavericks of the NBA and the Dallas Stars of the NHL, it was apparent how much work went into making sure that every conceivable minority group got a piece of the pie. Tom Hicks, owner of the Stars and baseball's Texas Rangers, was one of the developers who pushed for the new American Airlines Center by promising that at least 26 percent of the construction contracts would go to minorities.[18] But the developers overdelivered.

A third of the contracts went to minority- or women-owned businesses. At the time of the report, black-owned and Hispanic-owned businesses had each received about 10 percent of the total expenditures for the arena, Asians and American Indians got about 2 percent, and companies owned by white women got about 12 percent. Some two hundred minority-owned and women-owned companies were helping build the center.[19]

We've come a long way—or have we? Minority or not, how many of those companies were large and wealthy to begin with? In the case of the women-owned companies, how many men were in the background after having put the company in a woman's name in order to become a Historically Underutilized Business (HUB)? And what about Choctaw Erectors Inc., run by American Indian Kevin Ball? Choctaw, with its very PC name and minority status, received a contract for $100,000 worth of steel services, according to the report.

It's hard to imagine Mr. Ball at the construction site in full tribal head-dress. It's equally hard to imagine that Mr. Ball could be picked out of a crowd as an American Indian if he were dressed in a regular business suit, or that he is affected in any way by the remaining vestiges of slavery. But if Choctaw Erectors is able to pick up contracts by virtue of preference programs, it's hard to fault them for playing the game.

The game extends far beyond city construction contracts for local minority companies. Inside big government agencies such as the Federal Communications Commission (FCC), adversary diversity is practiced with a vengeance. The FCC fought hard to preserve an outrageous "equal opportunity" plan that is foisted upon radio and television stations, forcing them to jump through dozens of racial hoops before anyone can be hired. And the FCC has, from time to time, installed various programs designed to increase the diversity of broadcast ownership—naturally, at the expense of others.

The *Wall Street Journal* carried a story that contained two bizarre examples of how the FCC worked its diversity schemes, and who was standing by to take full advantage. In one case, a group of black investors formed in 1985 to purchase a television station in Buffalo. The investors—being black—were considered to be "economically disadvantaged" under the program. The group included O. J. Simpson, Colin Powell, Patrick Ewing, Julius Erving, and several members of Michael Jackson's family. After receiving the tax breaks from the program, they sold the station in 1995.[20]

The other case involved Harvey Gantt, who is black and was mayor of Charlotte when he and some partners picked up a television license under a minority bidding system. Four months later, they sold the license to a white buyer, making a $3 million profit. Since then, Congress has ended some of these programs, but as the *WSJ* column points out, "The track record of the FCC on racial preference programs is a virtual textbook on how such programs primarily benefit people and companies that don't need the help."[21]

Another interesting case is that of the Piscataway, New Jersey, School Board in 1989. This one almost backfired and had the diversity community biting its nails, hoping it would just go away. The case involved a budget shortfall in which one teaching position was going to be cut. It eventually came down to two teachers—one black and one white—and the school board retained the black teacher in the name of diversity. The white teacher sued and the case headed for the Supreme Court.

Bob Herbert, a liberal columnist, was worried that this case might end racial preferences in most cases. Here's the problem as Herbert saw it: First of all, the black teacher, Debra Williams, held an advanced degree, while the white teacher, Sharon Taxman, didn't. So the school board should have claimed that it was retaining Williams on that basis. But it didn't; it had flatly stated that Williams was retained because she was black. To further complicate the picture, the school board had never admitted that it had discriminated in the past, and therefore the application of diversity in this case was not for the purpose of redressing past abuses.[22]

The moral of this story, according to Herbert, was simple: Don't apply affirmative action to a case such as this if there's a chance that it might backfire. Others were worried about the same thing, and eventually the case reached a settlement without going to the Supreme Court. The settlement amounted to $433,500, with $308,500 coming from the Black Leadership Forum. Columnist Joan Beck said it was "hush money, collected to prevent the possibility of the high court ruling against affirmative action or even hearing oral arguments about it."[23]

(The element of "systemic racial discrimination" applies to government business contracts, as well. Dallas officials, who had overdelivered on minority contracts for the American Airlines Center, thought that the city's affirmative action plan might be in legal danger under a 1989 Supreme Court decision. So they brought in a consultant to conduct an "availability and disparity study." Not surprisingly, the consultant found enough discrimination to "legally bulletproof" the city's racial preference program.)[24]

The Piscataway case was unusual in that some people in government— namely in the George H.W. Bush Justice Department—actually noticed an abuse of adversary diversity. But when it takes place in elections, most people fail to see it. President George W. Bush signed a campaign finance reform bill, but the bill didn't address the main arena where elections are actually rigged: redistricting.

Understand that this little diversity scheme affects just about every election in the country except for the United States Senate, which is immune from redistricting. But state legislatures and U.S. representative districts are constantly gerrymandered for racial purposes.

Republicans and Democrats usually draw up maps that protect incumbents from their party, and civil rights groups chime in demanding more districts to be set aside for minorities. The argument is that blacks and Hispanics are "underrepresented" in state houses or in the United States House of Representatives. But consider this: When districts are drawn for racial purposes, they are always set up to benefit blacks or Hispanics, who usually run as Democrats. Is it any wonder that the Left is so excited about affirmative action in elections? It means free seats for their party.

In spite of how it looks, not all black people are sold on the idea of affirmative action. Some even believe that it is demeaning to blacks and other minorities because it makes it look as if they can't compete on a level playing field. Jackie Cissell, a black woman who works in public relations in Indianapolis, wrote an op-ed for USA Today saying that blacks can't afford the luxury of self-pity. Instead, she suggested that they work to remedy the "root causes" of their problems, including the failure of public education in black communities.[25]

Many black people who are celebrities or high-level officials hold similar opinions, and they often run afoul of the civil rights community. The highest-profile example is Supreme Court Justice Clarence Thomas, who has a track record of voting against affirmative action and racial gerrymandering.

In an attempt to embarrass Justice Thomas, a predominantly black school board in the Washington suburb of Landover, Maryland, abruptly withdrew an invitation for Thomas to address an awards ceremony at the Thomas Pullen Creative and Performing Arts School. The reason? A member of the school board charged that Justice Thomas's work on the High Court "had not represented the interests of black people."[26] Wire stories noted, however, that

Justice Thomas frequently plays host at his Supreme Court offices for informal meetings with local school groups—many of them black.

But Clarence Thomas is not part of the adversary diversity community. When he talks to students, he tells them to work hard in school to achieve their full potential—not to seek out government set-asides. And so, the AD community works to shut him up.

When the black National Bar Association asked Justice Thomas to give a speech, some members wanted to do exactly what the school in Landover had done—withdraw the invitation. The *Wall Street Journal* reported that Judge A. Leon Higginbotham, who "has made delegitimizing Clarence Thomas virtually his life's work" was one of those who wanted to un-invite him.[27]

If the adversary diversity community has, shall we say, distaste for Justice Thomas, it literally loathes Ward Connerly, the man Paul Gigot of the *Wall Street Journal* calls "a one-man melting pot." Connerly enjoys explaining that his father left when he was under the age of two; his father's mother was white; his father was black; his mother died when he was four; her mother was full-blooded Choctaw Indian; her father was white French.[28] And yet, does Mr. Connerly use any of this rich minority status for his own personal benefit? Not on your life! He is, in fact, the nation's single most effective opponent of AD in all its forms.

Mr. Connerly was the cover feature for *Parade* on May 31, 1998. In the article, he explained his vision of a colorblind America, saying that while America was using affirmative action to remedy racism, the country became "addicted to government and its occupation of our lives."[29]

How did a black man become such an ardent foe of adversary diversity? It really began when he worked for Assemblyman Pete Wilson in 1968. Later, as governor and under some pressure to make a minority appointment, Wilson named Mr. Connerly to the University of California Board of Regents. In 1994, he was approached by a couple, Jerry and Ellen Cook, who told him that their son had been rejected by the medical school in San Diego even though his grades were good enough for Harvard. When Mr. Connerly saw the numbers and realized that blacks and Hispanics were getting racial preferences, his eyes were opened. He told Governor Wilson that the practice should be stopped. Amazingly, it took just months to end the preferences, which the regents did on July 20, 1995. Suddenly, a twenty-nine-year policy of preferences in admissions, jobs, and contracting was gone.[30] Next, Mr. Connerly took on the Prop 209 initiative.

The *Parade* pull-quote pretty well summed up Mr. Connerly's objections to affirmative action: "I wouldn't accept a job or college admission based on color. I wouldn't want the stigma, the cloud hanging over me. There would be no greater insult."

And Ward Connerly isn't through yet. He wants a totally color-blind California—one that doesn't classify people by race at all. Mr. Connerly says that racial data doesn't help anyone and doesn't prevent discrimination. He points out that the NBA is disproportionately black, then asks, "Does that mean the NBA is discriminating against whites or Asians or Latinos?"[31]

His critics are vocal, charging that race-based data not only helps with anti-discrimination efforts, but also in other areas such as law enforcement and medicine. In reality, Mr. Connerly's proposal simply calls for no racial classification by the state in the operation of public education, public contracting, and public employment. If passed into law, private companies could still have all the diversity training they want, but diversity consultants who work with the state might lose a great deal of business.

Leonard Pitts, a black columnist for the *Miami Herald,* wishes Mr. Connerly would just go away. Pitts admits that there are valid reasons to question affirmative action but doesn't like Mr. Connerly's reasons, mainly the contention that it's "divisive." Pitts contends that white men have had a form of de facto affirmative action for years, while holding back blacks. But in a statement that could be taken two ways, Pitts writes, "Those who enjoy privileges seldom surrender them easily."[32]

What Pitts meant was that white males, with their "de facto" preferences, want to keep them. But the statement also conjures up images of Jesse Jackson's mob on the Golden Gate Bridge belly-aching about losing racial set-aides.

It's hard to convince minorities to give up preferences, even when those minorities are prominent Republicans. Former U.S. Representative J. C. Watts of Oklahoma is black, conservative, and convinced that it would harm the GOP if affirmative action went away. When Representative Charles Canady, R-Fla., and Senator Mitch McConnell, R-Ky., sponsored a bill that would have been a Prop 209 for federal programs, Watts opposed it. So did Representative Henry Bonilla, R-Tex., who said the bill would not help Republicans politically.[33]

Strange as it seems, adversary diversity in the form of affirmative action still exists today largely because of the Republican Party. The constant battle to win votes—especially in the wake of the Bush-Gore contest in 2000—has made the minority vote key. While the GOP has little hope of winning over large numbers of blacks, the party believes that the growing Hispanic vote is up for grabs.

When do we say when? With the nation divided almost exactly fifty-fifty, and with the minority population on the rise, Republicans are scared to oppose any racial preference that might hand the Democrats an issue. Ward Connerly will have a victory here and there, but as a nation, we're not going to say "when" anytime soon.

From Bakke to Hopwood: inequality in education

Dateline Amherst: About 150 students at the University of Massachusetts declared victory after occupying a campus building for six days. Student Government President Maurice Caston-Powe was ecstatic. "United we fought; together we won this," he bragged to three hundred students outside the building.[34]

What exactly did the protesters win? According to school officials, nothing that wasn't already a part of campus policy. Certainly nothing on the order of more qualified professors, or more courses on Western civilization. Nope; what they demanded was mostly related to adversary diversity:

· A 4 percent increase in minority enrollment, bringing it to 20 percent.
· More financial aid and more funding programs for minorities.
· More minority faculty and administrators.
· An end to all student late fees.
· Departmental status for Irish, Native American, Latin American, and Asian American studies.

In looking at college campuses today, one is compelled to wonder: What were these students thinking? Except for the demand on student late fees, the rest of their diatribe amounted to what passes for normal at most universities. Going as far back as the 1970s, the headlines have been full of stories about minority preferences on college campuses.

It was 1978 when the Supreme Court made its famous ruling in *Regents of the University of California v. Allan Bakke*. Bakke was a white man who wanted to attend the medical school at Davis. He sued after discovering that his test scores were higher than the scores of some minorities who had been admitted under a preference program. The case was a conundrum for the court.

Applying the Civil Rights Act of 1964 and the Equal Protection Clause, the justices ordered the school to admit Mr. Bakke. But Justice Lewis F. Powell Jr. issued a second ruling: schools could consider race and ethnicity in their admissions program, providing that it was one of several factors considered. The other four justices supported this part of the ruling. So while Mr. Bakke won his case, the dual decision really didn't decide anything.

That brings us to more modern times and the similar situation of Cheryl Hopwood, Ken Elliott, David Rogers, and Douglas Carvell. This time, it was 1992 and the school was the University of Texas at Austin's law school. In August, the four whites were denied admission, but as in the case of Bakke, the applications were not judged on an equal basis. The fall class boasted forty-one blacks and fifty-five Hispanics, but on a level playing field, it would have contained only nine blacks and eighteen Hispanics.[35]

In September, the four white people filed a lawsuit against the UT law school, charging discrimination in its admissions policies. The suit became known as "Hopwood." During the past decade, the case has been a roller-coaster ride of court decisions, rulings from state officials, and newspaper headlines warning that, from a minority enrollment viewpoint, the sky is going to fall.

In 1994, Federal Judge Sam Sparks cited the Fourteenth Amendment in ruling that the four whites were denied equal protection, but he also said that they hadn't proven that they would have been admitted even with a level playing field. Two years later, the 5th U.S. Circuit Court of Appeals reversed Judge Sparks by ruling that the Hopwood plaintiffs were discriminated against. On July 1, 1996, the Supreme Court refused to hear the case. On July 2, the *Austin American-Statesman*'s headline read: "Minority enrollment at U.T. expected to decline."[36] UT President Robert Berdahl (later to become chancellor at Berkeley) immediately met with faculty and students to assure them that diversity goals would not be abandoned.

In February of 1997, Texas Attorney General Dan Morales put forth his own interpretation of the ruling: He said it meant that race-based admissions were illegal statewide. Some four months later, a state law was passed to provide automatic enrollment to the top 10 percent of the graduating class of each high school.[37]

The *Statesman* was unrelenting in its coverage of declining minority applications in the wake of the court decisions. In an article about applications for the fall of 1997, the *Statesman*'s headline blared, "Texas college applications by minorities drop." The story explained that minority applications at UT were down by 52 percent; applications to the law school from minorities were in sharp decline; and at least one candidate for a faculty position at Texas A&M had turned down an offer out of concern about Hopwood.[38] A close reading of the story revealed that applications were down in general; white undergraduate applications at UT were off 32 percent. Those facts weren't reflected in the hysterical headline. Nor was there any explanation of why whites were not taking advantage of the court rulings by applying in even higher numbers than before.

As the school year opened, the headlines and the stories behind them were coming from a very set point of view. "U.T. reopens amid troubling racial shift," read one banner, as if the race-neutral decision was "troubling" to everyone. In truth, it was troubling to many in the education establishment and those on the Left, but to affirmative action opponents such as Ward Connerly, it was more hopeful than anything else. Even so, the *Statesman* article's pull-quotes came exclusively from those who opposed race neutrality on campus. "The issue for me is not if Hopwood is right or wrong, but it's how to have diversity in higher education," said Glenn West of the Austin Chamber of Commerce.[39]

The *Statesman* published a diatribe written by M. Michael Sharlot, dean of the UT law school, in which he seemed to be saying that without racial preferences, UT would lose "the diversity that was once our hallmark." Sharlot explained in typical educratic rhetoric, and with no substantiating facts, that race-neutral policies would prevent the law school from providing "opportunities for all students to benefit from the perspectives of society's traditionally marginalized groups."[40] But Dean Sharlot never explained just why he thought minorities couldn't make it on their own.

On April 28, 1998, Attorney General Morales, himself a Hispanic, drew the ire of university officials and the media by refusing to appeal the case. Mr. Morales was quite clear in his reasoning: "My office has identified no sufficient grounds upon which to base an appeal . . ." In a written statement, he affirmed his support for race-neutral admission criteria: "Racial quotas, set-asides, and preferences do not, in my judgment, represent the values and principles which Texas should embrace."[41] Critics immediately blasted Morales, and UT officials started making plans to appeal the suit with private attorneys. The *Statesman* editorialized against Morales, saying that he had decided to "abdicate his responsibility."[42] The editorial stated, "Locking the doors to the flagship universities to minorities would be bad policy." Exactly how a race-neutral policy amounted to "locking the doors" to minorities was not explained.

Morales, who later failed in an attempt to win the Democratic nomination for governor, left office and the new attorney general, Republican John Cornyn, rescinded the Morales opinion. Mr. Cornyn directed schools to stay the course until the courts made a final decision. Meanwhile, the State of Texas asked the 5th U.S. Circuit Court of Appeals to reinstate affirmative action. In December 2000, the court issued another one of those "divided" decisions. On the one hand, the court lifted the injunction against race-based admissions policies, citing the Bakke case. But the court sent the case back to the federal district court for more consideration.[43] UT officials considered it a win.

It was becoming more difficult to tell a win from a loss. In May of 2001, UT officials were giddy because of a ruling involving the University of Washington. Three white students there had sued, claiming that their rights had been violated because of racial preferences. But, citing Bakke, the 9th U.S. Circuit Court of Appeals ruled that race-based admissions policies were all right. The Supreme Court refused to hear the Washington case, letting the decision stand.[44]

The next month, the Supreme Court again refused to hear the Hopwood case. That meant two things. First, Texas schools would have to keep ad-

mitting students with no consideration of race. Second, diametrically opposite appeals court rulings were now in effect. The Supreme Court seemed to
say that race-based admissions were bad in Texas, but good in Washington.
University of Texas President Larry Faulkner made it known that UT would
do everything it could to get around the Texas ruling while waiting for a final
decision: "For now we will keep searching for creative and legal ways to serve
all the populations of Texas."[45]

The boom was lowered—at least for the time being—in July 2001 when
U.S. District Judge Sam Sparks declared the case "closed." He said that "no
viable issue" remained in the nine-year-old-case. Steven Smith, the lawyer
who represented some of the plaintiffs, said he agreed with the decision, but
UT officials were not happy. William Powers, now dean of the law school,
said, "We will continue our vigorous efforts to enroll students of all races
within the limits imposed by the courts."[46] It was clear by this time that Texas
schools were going to have to live under this ruling for some time. It was also
clear that they intended to live up to the letter of the ruling but that they
would violate its spirit every chance they got.

Schools in both Texas and California began to get creative. Texas A&M
announced that it would make a special effort to go after the "top 20 percent" of students at about 250 high schools that were deemed low-performing or disadvantaged. A&M would also place a special emphasis on high
schools that traditionally sent few students on to Aggieland. The students
would be admitted if they scored 920 on the SAT and took certain courses
while in high school.[47]

It was an end-run around the Hopwood decision and everybody knew it.
A campus activist group known as the Young Conservatives of Texas called
the plan "illegal, unfair, and academically indefensible preferential treatment."[48] YCT Chairman Mark Levin asked Attorney General Cornyn to dis-
allow the plan and threatened a lawsuit if he didn't.

The University of California had been thinking along these same lines
but approached the problem from a slightly different angle; instead of using
Texas A&M's "disadvantaged" approach, Cal would use a "victim" tactic to
get around Prop 209. Here's how it works: An applicant to Cal would have
a preference if he or she had been engaged in a "struggle" (a racially charged
word still used by the diversity industry) or had experienced difficult family
situations. California would give a few extra points to students who had
overcome a physical handicap, worked after school, were fired or laid off at
work, lived in single-parent or low-income homes, or came from a family
where neither parent went to high school.

John Leo, the writer for *US News & World Report,* called it a diversity
tactic used to evade laws or court rulings against quotas. "This means that

students are rewarded for their parents' failures and for their own psychological problems as well," said Leo. "If Dad walks out on Mom or beats her up, or if you have a few suicide tries on your record, you might improve your chances of leaping over more academically qualified candidates who are short of family turmoil."[49]

While all this was going on in Texas and California, other universities in other states were getting rulings that were more to their liking. The University of Washington was still openly practicing adversary diversity, and now the law school at the University of Michigan could follow suit. This time, it was a five-to-four decision by the 6th U.S. Circuit Court of Appeals that allowed race-based programs at Michigan to continue.[50] So as this is written, we have no fewer than four federal appeals court decisions on racial preferences for colleges—and the decisions are not in agreement.

The situation at the University of Michigan casts a bright light on a central theme of those who promote diversity for diversity's sake on campuses. To them, "nondiscrimination" means "we must discriminate." Columnist Steve Chapman took a look at Michigan's Web site and found this disclaimer: "[The university] is committed to a policy of nondiscrimination and equal opportunity for all persons regardless of race."[51] But as Chapman points out, the school had been fighting a court battle for years for a simple reason: The University of Michigan discriminates on the basis of race, and it has no intention of stopping.

On June 23, 2003, the Supreme Court finally issued a ruling in the Michigan case. The High Court upheld a race-based admissions policy for Michigan's law school by a vote of 5–4 with Justice Sandra Day O'Connor writing for the majority that the school has a "compelling interest" in attaining a diverse student body. However, the Court also ruled that Michigan must throw out its practice of awarding points to undergraduate applicants based simply on race.

Prior to the Michigan ruling, state schools weren't really sure where they stood. Adversary diversity was out in California because of Prop 209; it was out in Texas because of the Hopwood decision. It was OK in Washington and Michigan because of appeals court decisions. Following the Supreme Court ruling in Michigan, major universities immediately went to work to tailor their race-based admissions policies to be in line with the new standards.

It remains to be seen how the new decision will affect some programs that were already being implemented in some states.

In Florida, the State University System's board of regents voted 12–0 to pass Governor Jeb Bush's "One Florida" plan, ending racial preferences for the ten state schools. Governor Bush prefers to allow automatic admissions for the top 20 percent of each high school's graduating class. The reaction from diversity proponents was predictable. "You say 'Bush,'" shouted Tampa minister Frank Williams at the regents meeting. "I say, 'Heil Hitler.'"[52]

The message from the Left could not be clearer: If you oppose race-based admissions policies, you are a Nazi. If a court rules against them, the schools will find new ways to discriminate.

Church burnings and other hate crimes

It's well known that high blood pressure is more prevalent among blacks than whites. What do you suppose could be the cause of that? If you guessed "racism," move to the head of the class. Adversary diversity provides a convenient excuse for just about every problem that any non–white male could ever experience.

We're not kidding about the blood pressure thing. A study published in the *American Journal of Public Health* found that "racial discrimination, along with a person's method of coping with it, may be an important cause of high blood pressure in blacks."[53]

So, when a series of church burnings in the black community made headlines, could a racial hook be far behind? Of course not. The principles of adversary diversity dictate that there must be some sort of conspiracy against minorities.

In an op-ed piece, Hugh B. Price, president of the National Urban League, called the burnings "an absolute outrage" that must be stopped. He commended President Bill Clinton, who was playing along with the idea that white racists must be behind it all: "Clinton met with the governors of the southern states in a bipartisan effort to stop the burnings. He said, 'It is clear that racial hostility is the driving force behind a number of these incidents.'"[54] Price compared the burnings to the Oklahoma City bombing and opined that such events are fueled by rhetoric on (conservative) talk radio.

The rhetoric on the Left was getting as hot as any fire. A bevy of organizations fronted by the National Council of Churches took out a full-page ad in *USA Today* asking for donations to rebuild the burned churches. Beneath a huge photo of a burning church, the copy read:

"If just one church in America had been burned or desecrated by racists, all people of faith would have been affected. But, in the last 18 months, more than 40 church buildings in the United States have been burned or desecrated. Over 80 other attacks have been documented since 1990. These attacks aimed predominately at African-American congregations threaten all of us. The National Council of Churches is the oldest and largest religious ecumenical organization in America. Most of the burned churches were our churches."[55]

The coupon said, "Yes. I want to stand up against racism . . ."

For his part, Bill Clinton saw an opportunity to make a few political points with a key constituency. On his weekly radio address of June 8, he told us: "I have vivid and painful memories of black churches being burned in my own state when I was a child." But John Starr of the *Arkansas Democrat-Gazette* contacted every civil rights leader he could find. Not one of them could remember any church burnings in Arkansas during Clinton's childhood.[56]

The fact is that all the hysteria about black church burnings being racist was so much nonsense. Jim Johnson, a retired state Supreme Court justice, wrote to the president and demanded a retraction: "Name one black church which has been burned in the state of Arkansas or else apologize for the shame which you continue to bring to your native state."[57] Clinton backed off but still said he could remember fires at unnamed "black community buildings."

The cat was out of the bag. Stories were popping up everywhere disputing the claim of racism in the burnings. *USA Today* reported, "Federal investigators are probing nearly as many arson cases at predominately white churches as they are black churches."[58] The *USA Today* story also noted that about 1,330 fires strike churches each year. The Associated Press reported that nothing seemed out of the norm: "A review of six years of federal, state, and local data found arsons are up—at both black and white churches—but with only random links to racism."[59]

The *Wall Street Journal* ran a story attributing the origin of the church-burning hysteria to a group called The Center for Democratic Renewal. The group's mission was to work with liberal organizations to counter right-wing rhetoric and public policy initiatives—really, to uncover any resurgence in racist activity.[60] With the church arson story, CDR cooked the statistics and stepped over the line. But as is so often the case with the radical Left, none of that mattered; it was all for the cause.

It's easy to imagine how so many people in the black community could believe the poppycock about the church burnings. According to a Gallup poll, almost two-thirds of them believe that the criminal justice system is stacked against them. They point to harsher penalties for black crack offenders than for whites who deal in cocaine. And they note that black people receive the death penalty in disproportionate numbers.[61] (This is the reason given for so-called "jury-nullification," which produced the not-guilty verdict in the O. J. Simpson murder case.)

But is it true? An exhaustive study by the Center for Equal Opportunity looked at data from the Bureau of Justice Statistics from more than 55,000 state cases covering fourteen types of felonies. In only two of them—"traffic offenses" and "other felonies"—were blacks more likely to be convicted than whites. In categories such as murder, rape, robbery, assault, burglary, drug trafficking, and weapons charges, whites were more likely to receive a verdict of guilty.[62]

What exactly does this mean? The authors of the article, Linda Chavez (president of the Center for Equal Opportunity) and Robert Lerner (who conducted the study), say it could go one of two ways. Conspiracists will tell you that police departments routinely charge too many innocent blacks. Or, the high number of black acquittals could be the result of jury-nullification, something that Chavez and Lerner would call "a different kind of racism."

Whether perception or reality, many blacks—as well as some Hispanics, homosexuals, and members of various other groups—obviously feel that they deserve extra protection under the law. And that brings us to hate crimes legislation.

This is where adversary diversity gets truly bizarre. Every single law that applies to the protection and well-being of white people and straight people also applies to minorities and homosexuals. Federal law already allows for hate crime prosecutions on the basis of race, color, religion, or national origin—limited to crimes committed against people doing any of six protected activities, such as going to school or voting. But that doesn't stop the politics of race—and in this case, sexual orientation.

The push for new hate crimes legislation was spurred on by two heinous crimes: the brutal murder of a young gay man, Matthew Shepard, in Wyoming, and the dragging death of a black man, James Byrd Jr., in Jasper, Texas. In fact, both of these crimes were aggressively prosecuted under existing laws. Then why the need for racial or sexual-orientation-based set-asides in the law?

The case was made in an op-ed piece signed by four prominent United States senators, Robert Torricelli, Edward Kennedy, Barbara Boxer, and Ron Wyden—all of whom signed on as sponsors to the Hate Crimes Prevention Act (HCPA). Understand that federal law already encompassed crimes based on a victim's race, religion, national origin, or color. But the four liberal senators wanted more.

The two men who had allegedly killed Mr. Shepard had been charged with first-degree murder, but the prosecutor in the case had not decided on whether to seek the death penalty. Furthermore, they said, many states have no hate crime laws, and some that do are influenced by prejudice every step of the way. But the heart of the matter to the senators was their total support of special rights for certain groups: "Unlike other violent crimes, hate crime victims are selected simply because of who they are. Their victimization sends a message of fear and intimidation to an entire group or community and is designed to make the group feel isolated, vulnerable and unprotected."[63] The senators were concerned about how these groups "feel," and they wanted action.

They also mentioned FBI statistics that said 8,759 hate crimes were committed in 1996. The fact that there is no such thing as a "love crime" was not brought up, nor did the senators seem concerned that prosecutors in the O. J. Simpson case—a black man charged with the brutal murder of two whites—did not seek the death penalty.

President Clinton was all for the legislation. He talked about "the persistence of old, even primitive hatreds" in asking Congress to expand federal hate crime laws to include protection for homosexuals.[64] He did not mention any memories of predominately gay churches having been burned when he was a kid. However, he did link the debate to what was going on in Kosovo, where hundreds of thousands of people were being killed or expelled by the Serbs because they were ethnic Albanians. In June 2000, the Senate passed the bill.

Meanwhile, in Texas, things were heating up over the James Byrd dragging case. Liberals in the state wanted a double whammy: tough new state laws on top of what might be passed at the federal level. One interesting thing about the Texas situation is that the governor who might find a hate crimes bill on his desk was George W. Bush—who was making plans to run for president of the United States.

Governor Bush wanted no part of the hate crimes bill, and for the most part he just ignored it. This drew the ire of the chief sponsor of the bill, state Senator Rodney Ellis: "Since our governor is a leading presidential hopeful, the eyes of the world are on Texas," warned Mr. Ellis. "Everything we do now takes on national implications."[65] But the bill died when Republicans and Democrats could not reach a compromise, and Governor Bush never had to make the tough decision on whether to sign it.

The battle raged on. After Mr. Bush had moved to Washington and handed over the governor's mansion to Rick Perry, the new governor found himself in the same pickle. His conservative base was telling him to sign the legislation over their collective dead bodies. In March 2001, they descended on Austin to proclaim support for equal protection under the law—but not for the hate crimes bill. Kelly Shackelford, president of the Free Market Foundation, a pro-family organization, said the hate crimes bill would protect some people more than others: "The homosexual who leaves the gay bar should receive the full protection of the law, but so should your grandmother on her way to the supermarket."[66]

But Governor Perry, who very much wanted the support of the emerging black and Hispanic vote in his upcoming gubernatorial run, was beginning to weaken. In May, he caved. "All of us ... have always agreed on one thing: Hate and hate crimes are unacceptable in a state as great as Texas."[67] Senator Ellis was ecstatic.

Surrounded by liberal Democrats and other proponents, Governor Perry signed the "James Byrd, Jr. Hate Crimes Act" into law on May 11.[68] As he was signing the legislation, two of the white men who killed Mr. Byrd were already sitting on Texas' death row, and the third was serving a life sentence.

Back in Washington, the battle still rages. Senate Republicans have refused to add "sexual orientation" and "disabilities" to the list of protected groups. Democrats say they will not give up. "Senate Republicans made clear that they will not take action to fight terrorism at home," said Senator Kennedy.[69] The obvious implication was that while Republicans will fight radical Islam, they won't lift a finger to protect homosexuals here in the U.S.

The *Wall Street Journal* writer Dorothy Rabinowitz would take exception to Senator Kennedy's tirade. When Al Gore was saying that "hate crimes hurt the heart of America, the faith that we are one people with common values," Rabinowitz shot back. "To the contrary, those who hold to the faith that we are one people don't require two sets of laws—one for crimes against government-designated victim groups, the other for the rest of America."[70]

It's time to end racial politics in America

"Hell, I was born a minority," said John Goode, a black man who had been providing barbeque for city-owned venues around Austin. But Goode's contract was pulled when he refused to sign up for the city's affirmative action program. "I just want to be judged on what I provide. The irony is, here's a black man making it on his own, but now he's being told that if you don't ask for special privileges . . . we can't use you."[71]

Then there's the story told by the syndicated talk show host Neal Boortz, who despises such terms as "African-American." Two members of Mr. Boortz's audience became U.S. citizens in 1980. They received a book entitled *The Meaning of American Citizenship* when they took their oaths. Here's what appeared on page three of the booklet:

"Today you have become a citizen of the United States of America. You are no longer an Englishman, a Frenchman, an Italian, a Pole. Neither are you a hyphenated-American . . . a Polish-American, an Italian-American. You are no longer a subject of a government. Henceforth, you are an integral part of this Government, a freeman, a Citizen of the United States of America."[72]

Boortz says that statement is no longer in use. How could it be, in a nation so consumed with race and ethnicity that we have a racial aspect for everything from government contracts to school admissions to test scores to criminal charges?

One big government undertaking that failed to implement affirmative action was President Clinton's 1997 "national discussion on race." That is to say that the chairman of Mr. Clinton's National Advisory Committee on Race, John Hope Franklin, never got around to inviting people who disagreed with him. Franklin said that such people as Ward Connerly had "nothing to contribute."[73] After mounting criticism, affirmative action critic Abigail Thernstrom was brought in, only to be badgered by President Clinton: "Abigail, do you favor the United States Army abolishing the affirmative action program that produced Colin Powell? Yes or No."[74] She answered by complimenting the army for its equal treatment policies.

The big international conference on racism held in Durban, South Africa, a few years later was, if anything, worse. The conference turned into an Israel-bashing session so vile that the United States and Israel pulled out. In an editorial, the Wall Street Journal noted that everyone at the meeting already agreed that racism is bad, but they "also agree that it is others, not themselves who are the racists."[75]

And so it goes. There still has not been a serious national or international debate about race and affirmative action. Those who make the attempt at serious debate often get shouted down, while those who are the beneficiaries must continually charge that someone else is practicing racism in order to keep the preferences coming.

But perhaps it's time to "say when" when some of the wealthiest Americans get preferences because of the color of their skin. Or when it becomes necessary to bring in consultants to mount a search for racism so that city contracts can still be set aside. Or when those who favor preferences are forced to pay off a teacher because her case against affirmative action is considered dangerous. Or when an entire diversity industry has popped up, hawking everything from advice on how to apply for set-asides (on the one hand) to cultural sensitivity training (on the other hand). Or when entire segments of the population are held to lower standards.

Let's be clear. The term "affirmative action" is dripping with pleasantness; it sounds wonderful. It is wonderful to those on the receiving end. But as the minority population of the United States balloons, the percentage of those who are on the other end is falling. Sooner or later, there will be more minorities than majorities, and affirmative action will be crushed under its own weight. Let's end it now.

The place to begin is in grade school, where all the blathering about self-esteem should be replaced with character building and emphasis on our identity as Americans:

· Teach the kids that their skin color is not as important as the content of their character.
· Teach them that America is a nation of immigrants who formed a "melting pot" and emerged with a common culture and a common language.

- Teach them American history and the history of Western civilization so that they will have an appreciation of why they live in the greatest nation on earth.
- Instill in them the importance of a high-quality education, and train them to study hard and be prepared for class each day.
- Implement a policy of hiring staff and teachers based on their competence and ability without regard to race, color, or ethnicity.

Let's fire the "diversity police" that work so hard to preserve the carefully nurtured victim status of minority students so that they can leave school prepared for a workplace dominated not by government programs but by market forces. After all, how can the United States of America continue on a path of greatness if we merely exchange one form of discrimination for another?

Ward Connerly is right. We should stop classifying our citizens by race and stop the practice of taking away from one group in order to give to another. With abundant natural diversity in our country, businesses and corporations are eager to sell their products to minorities and to tap into the talents of minorities. That will be the case long after affirmative action is gone and forgotten.

CHAPTER 8

Keep America Strong

---

*We must declare that the United States of
America will always be the strongest military
power on earth, capable of waging two major
wars at once.*

On September 11, 2001, an airplane commandeered by extremist Islamic
terrorists was purposefully crashed into the Pentagon, killing 189 people. It is no accident that the seat of United States military power was selected as a target. The terrorists wanted to cripple the country by hitting the
headquarters of our Defense Department, the New York skyscrapers that
symbolized the American free enterprise system, and buildings that house
our national leaders. Three out of four of the attacks were successful.

The attacks on America made us realize that our military strength and
our military intelligence network may not be adequate for the challenges
that face us in the twenty-first century. Regardless, the United States found
itself embroiled in a War on Terrorism that it never saw coming. But why did-
n't we see it? After all, when the airplanes flew into the twin towers of the
World Trade Center (WTC) on September 11, it wasn't the first time those
buildings had been targeted.

The first attack on the towers came at 12:18 P.M. local time on February 26,
1993—just a short time into the Bill Clinton administration. A massive explosion erupted from a car bomb in a parking garage beneath one of the towers.
Walls collapsed, fires broke out, power was knocked out, telephone lines went
down, and a massive hole was ripped in the ground beneath the buildings. The
blast was so powerful that the crater it created ranged from three to five stories
deep. Six people died in the blast, more than 1,000 people were injured, and
some damage estimates exceeded $1 billion.[1] Still, it could have been worse.

The terrorists' idea likely was to topple one of the towers into the other one, causing them both to collapse. During the noon hour, with the buildings full of people, the death toll could have exceeded 50,000. However, the unusual load-bearing corner beams of the towers may have prevented that from happening, unlike on September 11 when the airplanes hit closer to the tops of the towers, igniting 2,000-degree infernos that eventually caused the collapse of both structures.

In the months after the 1993 explosion, the WTC was repaired and business in the towers returned to normal. Seven men were charged with participation in the bombings. They were all identified as Muslim terrorists. In August of 1993, it was disclosed that they and a few others also had plans to blow up several other New York City structures, including the United Nations building and two Hudson River tunnels. They also were concocting a scheme to assassinate Egyptian President Hosni Mubarak.

In March of 1994, four of the fundamentalists were convicted in a federal court. They were given 240 years each in prison, so that none would ever be paroled. A second trial was held, and ten more of the Muslim radicals were convicted. In addition to the charges already mentioned, the men were planning to bomb the FBI headquarters and the George Washington Bridge.

You would think that something like this would get the attention of the president of the United States. But Bill Clinton was president, and Bill Clinton always had something else on his mind. So did most Americans, few of whom worried much about the WTC bombings after the story cycle came to an end.

In 1996, author Steven Emerson warned in a *Wall Street Journal* essay that radical Islam was spreading across the United States. But he also warned that political correctness, enforced by American Muslim groups, was keeping the information from becoming public. He went on to charge that President Clinton was talking a good game in the battle against terrorism but "the administration's deeds do not match its words."[2]

As Emerson pointed out, the president of the United States seemed blind to the dangers of terrorists operating within our own borders. He did a few things, such as issuing an executive order in January 1995 to freeze assets of twelve terrorist groups. But the groups had tens of millions of dollars and the Treasury Department seized only about $800,000. Emerson said the administration had adopted "a policy of denial" toward Syria, which was harboring more than a dozen terrorist groups. Finally, he said, the Clinton administration had established close ties with groups like the American Muslim Council. Emerson was concerned because that group had connections to Hamas and other radical organizations, some of which were operating in the United States from San Diego to Houston to New York.

Emerson's words seem almost prophetic in light of the events of September 11, 2001. He warned that a strong policy to fight terrorism must begin with "the understanding that terrorism is the product of an extremist ideological culture, and it can only be fought using a complete moral, political, and military arsenal."

Let's be clear. These words were written five years before airplanes came crashing down on September 11. We knew the danger existed. President Clinton knew it. But there were too many fund-raisers to attend, and way too many scandals. Even though the name of Osama bin Laden was starting to come up, the president remained distracted.

Speaking of Osama, he may or may not have been involved in the first WTC bombing; some law enforcement officials believe that he may have helped with the funding. He may have been involved with the 1993 deaths of eighteen U.S. soldiers in Somalia. However, the evidence is stronger in the August 7, 1998, bombings of U.S. embassies in Nairobi, Kenya, and Dar es Salaam, Tanzania, in which hundreds were killed and injured, and bin Laden is under indictment for those attacks. The State Department also believes that bin Laden's fingerprints are on the bombing of the USS *Cole*, which took the lives of seventeen U.S. servicemen in Yemen on October 12, 2000.

All of these things took place during the Clinton years, and yet the president, who was said to "loathe" the military, never made terrorism a priority. The American people who elected him and then reelected him didn't seem to notice.

Eisenhower to Clinton: military hero to military zero

Dwight David Eisenhower was an American war hero, elected to the presidency in 1952 on the strength of military popularity. Eisenhower had been leader of the Allied Forces in Europe during World War II and had thirty years of military training and experience under his belt by the time he entered the White House.

However, Mr. Eisenhower, by all accounts a gentle and thoughtful man, believed in less government spending, and one of the things he cut was the military budget. With indications that the Soviet Union was not about to start a war in the foreseeable future, he cut back the previous administration's defense budget by $5.2 billion. Mr. Eisenhower's "New Look" armed forces had fewer ground soldiers but more nuclear weapons.

The contrast between Mr. Eisenhower and Mr. Clinton is this: the American people elected "Ike" precisely because of his military background. The political landscape had changed so much by 1992 that a war hero who was already in office, George H. W. Bush, was swept out in favor of a man

with no military service at all. In fact, Mr. Clinton had avoided military service and had protested against America while overseas.

By the time Mr. Clinton was elected, the all-volunteer nature of the
armed forces had led to a situation where millions of voters had never
served, and they didn't seem to mind that the Democratic nominee had
never served, either. There was a new casualness about military service.
Never mind that President Bush had presided over Desert Storm—perhaps
America's most successful war ever. The Arkansas governor was young and
handsome and had new ideas and a brainy wife—and he had a catchy slogan: "It's the economy, stupid!"

The slogan summed up Mr. Clinton's policy about the military and foreign
affairs. Ignore them; the American people vote their pocketbooks. Mr. Bush
had broken his promise not to raise taxes, and he had the misfortune of a small
recession as he was running for reelection. So, on the strength of his domestic
agenda (with some help from third-party candidate H. Ross Perot) Mr. Clinton
assumed office. He had lots of ideas for social programs and new spending, and
he needed money. To get it, he looked at the military budget.

Clinton and the decline of the military

On March 27, 1993, the new president released his first Department of
Defense budget, requesting $263.4 billion for fiscal year 1994—some $10 billion less than the final budget under the first President Bush. This budget
scrapped some of the funding for President Reagan's Strategic Defense
Initiative, dubbed "Star Wars" by the mainstream media, effectively ending the
program. There were also signals in that first year of the new administration as
to what type of leadership Mr. Clinton might bring to a crisis overseas.[3]

The United States was involved in a humanitarian mission in Somalia to
provide food to thousands of people who were starving due to anarchy
brought on by tribal warfare. The mission, started under President Bush, had
sent 28,000 troops to the African nation, however, all but about 3,000 had
been withdrawn. Those remaining were acting as security for United Nations
peacekeeping forces.

It got nasty on October 3 and 4 when the U.S. troops engaged in a gun
battle with supporters of the Somali warlord, General Mohamed Farah
Aideed. Eighteen U.S. soldiers were killed, and American television showed
images of a dead American solider being dragged through the streets of
Mogadishu.[4]

The American people were not happy with what was happening in
Somalia. So on October 7, Mr. Clinton pledged to withdraw our troops by
the end of March 1994, which he did. At the same time, he sent in another

1,700 soldiers, and then an additional 13,000 to be stationed offshore. The death toll of American servicemen in Somalia had grown to 29 by the end of the conflict.[5]

The president-who-loathed-the-military deployed American troops and weaponry in several other trouble spots around the world, including Haiti, Bosnia-Herzegovina, and the former Yugoslavia. The president also launched twenty-three Tomahawk cruise missiles at Iraq, with the stated reason being retaliation for an attempt on the life of President George H. W. Bush.[6] Mr. Clinton would utilize American military might many more times during his eight years in the White House—sometimes coinciding with news about his various scandals and raising the eyebrows of his political opponents.

In 1994, President Clinton sent troops to Haiti, Saudi Arabia, and Kuwait. For fiscal 1995, he asked for an increase of $2.8 billion for the defense budget, but Congress approved $243.7 billion, a decrease of $17.1 billion from 1994. The shrinking budget caused sharp reductions at the Pentagon. By year's end, United States troop strength in Europe was at 140,000, down from 340,000 in 1990.[7]

There were more peacekeeping and humanitarian missions in 1995, including operations in Bosnia, Haiti, and Somalia, where 1,800 Marines provided cover for the withdrawal of the last U.N. peacekeepers. With no threat from the Soviet Union, the downsizing of the military continued and another 40,000 troops were withdrawn from Europe. Base closures that had begun under President Bush continued. This time, the nonpartisan committee recommended shutting down seventy-nine bases and realigning twenty-six others to save $19.3 billion over twenty years. Mr. Clinton's budget request for fiscal 1996 asked for just $261.4 billion, a $10.2 billion dollar decrease from the prior year. Congress approved $243.3 billion.[8]

So now we're well into the Clinton presidency and the eleventh straight year of declining military budgets. The president and the Congress have slashed the defense budget to the point where, after adjusting for inflation, it is some 40 percent less than it was for fiscal year 1985 during the second Reagan administration.[9]

The year 1996 saw cruise missile strikes against Iraq and 18,000 U.S. troops stationed in the Balkans as part of a NATO peacekeeping effort. The president sent the U.S. aircraft carrier *Independence* and three other ships to the Taiwan Strait because of tensions between Taiwan and China. The budget request from Mr. Clinton for fiscal year 1997 saw another decrease—this time a reduction of about $10 billion from what the Congress had approved for the prior year. The final bill signed by the president set aside $244 billion for defense. This finally halted the long string of declining military budgets, but not by much.[10]

The year 1997 was calmer for overseas operations, though 8,500 American troops were still keeping the peace in Bosnia. President Clinton recommended closing several more military bases, but the Senate rejected the plan, and that blocked efforts to proceed with some already approved base closings. For fiscal year 1998, the defense budget request was $259.4 billion, with Congress finally approving $268 billion.[11]

On December 16, 1998, the U.S. and Great Britain began four days of strikes against military targets in Iraq because Saddam Hussein wouldn't cooperate with UN weapons inspectors. Earlier in the year, Mr. Clinton launched missiles against terrorist targets in Afghanistan and the Sudan. These attacks came on August 20, three days after the president had gone on TV to admit that he had "misled" the nation about his sexual relationship with "that woman" Monica Lewinsky. Defense Secretary William S. Cohen wanted two more rounds of military base closings so that the Pentagon could stay within its budget.[12] He wasn't kidding. The U.S. armed forces were pushed to the limit in 1998.

With all the peacekeeping duties overseas, and some grumbling within the ranks about readiness, Mr. Cohen decided that the military needed more money. The joint chiefs of staff said that unless funding levels could be increased, some weapons systems or overseas deployments would have to be eliminated. So at budget time, the Defense Department asked for $257.3 billion for fiscal 1999. What it got was a final bill in the amount of $250 billion, including some money for peacekeeping and a missile defense system.[13]

In 1999, NATO forces were attacking Yugoslavia to stop Slobodan Milosevic from committing "ethnic cleansing" of ethnic Albanians in the province of Kosovo. Hundreds of U.S. aircraft participated. About 6,000 U.S. troops were keeping the peace in Bosnia, and U.S. fighter jets were patrolling no-fly zones in Iraq—and dropping a few bombs here and there on selected military targets. This time, Defense asked for $267.2 billion for fiscal 2000, including a $4.4 billion pay increase for soldiers.[14]

In 2000—the year the USS *Cole* was bombed—U.S. military strength was at 1.383 million soldiers. About 16,000 troops were stationed in the Middle East, and peacekeeping efforts continued in the usual trouble spots, including Kosovo and Bosnia. President Clinton, winding down his presidency, decided to punt on the final decision regarding a missile defense shield, leaving that to his successor. The Defense budget request amounted to $291.1 billion—up $11.2 billion from the prior year. The final bill, signed by Mr. Clinton, totaled $288 billion and provided a 3.7 percent military pay raise. There was also a supplemental spending bill for $6.5 billion to pay for ongoing peacekeeping missions.[15]

In the year 2001, with a new president and a new War on Terrorism, humanitarian and peacekeeping efforts continued and the troop numbers were sustained in the Middle East. But the new President Bush had lots of decisions to make regarding the military. He ordered a review of the nation's strategy and put some spending decisions on hold until he got answers.

So fiscal 2002 got an "on-hold" budget of about $310 billion. Later in the year, Mr. Bush asked for an additional $18.4 billion for defense. In December, the Congress handed Mr. Bush a bill in the amount of $343.3 billion, tacking on $15 billion to fight the war against terrorism. Also tacked onto that bill was the creation of another independent commission to find more military bases to close.[16]

For fiscal year 2003, both the House and the Senate were in a pro-defense mood, considering bills that would provide the military with an additional $34.4 billion, while denying the president a $10 billion war contingency fund.[17] Finally, in late October, George W. Bush got almost everything he wanted—with the exception of the fund. With the War on Terrorism underway and the Iraq situation red hot, Mr. Bush signed a spending bill amounting to $355.5 billion—the largest since the Reagan era.[18] Included in the measure was a 4.1 percent salary increase for military personnel and $72 billion for new weapons. $7.4 billion was earmarked for continued development of the missile defense system.

Clearly, the 9/11 attacks had intensified support for the military, producing a marked turnaround from the low-priority military of the Clinton years.

According to former Defense Secretary Caspar Weinberger, Mr. Clinton had cut back the military so much that the United States might not be able to fight a war against terrorism on several fronts. Mr. Weinberger told Sean Hannity on WABC that "just the Army alone" that won the Gulf War was over 900,000, "and now it's under 400,000, which is a tremendous drop." And that's just one service, said Weinberger.[19]

The former defense secretary listed the problems brought on during the Clinton administration. They included lost air and sea lift capacity, two or three years during which nothing was procured for the military, and cuts in research and development. Mr. Weinberger said that Clinton may not have set out to harm the military, but he cared so little about it that the deterioration was inevitable.

But it wasn't just monetary cuts that harmed the military during the Clinton years. There was a wee bit of social engineering, too.

The new touchy-feely military

The history of the gender-neutral, politically correct armed forces is not a long one. In 1975, the service academies were opened up to women. The world didn't come to an end, and in the early '80s, the army decided to grant women additional "equal rights." So the army experimented with co-ed training for recruits. It didn't work; the women couldn't keep up with the men, so the effort was abandoned, and you would think the story ends there.

However, facts and logic about the emotional and physical differences between men and women failed to get in the way of ideologues like former U.S. Representative Patricia Schroeder, who once lamented that the structure of the military was a top-down hierarchy with nothing but males at the top.

And so it was—and had been for two centuries. The purpose of an army has often been cited as twofold: to kill people and break things. That's oversimplification, but the military is supposed to protect the security of our nation and preserve our freedom by laying waste to our enemies and destroying their infrastructure and their weapons. So "killing people and breaking things" is not too far off.

In order to best accomplish that mission, recruits are put through tough training exercises. They have to know how to do such things as load and fire weapons, drive tanks, pilot combat helicopters, and parachute from airplanes. Some of them will be ground troops, and they have to be strong, durable, and physically fit. So the move by Ms. Schroeder and the radical feminist movement to have a kinder, gentler, sexually mixed army was a basic culture change for the military that was bound to cause problems.

Keep in mind that this "sensitive" armed forces is being brought into play on top of two other major challenges being confronted by the military that we've already discussed: increased peacekeeping missions and severe funding cutbacks.

But those who wanted to social-engineer the military were not to be denied. Little thought was given to whether a gender-mixed military would be as strong, or to what the ultimate result of such an experiment might be. The only thing that mattered was advancement of the radical feminist movement through sexually integrating the military.

In the 1990s, most of the bad things that you might imagine actually came to pass as male soldiers began to get their "sensitivity training." E. Thomas McClanahan of the *Kansas City Star* noted in his column that obstacle courses once run by navy recruits became known as "confidence courses." The army tried to set up gender-neutral strength standards, but the *Army Times* reported that most of the women couldn't meet the standards for "nearly 70 percent of the Army Specialties." [20]

Then there's the story of former marine Lieutenant Adam Merserau, who wrote about diversity in the *Wall Street Journal* and was quoted in McClanahan's column. Merserau explained that a woman marine was supposed to pick up and carry a "wounded" comrade during a training exercise.

He even stood up and draped himself over her shoulders, but she still was unable to hold him. He said, "The Marines who saw her knew that they would perish if they ever had to rely on her in a life-or-death situation."[21]

Stephanie Guttmann researched the subject for her book *The Kinder, Gentler Military: Can It Fight?*[22] and wrote extensively in the *Wall Street Journal.* She says that sex integration in boot camp has devastated morale and harmed recruitment. Ms. Guttman says it goes back to the early '90s, when military budgets were on the way down and there were sexual harassment issues within the military. Congress was told that the "warrior culture" had to be reformed—"not just behavior, but attitudes."

That's where the sensitivity training came in. The good old boys who still believed that their military was supposed to kill people and break things would require an attitude adjustment. What better place to start than in boot camp, where the initial attitudes were formed? Ms. Guttman points out that there could be no dissent. If a general were to speak up about differences in the sexes as they apply to a combat situation, he was simply considered a sexist.[23] So the military got its sensitivity training, along with constant monitoring by equal opportunity officers. Women also got bigger roles to play within the hierarchy.

Meanwhile, back at the more sensitive boot camp, drill sergeants were faced with all kinds of new problems because the women were generally smaller, weaker, and—well, built differently. The women got injured more often, and they tended to drop out. This was not acceptable to the Schroeder-ites.

So, Ms. Guttman stated in her op-ed piece, the army's manual had to evolve such entries as "It is essential that the cadre develop the soldier's self-esteem, self-confidence, and positive attitude toward Army service . . . Leaders help soldiers cope with unnecessary stress by . . . conducting periodic morale/feedback sessions and conducting and requiring effective counseling . . ." Recruits could no longer go on the "confidence course" without watching a safety video first.[24] Ms. Guttman reported that this type of sensitivity seemed okay to the girls; the boys didn't care for it much.

In addition to loss of morale and fighting edge, a mixed military opens the door to another major problem: sexual harassment. You would think that those who advocate putting young men together with young women would have thought of this—but no. The idea here is to provide "equality" for the women while adjusting the men to view the women as anything but females. But that's not going to happen.

In 1997, Lt. Gen. Claudia Kennedy—who had charged a male general with harassment—was part of a panel set up to study the problem. It found that 47 percent of women in the army had experienced sexual harassment, especially if you defined harassment as being touched in a way that made you feel "uncomfortable."[25] Again, the men were supposed to train with the women—not look at them!

All this feminizing of the military comes on top of President Clinton's early attempts to overturn the ban on homosexuals serving in the military. If Clinton had prevailed, morale would have dropped even further, with macho soldiers being forced to shower and bunk with men who might have a sexual interest in them.

Cooler heads prevailed and Mr. Clinton was only able to change the existing policy slightly. Recruits would no longer be asked anything at all about their sexual preference. That meant that gays could serve—as long as they didn't "come out" and openly practice their homosexuality.

The compromise followed strong objections from the joint chiefs of staff and from Sam Nunn, who in 1993 was chairman of the Senate Armed Services Committee. It was a major win for a troubled military that would still have to deal with the gender issue.

The two-war strategy: are we prepared?

In January 2002, President George W. Bush asked for an additional $48 billion in the coming year to help fight the war against terrorism. Speaking to the Reserve Officers Club in Washington, the president outlined the largest increase in military spending in twenty years, saying, "I have a responsibility to prepare the nation for all that lies ahead. There will be no room for misunderstanding."[26] Mr. Bush told the group that once Congress approves the request, it will be spent for missile defense, pay raises for service personnel, acquisition of precision weaponry, unmanned vehicles, and high-tech military equipment.

The request was not met with enthusiasm by all members of Congress, particularly Democrats. Senator Daniel Inouye, D-Hawaii, told reporters that as defense chair of the Senate Appropriations Committee, he would not want to approve the spending unless it was justified.[27]

Congress, and again, particularly Democrats were loathe to watch the big surpluses begin to dry up in the wake of the September 11 attacks. Mr. Bush was proposing deficits again, while Democrats and some Republicans wanted to add new social programs, such as a pharmaceutical benefit. But the fact that Mr. Bush had to ask for such a large increase was emblematic of the decline of the military under Bill Clinton.

Ironically, the Pentagon had issued a routine military-readiness report that hit the papers just a year and ten days before the terrorist attacks. The story reported that most U.S. combat forces were ready to perform wartime duties, but if the country was forced to fight two major conflicts at one time, the risk of casualties would be high. The problems were shortfalls in the ability to move and protect troops and keep them supplied.[28]

The Pentagon makes such a report fairly often, but this one was important because it came during the time that Vice President Al Gore and Governor George W. Bush were in a heated battle for the White House—with military strength as a major issue.

Mr. Bush kept charging during the campaign that the military was in decline and morale was low. If you've read this chapter up to this point, you know how true that was. That left Al Gore to defend the policies of the current administration, usually saying something like "We've got the best fighting force in the world."

Given the situation, Gore was smart to attempt to twist the facts and try to make it seem as if Mr. Bush was criticizing the armed forces, when in reality it was Clinton-Gore policies that Mr. Bush wanted to change. Mr. Bush was concerned that budget cuts during the Clinton years had sapped the military to the point where it could no longer maintain its duties as the world's last remaining superpower.

After the Pentagon report was issued, Defense Secretary William Cohen could only say, "Things are on the upswing." But, he noted, there was a lot of room for improvement. The Gore campaign also trotted out William Perry, the defense secretary during Mr. Clinton's first term, who said that two-thirds of the military cutbacks came under prior Republican administrations.[29]

The Bush campaign responded by bringing out the retired joint chiefs chairman who had served under the first President Bush. General Colin Powell, who would become secretary of state under George W. Bush, said, "Readiness has declined, investment has declined, maintenance has declined." Powell placed the blame for a weakened and overextended military squarely on President Clinton.[30]

Democrats were still blaming prior Republican administrations and pointing out that spending was up under the last two years of President Clinton. General Powell countered that that was because of pressure from a GOP-controlled Congress which had been hearing complaints from the military brass.[31]

The *Dallas Morning News* provided additional coverage of the dispute. The newspaper quoted Mr. Bush, who had told the VFW that the next president would "inherit a military in decline." The *News* also quoted Mr. Gore's comeback: "Our military continues to be the best-trained, best-equipped, best-led fighting force in the world."[32]

The *News* also interviewed Joseph J. Collins, a retired army colonel who had once been a strategic planner for the Pentagon. Collins said that to some degree, both sides were right. The U.S. military still was the best, as Gore was saying—but as Bush pointed out, it was just a shell of what it had been a decade ago. But Dr. Collins' organization, the Center for Strategic and International Studies, had surveyed service members and found them to be uneasy. The most frequent complaint: a shortage of people and resources.[33]

What about the two-major-conflicts doctrine? Let's go back to February of 1997. Adjusting for inflation, defense spending had fallen by about 18 percent under President Clinton, and the belt was pretty tight at the Pentagon. Military brass were rethinking the two-war strategy.

Following years of cuts, Defense Secretary William Cohen said, "We are perhaps at the limit of our ability to do that." But the doctrine was never set in stone, and it was beginning to seem that it might be easier to change the doctrine than to beef up the military. After all, the doctrine had been adopted under President George H. W. Bush and was just a starting point anyway. With the Cold War over and the War on Terrorism still years in the future, all it would take to justify the current state of readiness was to proclaim, "There'll never be two major conflicts at the same time."[34]

Besides, the Clinton motto was "It's the economy, stupid." It was never the military. So the brass took to discussing what constituted "major conflicts" and came up with some examples. Suppose a half-million U.S. troops were called out for a Gulf War scenario and at the same time a war started in North Korea. That country has a big army, and things could get out of hand pretty quickly.

Then the questions became: What constitutes victory? How much risk could the U.S. assume? How much help can we count on from allies? Does high-tech weaponry reduce the need for troops? This is the point where clear thinking can suffer. After all, if the funds weren't there, the mission of the military could simply be downgraded.

Under the current two-war strategy, the army maintains ten active divisions (two of them at Fort Hood, Texas), at a cost of more than $2 billion per year—not counting a lot of expenses such as moving the divisions around. During the Cold War, there were eighteen divisions. But Pentagon studies showed that for a single major conflict, only five divisions, or about 100,000 troops, would be needed.[35] Think of the savings.

Cutting back to even seven divisions could save billions; it would just take a rethinking of the two-war scenario. And the Pentagon could use the savings for procurement or development of new weapons systems.

We might mention, too, that the armed forces were definitely getting certain equipment—provided that it came from the right state or congressional district. Retired army colonel David Hackworth complained in his column that too much military spending was buying political pork—"for racketeers like Sen. Trent Lott to buy ships the Navy didn't need, Congressman Newt

Gingrich to buy C-130 cargo planes the air force didn't want, and President Bill Clinton to buy Sea Wolf submarines and B-2s the Pentagon didn't want in the first place." Hackworth charged that these projects and more like them were solely for the reelection chances of the incumbent politicians and did little to strengthen the military. He called it a dereliction of duty.[36]

Hackworth talked about infantry leaders who believed that we would lose the next major conflict and who worried about President Clinton being so quick to commit our forces in situations that don't threaten our national interests. And yet, said Hackworth, no general or admiral would come forward to talk about the lousy conditions.

Toward the end of September 2000, the presidential campaign was finally bringing all this out, and the nation's military leaders made an appearance before Congress. They said that whoever was elected president, he would need to pump tens of billions of dollars into the defense budget or keep more of our troops at home.

Army general Henry H. Shelton, chairman of the joint chiefs, told the members of Congress, "We must find the resources necessary to modernize the force." He said that combat readiness was suffering because it was hard to prepare for major wars while focusing on all the peacekeeping missions. "Our equipment is wearing out at a much faster rate than expected," he said. "Consequently, our troops are paying the price by spending more time fixing mechanical problems instead of training for war."[37] Shelton also suggested more base closings.

So, can the United States wage two major wars at one time? As of the year 2000, the answer was no. A General Accounting Office (GAO) report issued in July concluded that the U.S. armed forces were hurting from a serious personnel shortage. A separate GAO report revealed that the military was short of aerial tankers and transport aircraft. That meant that the two-major-conflicts doctrine could not be carried out.[38]

In the year 2001, two major events signaled changes. One was the inauguration of George W. Bush as the forty-third president of the United States; the other occurred on September 11.

The world today

The military preparedness of the United States of America has never been more important than it is now. The world is literally simmering with disputes, conflicts, and full-scale war. About half a dozen bear watching. Some already involve the presence of United States troops; others could at any moment.

The primary conflicts on George W. Bush's table are the War on Terrorism and keeping the peace in Iraq following the ouster of Saddam Hussein. The

War on Terrorism goes well, but it's not a traditional war and, as Mr. Bush keeps telling us, it could continue for years. Already, two regime changes have taken place due to U.S. military missions to remove the Taliban from Afghanistan and to crush the administration of the brutal Iraqi dictator. The hunt for Osama bin Laden and the al-Qaeda terrorist network will continue for the foreseeable future.

The situation with Saddam Hussein in Iraq grew tenser in 2002, grabbing headlines away from the War on Terrorism. President Bush, demanding a regime change for this "Axis of Evil" nation, worked through much of the year to build an airtight case for Saddam's removal—even though most of Europe, with the notable exception of Britain's Tony Blair, was skeptical. Mr. Bush and Mr. Blair insisted that Saddam already had chemical and biological weapons and was close to realizing his dream of deploying nuclear weapons. They insisted that if Saddam obtained them, he would use them or hand them over to terrorist enemies of the United States.

Many Saddam-watchers also believed that the "Butcher of Baghdad" was fanning the flames of the Israeli-Palestinian conflict by sending money to help finance the Palestinian suicide bombers. Some believed that there was an Iraqi connection to the events of 9/11 and that members of al-Qaeda might be holed up in Iraq. In the past, Saddam has held military parades to show off conventional weapons, some of which are Russian-made surface-to-air missiles. Mr. Bush and Mr. Blair were determined to make sure that nothing in Saddam's arsenal would be turned on his Arab neighbors—or on the Western world.

On February 5, 2003, U.S. Secretary of State Colin Powell presented his case to the United Nations that Saddam must cooperate fully or be overthrown by the military might of a "coalition of the willing." France, Germany, Russia, and China were still unimpressed. Finally, after Saddam missed a deadline imposed by Mr. Bush, the United States rolled into action on March 19, with a strike on what the military referred to as "targets of opportunity." In essence, the strategy was to go after the Iraqi leader himself, cut him off from his senior military commanders, and destroy the morale of the Iraqi military. That was followed by the now-famous "Shock and Awe" air campaign and the march on Baghdad. About three weeks later, on April 9, the regime of Saddam Hussein was in tatters and the world watched with amazement as the Iraqi people, aided by the U.S. military, brought down the big statue of Saddam in downtown Baghdad.

With the situation in Iraq on the front burner, nerves were still on edge in our third trouble spot—the Middle East. Palestinian suicide bombers had a banner year in 2002, repeatedly entering civilian areas with the goal of blowing up as many Israelis as possible. Israeli Prime Minister Ariel Sharon sent troops into Palestinian strongholds, and Palestinian Authority leader Yasser Arafat was bottled up in his own headquarters. Then, after a period of relative calm, more suicide bombers struck, and so the Israelis fired again on buildings near Arafat's headquarters. (Ironically, the prior prime minister, Ehud Barak, had offered up most of what Arafat wanted, but when the time came to decide, Arafat turned the offer down.) However, with the Saddam Hussein regime toppled in Iraq, and with Mr. Arafat's authority dwindling, the Bush administration offered up a "roadmap to peace" in late April of 2003 that called for a new Palestinian state in return for Israeli security. But sporadic suicide bombings continued into 2003 and the situation remains uncertain. And don't forget—Israel has a formidable nuclear arsenal.

We'll place the conflict between North and South Korea fourth. Experts fear that fighting could break out in the Korean Demilitarized Zone (DMZ), with the North attempting to reunite the two Koreas by force. In October 2002, the North Koreans admitted that they had an ongoing nuclear program after the United States confronted them with evidence. President Bush has repeatedly warned North Korea not to proceed with the program, but indications are that the country already has at least a few nuclear weapons. North Korea has also clashed with the United States and with the United Nations over the issue of nuclear inspections. Inspectors who had been keeping watch over nuclear power plants were expelled from North Korea in December 2002. Dictator Kim Jong Il began some serious saber-rattling just as the United States was about to go to war in Iraq, testing America's capacity to fight two major battles at once. President Bush did not take the bait and instead concentrated on the Iraq situation. The biggest fear regarding a possible nuclear program in North Korea would be the apparent willingness of the government there to sell such weapons to anybody and everybody. North Korea is one of the three nations named in Mr. Bush's "Axis of Evil" speech.

Fifth on the list of world conflicts is the festering disagreement between India and Pakistan over disputed regions of Kashmir. The positioning of these countries adds fuel to the fire. Pakistan is next door to Afghanistan, and the military government of General Pervez Musharraf has been a tremendous help to the Bush administration in the War on Terrorism. It's highly likely that members of al-Qaeda have crossed the border and might be hiding out in Pakistan, and that means the U.S. could someday go after them. India has military superiority over Pakistan already and is modernizing its forces. Both countries have nuclear weapons. And just to the north sits China. Anything could happen in this region.

Sixth is the always-brewing war of words between the mainland Chinese and the island of Taiwan. After the incident in which the Chinese captured a U.S. surveillance airplane, President Bush authorized a huge arms sale to

Taiwan. Mr. Bush also made commitments to defend the Taiwanese if necessary. The Chinese continue to assert that Taiwan is part of China. But Taiwanese President Chen Shui-bian made a speech that asserted that Taiwan and China are separate countries, and he endorsed legislation to allow a referendum on the issue. China issued a statement calling the speech "a brazen provocation."[39] Taiwan continues to build its defenses, and from a military standpoint, things are calm. But you never know.

There are other spots around the world where conflicts could break out, but these are the main ones. What if a two-major-conflicts scenario was being a bit optimistic?

In support of a missile defense shield

When President Ronald Reagan wanted to use American technological know-how to build what he called a Strategic Defense Initiative (SDI), the mainstream media ridiculed the plan and dubbed it "Star Wars."

Liberal Democrats looked at several failed tests of the system and said that we shouldn't spend money on it because it doesn't work. (However, they wanted to continue spending money to find a cure for AIDS even though there's no working cure so far.)

The up-and-down missile defense system got a new breath of life in January 1999 when President Clinton decided to ask Russia to renegotiate the Anti-Ballistic Missile (ABM) Treaty so that such a missile shield could be built. Mr. Clinton made the request after being convinced that a rogue state like North Korea could develop a missile and the delivery system to strike the U.S. or its allies.

The Russians, of course, objected, and on September 1, 2000, Mr. Clinton announced that he would leave the decision up to his successor. Mr. Clinton said that he was unsure whether the technology and the ultimate effectiveness of such a system were sufficient to warrant the expenditures.[40] In any case, Mr. Clinton's vision was a far cry from the thousands of space-based interceptor missiles that President Reagan had in mind. President Clinton was thinking only of a modest 100 or so interceptors based in Alaska, and maybe later a couple of sites with up to 250 total missiles.

But George W. Bush was thinking bigger. He urged world leaders to "rethink the unthinkable," and he began making plans to ditch the ABM treaty. In doing so, the president pointed out that "Russia is not our enemy" and that threats to U.S. security are now less certain and less predictable—but just as dangerous. On December 14, 2001, Mr. Bush formally notified Russia that the United States would withdraw from the treaty.

Russian President Vladimir Putin called the withdrawal "a mistake," but he didn't seem to be bothered by the prospect of a U.S. missile shield. Putin had been kept fully informed by Mr. Bush, so none of this came as a shock. And Putin was quick to point out that Russia had enough missiles to overcome any shield.[41]

That means that the system will be used to ward off strikes that might come from smaller, rogue states, perhaps members of the "Axis of Evil." The vision of Presidents Reagan and Bush will come to pass and will make the world just a little more secure.

The United States of America: still the strongest nation on earth

September 11 was like a wake-up call. Sure, George W. Bush had been focusing on military shortcomings during the election, but did anybody really think we'd be attacked on our own shores?

Things had gotten too easy for the big spenders on Capitol Hill. The cuts in military spending had combined with the dot-com boom to produce huge surpluses, and Congress couldn't wait to spend it. After George W. Bush was elected, he proposed a meager tax cut, and it was demonized by the Left as being "massive" and for "the wealthiest one percent of Americans." Members of Congress wanted more social programs and more bike trails to take back home to the district.

The world was essentially at peace. There were cries of "it's *still* the economy, stupid." The two-major-conflicts doctrine was in big trouble. We know better now. In this post-9/11 world, it's easier to imagine more wars breaking out in the trouble spots we've discussed.

Let's be clear. There will always be people and nations that hate us. The potential for armed conflict will never cease. The United States is the remaining world superpower, but Communist China is an emerging giant, and many nations now have nuclear weapons—perhaps even the North Koreans.

The military needs to utilize high-tech weaponry that makes us stronger, but troop strength must remain at formidable levels. The army doesn't need to lose any more divisions. The mission of our fighting forces must be clearly defined so that eternal peacekeeping missions with no real U.S. interest at stake come to an end. Those parts of the world that would do us harm—including the remaining "Axis of Evil" nations—should be made to realize that the United States does not deploy its military without due consideration. But when we do, we mean business.

In "Operation Iraqi Freedom," also known as Gulf War II, the United States faced the task of fighting a war with far fewer troops than had been available in the first Gulf War. Rather than resort to the old "overwhelming force" doctrine, our military planners concocted a "Shock and Awe" campaign that would demoralize the Iraqi military. When new intelligence indicated that Saddam and his two murderous sons might have survived the opening-night salvo, the U.S. military went after him again. Some called it a PC war, but the idea was to kill the leaders and spare the Iraqi people and as much of the infrastructure as possible. By the time U.S. troops were ready to march toward Baghdad, many Iraqi soldiers were ready to give up. The strategy was brilliant and worked almost to perfection—though at this writing there is no firm conclusion as to the fate of Saddam Hussein, and the search is ongoing for his weapons of mass destruction. The bottom line is that, due to downsizing and new technology, we saw a very different Gulf War this time.

President George W. Bush and the United States fighting forces proved that we are still the strongest nation on earth. But even so, there were controversies, such as women being taken as prisoners of war by the Iraqis and famous declarations by some reporters and writers, such as Peter Arnett of NBC, that the U.S. war plan was a failure. Arnett was dead wrong and lost his job due to a gigantic backlash that was well documented by rival networks.

The lessons we're learning from the attacks of September 11, the campaign in Afghanistan, and Gulf War II are many and varied. Thankfully, the touchy-feely "feminized" military never showed up in Iraq; instead we saw a tough-as-nails, hard-trained fighting force. That's good news for freedom and bad news for rogue nations. Still, we are a country that's been softened by the forces of political correctness, and those forces must not be allowed to impact our military. Women who want to serve their country but who don't measure up physically should be assigned appropriate duties. We should state with moral clarity that war is hell. It's a messy business that involves killing people and breaking things, and there is no room for sensitivity training.

We should also reevaluate who our friends are. When a crisis situation emerges, the United States needs allies that it can count on to do the right thing. Britain is such an ally; France, Germany, and Russia are not. Turkey may even have cost coalition lives with its refusal to allow troop movement through its territory. The United Nations proved itself too weak to enforce its own resolutions.

So where do we go from here? "Shock and Awe" might not work in North Korea, and Lord forbid that we ever engage in an armed conflict with the communist Chinese. There are terrorist regimes in Libya, Syria, and Iran, and the leadership in Egypt isn't much better. No one knows how Mr. Bush's "roadmap to peace" for Israel and Palestine will play out. There is no peace dividend on the horizon.

We should have learned by now that much of the world thought we had softened and that we were afraid to defend ourselves. We've proven them wrong, and in the process we've reaffirmed the historical truth that peace comes only when freedom-loving nations are strong.

So let's build that missile-defense shield. Let's keep working to develop smarter ways to do battle with high-tech weapons. Let's keep our troop strength at levels that will provide a strong deterrent. Let's make sure that the fighting forces of the United States of America always have the full support of our government and our people.

The security of the United States, and the rest of world, depends on it.

CHAPTER 9

Take Back Our Schools

We must declare that our educational system will be the world's best, by ending federal involvement, stopping the political correctness movement, and instituting a strong core curriculum.

An episode of the now-defunct newspaper strip "Sibling Revelry" had the little boy, Stew, discussing school with an adult. Stew said, "This year I haven't learned one thing about the Gettysburg Address, or Edison, or D-Day." In the second and third panels he continued, "Instead, I've been told about diversity, gender roles, and the National Organization for Women. What do you call that?" The lady raised her hand to make a point in the final panel and said, "Standards."[1]

Parents across America may have chuckled at this little cartoon—many of them not realizing that the joke was on them and their children. Schools today are not about the "three R's" of reading, writing, and arithmetic—even though those subjects are still taught. Campuses, whether they are grade schools, colleges, or major universities, have become places where certain types of values are taught, much like the ones mentioned in the comic strip.

In the grade schools, diversity, multiculturalism, and self-esteem have trumped math, science, and American history in importance to educators. On college campuses, a strident leftist agenda has taken hold, and it will not allow dissenting voices to be heard for fear that a member of some victimized group might be offended.

In a word, education in the United States is all about feelings.

In a particularly damning article in *Investor's Business Daily*, it was revealed that polls show disturbing trends at America's teachers' colleges.

These colleges—charged with producing our teachers, administrators, and school superintendents—don't seem to be interested in basic skills and tougher standards. The article quotes Patrick Gross, professor emeritus of education at San Diego State University: "The average professor of education's notion of research and teaching is mostly ideological and idealistic. They have a soft-hearted but scientifically unsound approach to education."[2]

New York–based Public Agenda polled 900 education professors, finding that they are more likely to favor the "process" of learning over actually teaching facts and figures. They are more likely to use techniques to boost self-esteem than to actually implement a system of instruction. Eighty-six percent of education professors told the polling firm that it's more important that the kids "struggle with the process of finding the right answers." Only 12 percent thought it was important that students actually ended up knowing the right answers.[3]

Let's be clear. If these are the predominant attitudes in institutions that produce what are now known as "educators," then it's no wonder that our schools are in a mess. The poll went on to show that a great majority of professors are not concerned with a rigorous core curriculum and are not particularly concerned with reading, writing, math, and grammar.

A book called *Bad Teachers* sums up how these attitudes have made it into the classroom. Author Guy Strickland, himself a teacher, principal, and now education consultant, does not buy the argument that teachers always know best. Out of 145 goals, none of the top 8 selected by teachers had anything to do with learning. Self-esteem was at the top, followed by "attitude" and "socialization."[4]

These attitudes have led to a new vocabulary within the education establishment that replaces old terms such as "teacher." Teachers are now "facilitators" whose job it is to guide students toward learning on their own. Administrators now see themselves as "educators"—a select group of individuals who always know best and whose education models may not be challenged by lesser beings who are not part of the education establishment.

In the classroom, diversity, multiculturalism, and self-esteem are joined by such education fads as "values clarification," which allows students to work out their own values (which may be in opposition to those of their parents), and "whole language," which seeks to teach students to read without the old tried-and-true phonics. Kids simply look at pictures and try to figure out what the text is saying. "Outcome-based education" aims at certain outcomes, regardless of how they are attained. No need for standards or grades or failure. With OBE, everyone's a winner; everybody can feel good!

Needless to say, with these new trends in effect now for going on forty years, our public schools are massively screwed up—and that's especially true in poorer, inner-city schools, where low pay and declining expectations have resulted in a teacher shortage.

To attract highly qualified teachers is going to take more than money according to correspondent William Lutz, writing in the *Dallas Morning News*. Lutz says it's going to take an attitude adjustment within the education community: "It means junking the idea that teachers are 'facilitators' whose most important job is to develop 'high-order thinking skills' and returning to the view that teachers are authority figures in the classroom whose primary goal is to teach important facts and skills."[5]

Lutz was talking about real facts and skills—such as teaching algebraic formulae, the causes of World War II, the physics that make airplanes work, and the basics of cell structure. What constitutes "important facts" may be different when left to today's new education bureaucracy. Such "gender issues" as "the glass ceiling," and "a woman's right to choose," and diversity issues like "hate crimes laws" and "reparations for slavery," are often deemed more important—especially on college campuses. In some school districts, it's more important to conduct math class in Spanish than simply to teach math.

This is not to say that there aren't any good teachers in our schools today. On the contrary, there are many who labor in the classroom day to day, trying to teach real facts and skills while not running afoul of the educators who run the district. Sometimes, they find themselves at odds with not only the administration, but with parents as well.

A case in point is the strange saga of high school teacher Christine Pelton in Piper, Kansas. She failed twenty-eight sophomores in her biology class when she discovered that they had plagiarized their semester projects from the internet. The principal and school superintendent agreed that students who simply used computers to copy their reports—that's why all twenty-eight of them were just about the same—should not be passed. But parents complained, and the school board ordered her to change the grades.[6]

Ms. Pelton was not a happy camper. "The students no longer listened to what I had to say. They knew if they didn't like anything in my classroom from here on out, they can just go to the school board and complain." She resigned in protest.[7]

This incident points out how the decline of our educational system has come full circle. Even parents get incensed when standards are applied and their kids fail to meet them. To many of today's parents—themselves products of the watered-down educational system—it's better to pass with excellent grades and low standards than to keep the standards high.

On college campuses, diversity, multiculturalism, and political correctness are even more in evidence and lead to garbage courses such as "Hip-Hop Culture" at Texas A&M. The class is taught by a black professor named Finnie Coleman who asked, "Is hip-hop culture more diverse or less diverse than Aggie culture?" Ignoring the total irrelevance of the question, the Texas A&M

English Department "bent over backwards" to help Professor Coleman implement the course.[8]

Naturally, the English department would want to help. Even though this
course was akin to Basket Weaving 101, any resistance to it would have been
played out as racism. It's easier to take a little heat over a silly course than
to take a lot of heat over a racial issue. As we will see later, that's how many
decisions on college campuses are now made.

The Congress, which has no constitutional role in all this, has reacted to
deterioration of the public schools by increasing its own importance. New
legislation proposed by President George W. Bush, with the cooperation of
such liberal icons as Senator Edward M. Kennedy, has been passed into law,
expanding federal involvement. This means a continuation of the government monopoly on education at the grade-school level, with little choice for
those kids who are stuck in low-performing schools.

Members of Congress (as well as former President Clinton and former
Vice President Gore) often elect to take their kids out of the public schools.
An analyst at the Heritage Foundation did a survey of the Congress, finding
that 34.4 percent of the U.S. House and 50 percent of the Senate (with
school-aged children) have sent their kids to private schools.[9]

But by passing laws that discourage voucher programs and limit school
choice, they've made it very difficult for most parents and kids to escape
from the same bad schools that they are able to avoid.

Public schools: OBE makes classrooms PC

Have you ever wondered how the public schools transitioned from emphasis on traditional education (known in some education circles as ABCs)
to today's emphasis on feelings? To understand this trend, you have to examine the rise of an education fad known as "outcome-based education"
(OBE), which, as we said earlier, is not based on standards of learning.

In an ABCs classroom, a teacher monitors attitudes but assesses and
grades what students are learning. He or she is concerned with making sure
that kids know that two plus two equals four and that George Washington
was the first president of the United States. Students' comprehension and
knowledge are all-important.

Priorities are flip-flopped in the OBE classroom. Here, the facilitator
monitors knowledge and comprehension, but those are not the most important things. Group learning is implemented, with the ultimate goal being certain "outcomes" that must remain constant, regardless of how the students
reach those outcomes or how long it takes them to get there.

OBE is the teaching of "attitudes," the science of "adjustment," the precursor to brainwashing. It's all about feelings—but only the correct feelings. And so, instead of the basics that were being taught in the '50s and '60s, OBE has taken American education to a netherworld of touchy-feely "higher order thinking skills" that are largely related to the political goals of the Left, including multiculturalism, radical feminism, and radical environmentalism. OBE is political correctness, institutionalized in the classroom.

In their book *Outcome Based Education: The State's Assault on Our Children's Values*, Peg Luksik and Pamela Hobbs Hoffecker explain that OBE schools mandate that a student must show a "mastery" of certain outcomes. The problem is that those outcomes are mandated by the state, and they often have little to do with actual learning. They list some typical outcomes, in this instance, from the state of Arkansas:[10]

· Exhibit personal adaptability to change.
· Accept the responsibility for preserving the earth for future generations.
· Realistically assess personal strengths and weaknesses.
· Appreciate racial, ethnic, religious, and political differences.
· Function effectively in a multicultural environment.
· Exhibit positive self-concept and a sense of self-worth.

So these are the "higher order thinking skills" that are so important to today's educators. As you can see, they relate directly to attitudinal concepts while having little or nothing to do with real learning. If students are to "master" such concepts, they must be "taught" in a certain manner. That means making sure that kids understand that the rainforests are being assaulted, that the earth is becoming overpopulated, and that traditional gender roles are oppressive to women.

It also means making sure that textbooks are on board with OBE-style thinking. Marianne Jennings, director of the Lincoln Center for Applied Ethics at Arizona State University, was appalled when her daughter brought home a math text entitled *Secondary Math: An Integrated Approach: Focus on Algebra*. It contained "color photos, essays on the Dogon tribe of Africa, and questions such as 'what role should zoos play in today's society?'" The book contained photos of Bill Clinton, poetry from Maya Angelou, and insights on cultural differences. Jennings called it a "pedagogical nightmare."[11]

So where did this nonsensical approach to education begin? Luksik and Hoffecker attribute the movement to two educators: B. F. Skinner and Benjamin Bloom. Skinner's "Mastery Learning" worked with operant conditioning—assess, teach, reassess, re-teach, etc.—and held that all children can learn, but not on the same day. Bloom's theories, from his book *Taxonomy*, added the concepts of feelings, beliefs, and attitudes. Bloom defined good teaching as "a teacher's ability to ... challenge students' fixed beliefs."[12]

Mastery Learning—now known as OBE—slowly crept into classrooms, and at least some aspect of it is present in virtually every school in the United States. For example, even if your child isn't being given a test on attitudes with blanks to fill in for "my beliefs" and "my parents' beliefs," he or she is most certainly drilled in the holy grails of multiculturalism and self-esteem.

OBE concepts have left our education system in a shambles. In order to get into college, where it is reasonably important to know how to read, many young people must take remedial courses. The taxpayer is left to wonder why those remedial courses aren't part of the standard curriculum. Perhaps it's because those types of courses are too basic and they don't challenge such concepts as the nuclear family and pledging allegiance to the flag—you know, those "fixed concepts" that Professor Bloom worried about.

So here we are in the twenty-first century, and Johnny can't read. The schools, however, are not admitting failure, because Johnny is a good "global citizen." OBE has modified Johnny's thinking so that it may be quite different from that of his parents. Johnny has a full understanding of what socialism is all about—the common good, as opposed to individuality. As Thomas DeWeese writes, "He would believe that there are no absolutes, no real morality, and no religion. He would have no modesty and would accept any lifestyle or perversion. He would have few individual options and would not hold allegiance to family or nation. He would believe that competition is evil and that private property, wealth, materialism, or personal wants are selfish."[13]

From time to time, educators conspire with certain administrations or members of Congress to make an attempt to address the fact that our new global citizens are not performing well in math, science, and reading. These attempts usually involve calls for hiring more teachers, limiting the size of classrooms, and spending lots of money, but they rarely involve core-curriculum adjustments.

In 1994, the Senate enacted the "Goals 2000" program to define what schools must do to qualify for new funding. DeWeese says that there was specific funding for programs like "school to work" and "one stop social centers," and that even though the legislation never mentioned OBE, it made funding dependent upon it.[14] George Will notes that only two goals in Goals 2000 were quantifiable:

· By 2000, America's high school graduation rate would be at least 90 percent.
· Students will be first in the world in mathematics and science achievement.

Senator Pat Moynihan stated mater-of-factly: "That will not happen." [15]

George Will tells us that Senator Moynihan was right on target with his prediction. The graduation rate in 2000 was about 75 percent, and even that was inflated by social promotions. American students ranked nineteenth in math among thirty-eight nations that were surveyed—right below Latvia. In science, the U.S. came in eighteenth—right below Bulgaria. [16]

So, stuck with the concepts of OBE and the failure of Goals 2000, what else has the government done to "help" our schools? In 1998, the focus was on President Clinton's plan to spend $1.2 billion on new teachers in order to reduce class size in grades one through three. The Clinton administration and many educators felt that reducing class size from about twenty-three to eighteen would improve reading skills. As *Investor's Business Daily* reported, there were two gaping holes in the plan.

First of all, the president's plan didn't contain funding to do what Mr. Clinton wanted. It was just about enough to pay for 27,000 new teachers for only one year. Yet, Mr. Clinton was talking about 100,000 new teachers who, presumably, would be permanent. To hire them for even five years would cost $20 billion, according to *IBD*. [17]

The second flaw was the fact that research was showing that reduction in class size was not producing the intended results. A May 1998 press release from the Education Department contended just the opposite: "Studies confirm what parents and teachers know from experience—small classes promote effective teaching and learning." But most documented research suggested that class size had little effect on learning. University of Rochester researcher Eric Hanushek looked at 277 studies on student-teacher ratios and how they affected performance in the classroom. His conclusion was that no matter how you look at it, "Broad policies of class-size reduction are very expensive and have little effect on student achievement." [18]

The *IBD* story also pointed out that a three-decade spending spree on schools wasn't reaping major benefits—even with per-pupil spending up 150 percent from 1982 to 1995 (to about $7,000 per pupil). Even so, this type of thinking would prevail for the rest of the Clinton administration and into the George W. Bush years, when the federal role would be further expanded.

While the president and lawmakers fretted over class size and how much money to spend on education, the principles of outcome-based education were alive and well in the classroom.

The myth of self-esteem

The story of Anne Tyler as recounted in the September 1996 edition of *Family Voice* is an amazing example of how OBE has dumbed down our educational system. Mrs. Tyler, a former teacher who had lived abroad for several years, decided to get back into teaching after returning to the States. Fifteen years had passed since she taught fifth grade at a small academy founded by parents who were unhappy with public education. The academy was now defunct, and so she decided to try the public schools.

When Mrs. Tyler saw the latest textbook, she was aghast. The reading program now depended on pictures and guesswork—whole language—and she wondered if the kids were supposed to learn reading through osmosis. This passage from the magazine is the essence of OBE: "Creative writing lessons were designed to help students center in on their feelings. Spelling and grammar were not graded. The math program used manipulatives (counting with beans, etc.) instead of multiplication tables. Children used calculators on tests. History was especially disappointing, for every lesson seemed to denigrate democracy, capitalism, and Western civilization." [19]

But nothing could have prepared Mrs. Tyler for the extraordinary importance that was now placed on self-esteem. The kids—apparently no longer emotionally equipped to handle criticism—expected classroom assignments to be handled by the entire class and they expected to be graded as a group. Mrs. Tyler would have none of it. She avoided grade inflation, made individual assignments, and tried to work around the system. She was handed grief by the principal on behalf of the parents: "Mrs. Tyler," he would say, "parents are complaining that their children's grades have dropped drastically since coming into your class. You're too hard on them. Have you thought about the damage you may be causing them emotionally? Children need to feel good about themselves—and it's up to you to build their self-esteem." [20]

After one year back in the classroom, and after hearing that the National Education Association was promoting "Lesbian and Gay History Month," she quit teaching.

Was Mrs. Tyler's principal out of touch with reality? In one sense, he was; in another, maybe he wasn't. The parents who objected to Mrs. Tyler's traditional ABCs approach to teaching, and that of Christine Pelton in Piper, Kansas, may very well be in the majority. Jerry Jesness, writing in the *Dallas Morning News*, says that teachers know full well that self-esteem is junk psychology. Jesness, a teacher from Harlingen, Texas, says the public demands it. "Like many teachers, I learned early in my career what happens to those who grade harshly or even by the book. I once gave a failing grade to a star fullback who also was the son of a prominent businessman and the nephew of a school board member. That same year, I gave an administrator's daughter her first C. I was lucky to keep my job." [21]

Regardless, there are thousands of teachers who swear by the principles of self-esteem and its feel-good companion, whole language. When the

Austin American-Statesman applauded the return of phonics to Texas schools, it noted that whole language just wasn't working—25 percent of Texas kids were failing the reading portion of the Texas Assessment of Academic Skills (TAAS) test.[22]

That brought an irate reaction from Dianne Haneke, an adjunct professor of literary education at Concordia University. In explaining how no two children learn the same way (a principle of OBE), she lapsed into extreme edu-speak: "In the example of learning modalities, some learn through listening, some through seeing and some through touch. In the learning-style model, learners' thinking is either concrete or abstract, and either random or ordered. In the paradigm of multiple intelligences, individuals learn better through one of the following ways: verbal, mathematical, musical/rhythmic, spatial/artistic, kinesthetic/movement, interpersonal and intrapersonal."[23]

So, after reading that, how would you like for your kids to be taught to read? The phonics method? Or the kinesthetic/movement method?

If you're still wondering why Johnny can't read, and you don't buy the arguments of the Department of Education that it's simply due to a lack of funds and overcrowded classrooms—then lay the fault at the alter of self-esteem. Johnny can't read because whole language won't teach him to read, no matter what "learning modality" he's a part of, because whole language is only designed to make him feel good about himself.

And yet, after decades of feel-good methodology, the education community can't point to any real evidence that it works. The California Task Force on Self-Esteem spent $750,000 on research before admitting "how low the association between self-esteem and its consequences are in research to date."[24]

On the other side of the self-esteem bandwagon, there is some evidence that the movement could have harmful effects. The *Family Voice* article details a study by Roy F. Baumeister and Laura Smart of the University of Virginia, published in the *Psychological Review*, 1996, Vol. 103. The study points out that self-esteem has some less-than-desirable synonyms: pride, egotism, arrogance, conceitedness, narcissism, and a sense of superiority. Noting that gang members often have inflated egos, the report states that "People who perceive themselves as 'superior' may feel it is their 'right' to take what belongs to someone else—or attack an 'inferior' person without remorse."[25]

That view is also held by the family psychologist John K. Rosemond, who tells the story of a banner placed over a mirror in an Alabama elementary school. It says: "You are now looking at one of the most special people in the whole wide world."[26] You've probably seen this type of thing if you've visited your child's school. It's self-esteem, run amok.

Dr. Rosemond explains that the sentiment simply isn't true. "The truth is, no one is 'special.' By virtue of being human, one is fraught with fault." Dr. Rosemond asks you to consider this question: "Is an adult who thinks he or she is one of the most special people in the whole wide world charming?" Most people would answer "no" without hesitation. The fact is that most of the people we know who genuinely believe themselves to be special are impossible to be around. And yet, schools are intent on convincing kids that they are special.

There is one aspect of schools that doesn't pay as much attention to education fads such as self-esteem. Visit the locker room of your local middle school or high school and you're more likely to see a sign that reads "school pride." There are reasons why coaches are more interested in pride than self-esteem.

While self-esteem may be defined as "self-conceit" or even "self-worship," the dictionary says pride is "a reasonable or justifiable self-respect." A winning football coach does not care about self-esteem.

A coach who wants to keep his job knows he has to win. He selects his starting lineup based on what accomplishments his players have made in past games, or how well they've done in practice. Only when his team is ahead by forty points with time running out does he think about putting his second- or third-stringers into the game.

Over in the losing locker room, the coach is raising heck with his players. He's telling them that they will be running more track, doing more pushups, and working on the basics of blocking and tackling. He's telling them that there's another game next Friday and that they've got one week to get their act together. He talks about pride, all right, but he doesn't mention anything about anyone being "special."

Dr. Rosemond is right. Few people are truly special. Only a few will grow up to become president, or invent some life-saving drug. With rare exceptions, school kids are "gifted and talented" only in the minds of their own parents. Even on the football field, only a small number of players will be offered college scholarships, and fewer still will graduate to the professional ranks.

Now let's take a peek into that winning locker room. There, the coach is most likely bragging to his kids about the way they executed the plays and worked as a team. He's talking about individual accomplishments, such as that clutch reception on 4th and 1, and the big hole the line opened up for the winning touchdown. He's telling his team to have pride in what they accomplished.

In the classroom, sadly, accomplishments mean less. Students who are told they are special for no reason at all may come to believe it, and that is a recipe for disaster.

Still, it's hard to convince the education establishment, which has over four decades invested in self-esteem. When a group of parents and teachers called the "Texas Conservative Academic Network" began advocating a focus on reading, writing, and arithmetic instead of self-esteem, the teachers' unions accused them of being a front for the voucher movement. "They are not being straight with their total agenda," said Annette Coots of the Texas State Teachers Association. And the daughter of former Texas Governor Ann Richards agreed: "These are not mainstream Republican leaders," said Cecile Richards, president of the anti-religion group Texas Freedom Network. "This is not a moderate group." [27]

The lesson here is simple. Self-esteem, whole language, and other aspects of outcome-based education are sacred cows in public schools. Anyone who objects to those teaching methods, or who actually wants to do away with them and return to the basics, will be demonized and characterized as an extremist.

The Bush Plan: "No Child Left Behind"

During the 2000 election campaign, Texas Governor George W. Bush made education a big part of his stump speeches. Mr. Bush had seen the failures of the Clinton administration in the area of education, and he was promising to make major repairs to the system.

In Reston, Virginia, candidate Bush outlined his reading initiative, "Reading First," modeled after the one in Texas: [28]

· Early diagnosis of reading skills in kindergarten and the first grade.
· Teacher training for reading instruction for kindergarten and first grade teachers.
· Intervention funds to help children learn to read—such as tutoring, after-school programs, or summer school.

There was mention of returning to the basics and getting rid of education fads such as self-esteem and whole language programs. Mr. Bush wanted to earmark yet another $5 billion to combat the "national crisis" of illiteracy in the schools. It was more of the same, and none other than Al Gore was quick to point that out.

Mr. Gore's press office said that Mr. Bush was taking credit for a plan that simply copied what the current administration was already doing. "George W. Bush must have learned his ABCs from the Clinton-Gore administration," said a spokesman, Douglas Hattaway. "Bush's idea of leadership is to follow up on good ideas that have already been enacted."

Amazingly, Mr. Bush was not proposing any new ideas, and Mr. Gore was mad that Mr. Bush was staking claim to the status quo. Mr. Gore's statement touted how much money the current administration had thrown at programs designed to help kids learn to read by the third grade. "'The Reading in Excellence Program,' a $260 million federal grant program, competitively awards grants to states to improve reading," the Gore campaign bragged.[29]

Neither campaign seemed to grasp the surrealistic quality of fighting over authorship of programs that had the public schools mired in mediocrity. In fact, Mr. Bush's only real reforms were his ideas to consolidate about sixty federal education programs into block grants, annually test students in grades three through eight, and allow low-income kids trapped in bad schools to use public money to go to private schools. That last proposal was a violation of a leftist sacred cow; it would later be negotiated out of the Bush proposal, leaving most of the status quo intact.

Once Mr. Bush assumed the presidency, his plan and that of the Democrats began to come together. Senator Kennedy met with the new president in the Oval Office and said that the big difference continued to be Bush's position on using federal funds for private schools. But things were happening. Senator Joe Lieberman said that Democrats were willing to work with Republicans, and Mr. Bush openly praised him for that. The Bush plan and the Senate Democrats' plan looked astoundingly similar. Mr. Bush wanted failing schools to have three years to improve, after which kids could transfer out; the Democrats wanted failing schools to use new curriculum, be reconstituted, or changed to charter schools. Both sides wanted to spend a lot more money, with the Democrats estimating the cost of their plan at $35 billion over five years.[30]

As the debate moved forward, conservatives, who questioned the federal role in education at any level of spending, were shocked to discover that President Bush was intent on expanding the Department of Education. In late February, he visited an elementary school in Tennessee, saying that he was going to increase federal aid to public schools by $1.6 billion in the next fiscal year. That would give the DOE the largest percentage increase in budget of any cabinet-level agency. He also announced plans to shift a revamped Head Start program from the Health and Human Services Department to the DOE.[31] Education bureaucrats must have been all smiles; their jobs were secure for as far as the eye could see.

A few days later, conservatives, who had been uneasy with the way "education reform" was playing out, hit the ceiling. The House Education Committee voted 27–20 to strip the bill of its one main attraction to conservatives—the voucher provision. All of the committee's Democrats voted against the vouchers, joined by five Republicans. The vote would still allow low-income students to transfer—but only to other public schools.[32] Now Senator Kennedy had a bill that he could work with.

The Bush administration realized that the voucher issue was too important to core constituencies of the Democratic Party for them to allow it to pass. Since Mr. Bush badly wanted a legislative victory, he decided that he'd rather have a bill to sign without vouchers, than to have no bill at all. Thus, any protests from the White House were muted and frail. Conservative pundits accused Mr. Bush of caving in.

In the magazine *Sentinel,* published by Citizens for a Sound Economy, William J. Bennett (former secretary of education under Ronald Reagan) and Chester E. Finn Jr. (an assistant secretary of education under Mr. Reagan) blasted the new plan as "hardly worth enacting." The original plan, they said, was almost bipartisan, including school choice and more money for various projects such as teacher training. But Bennett and Finn charged that the education establishment struck back to defend the status quo: "Vouchers vanished, and school choice was limited to public schools—cold comfort for many children trapped in urban school systems. State flexibility was scaled back. Deadlines for 'punishing' failed schools were lengthened; the definition of 'adequate yearly progress' was blurred. And almost every special interest got yet more money for its favorite project." [33]

Mr. Bennett was also writing op-ed pieces for newspapers. In the *Dallas Morning News,* he urged the president to fight for his original plan—especially vouchers—"because school choice isn't simply an accountability issue. It's about empowering poor parents with the option of a better education when their children are trapped in schools that repeatedly fail to meet basic standards." [34]

Robert Novak, too, was writing about the Bush surrender. "The problem for conservatives was the president's determination to deal with two Democrats who are very unpopular with Republicans: Senator Edward M. Kennedy of Massachusetts, the roaring lion of the old liberalism, and Representative George Miller of California, the belligerent prototype of House Democratic partisanship." Novak spelled it out for those who might not understand; he explained that these two status-quo liberals had defeated George W. Bush. "To satisfy Kennedy and Miller, flexibility and choice were stripped from the bill while the controls and money remained." [35]

Only days later, Novak was engaging in a tête à tête with the secretary of education, Rod Paige. While Paige was denying it, Novak was asserting that the secretary was not happy with the education bill. Novak said the bill was not what Paige signed up to support. He claimed that two White House aides brought in from Texas—Margaret LaMontagne and Sandy Kress—convinced the president to "build this bridge for the enemy." Kress was once a Democratic activist who supported Michael Dukakis for president. [36]

Bad advice or not, Mr. Bush was on board with the liberal backers of the bill, and it was steamrolling through Congress.

It passed the House first, with representatives defeating two Republican tries to tack on vouchers once again. Minority Leader Richard Gephardt still had some problems with the bill, saying that it didn't spend enough: "Our greatest concern is that while everyone is talking about leaving no child behind, the Republicans are not backing up that commitment by devoting enough resources to achieve this goal." The bill passed 384 to 45.[37]

In mid-June, the Senate followed suit with a vote of 91–8. If Bob Novak had been correct about Secretary Paige, the secretary had been attitude-adjusted by now. "I thought we'd get a strong margin, but this is really beyond my belief," Mr. Paige gushed. "I didn't think it would be this strong. I'm really excited about it." There was still some work to be done. The House version called for about $23 billion in spending for the next year, but the Senate version called for $41 billion.[38]

As the final accord was reached, there was some truly bizarre rhetoric coming from both sides of the aisle. It was weird enough to hear President Bush and Senator Kennedy praising each other ("We really would not be here had it not been for President Bush," said Mr. Kennedy), but even weirder to hear the comments of Jim Jeffords, the former Republican. Spending had been drastically increased, but it wasn't enough for Mr. Jeffords. Upset that federal subsidies for the handicapped (known as "special education") hadn't gotten bigger increases, he said, "The administration is unwilling to support the funding that is essential to successfully carrying out its own education reform package."

And Senator Tom Harkin (who once called impeachment charges against Bill Clinton a "pile of dung") suggested that the administration resisted boosting special-education spending as a way to punish Jeffords for jumping ship.[39]

The fact is that the Democrats had gotten most of what they wanted— continued federal control and more spending—and most of Mr. Bush's conservative elements had been cut from the final bill. Federal aid to public schools would jump to $26.5 billion the next year, an increase of $8 billion over the current year and $4 billion more than the president had asked for. Still, it was billions[40] less than what the Democrats in the Senate had wanted.

And so, Mr. Bush got his wish and signed the bill in early January 2002. When all the compromising was said and done, the bill was a bloated statement of just how bad government can be when it treads into what ought to be forbidden waters. The federal government—with no constitutional authorization to do what it had just done—was back in the education business big-time, including more bucks for early reading education, teacher training, school safety, after-school programs, and even college tuition grants.

At the signing ceremony, President Bush proclaimed that the education problem in America was now solved: "As of this hour, America's schools will be on a new path of reform and new paths of results." He joked about the complexity of the bill, saying, "it's not exactly light reading."[41] It never is when the federal government is involved.

While it didn't address the major mistakes of our educational system—such as outcome-based education, whole language, bilingual education, and all the other feel-good aspects now ensconced in the system—the signing of the education bill did accomplish two very important things. It gave President Bush a major political victory, and it made Senator Kennedy very happy.

College campuses: resistance is futile

Perhaps the Bush "reforms" will work their magic in the public schools and send a new generation of high school graduates to colleges, prepared to do college-level work. That would be a good thing, since most college professors don't care a whit about self-esteem.

What they do seem to care about is correct thinking. After all, many leftist campus radicals from the 1960s went on to become educators or college professors, and many of them seem to have a deep-seated allegiance to the ideals of the American Left. Add to that the fact that OBE-adjusted kids now head for college with many of those same attitudes in their heads and you have a formula for today's campus thought-control.

You might think that college campuses are some sort of incubators of free speech and diversity of opinion. You would be wrong. On major college campuses from Berkeley to Ann Arbor to Austin, you can count the conservative professors on one hand.

Ironically, the big universities are consumed with the idea of diversity. They will go to any length and spend any amount of money on high-priced lawyers to preserve their race-based admissions policies. But while they desire to see students of all skin colors, that's where diversity stops. If a student or a campus speaker strays from approved patterns of thought, he soon learns that there is no diversity of opinion.

College campuses have become "Constitution-free zones" where the First Amendment is suspended and independent thought is forbidden. As the Borg used to say on Star Trek, "Resistance is futile; you will be assimilated." If you don't think good thoughts and say the right things, you will be banished to the proverbial cornfield—shouted down, demonized as a racist, and often threatened with physical violence.

In many cases, all this goes on while the campus administration stands idly by or even voices its approval.

Approved "campus-think" is that racial preference in college admissions is highly desirable and that race should be placed ahead of individual ac-complishment and credentials. (Remember that one of the basic tenets of the Left is that group rights are more important than individual rights.)

So when Ward Connerly, the black University of California regent who led the fight for Proposition 209 to end official state racial preferences, came to speak at the University of Texas, he experienced a "verbal lynching." UT professor Marvin Olasky wrote: "Sadly, the Austin Left once again tolerated only those who share its prejudices. We all lost the chance for dialogue on an important question: What will happen to African American and Hispanic students if racial preferences disappear?"[42]

Connerly tried to answer that question and others by contending that bet-ter schools would help solve the problems that minorities have with schools. As is the case with most conservatives—even black conservatives—who at-tempt to bring their ideas to university campuses, Connerly got nowhere.

Even Austin's daily newspaper, the American-Statesman, did not want to hear what Connerly had to say. They called his followers "anti-affirmative action zealots" and had only a mild rebuke for those who tried to prevent Connerly from speaking: "Only the obligatory protestors at the University of Texas who unwisely planned to shout him down during his speech at the law school Monday night considered Connerly's message important to Texas."[43]

The editorial pointed out that Governor George Bush and Lieutenant Governor Rick Perry ignored the speech. At least the Statesman's editorial board made some attempt—feeble though it may have been—to answer Connerly and justify the continuation of institutionalized racism at the University of Texas. The hecklers who showed up at the law school only wanted to shut him up.

Another example of campus-think occurred just a hundred miles north of Austin, in Waco, famous for the Branch Davidian compound and the world's largest Baptist university, Baylor. Within the comfortable confines of "Bear Country," you would think that more conservative viewpoints such as a belief in God and opposition to abortion might be at least tolerated. Again, you would be wrong.

When Robert Sloan assumed the presidency of BU in 1995, he wanted to pursue both academic excellence and Christian commitment. He had read a paper by Dr. William Dembski and was very impressed by the writing, as well as by Dr. Dembski's credentials.

At Sloan's urging, Baylor officials contacted Dr. Dembski and discovered that he was pursuing the idea of assembling a research center to test the the-ory of intelligent design.[44]

This fell right in line with what President Sloan considered Baylor's mis-sion to be. So they made an offer, and soon Dr. Dembski came to Baylor and founded the Michael Polanyi Center. He then set about the task of using mathematics to find out if intelligent design could be tested scientifically. As the news spread, papers in Waco and Houston began to quote some Baylor professors who were "appalled that such a monstrosity such as the Polanyi Center should be found on their campus."[45] The charge was that Dr. Dembski was using the Polanyi Center as a front for creationism.

Dr. Dembski, a scientist with Ph.Ds in mathematics and philosophy, was trying to set up methods for detecting intelligent design (the idea that a sentient force was involved in creation) if such evidence were to be found in nature. But eight members of Baylor's science department thought the research was "dangerous," and the faculty senate voted twenty-six to two to recommend that the think tank be dismantled.[46]

The question here isn't the veracity of any conclusions that might have arisen from this research. Intelligent design either exists or it doesn't, but proving it one way or the other was not acceptable to the closed-minded professors at Baylor. All they could see was that Dr. Dembski was heading in a forbidden direction. He had committed the sin of independent thought on a college campus, and he had to be stopped.

Before we leave the halls of Baylor, let's examine another situation involving another sacred cow of campus-think: "abortion rights."

In November 2001, an anti-abortion display sponsored by the student organization "Bears for Life" made its way to the Waco campus. The three-sided, eighteen-foot-tall display asked the question "When are we human?" and showed a variety of human embryos and aborted fetuses—all in living color. Some Baylor students were outraged.

A group of thirty students descended on President Sloan's office to demand that the display be removed. "If you can't avoid something, by either hearing it or seeing it, then it's oppressive," said junior Ashleigh Stokes.[47] For the next several days, the campus newspaper, the *Baylor Lariat*, was full of letters, op-eds, and editorials about the display.

Most bizarre was a *Lariat* editorial that flat-out rejected the idea that anti-abortion views should be expressed through such an exhibit. The *Lariat* first noted its support of freedom of speech but then lashed out at the administration for allowing such freedom in this particular case: "Baylor never should have allowed this display. Whether one is anti-abortion or pro-abortion rights is not at issue, nor is whether Justice for All and Bears for Life have a right to express their opinions. What is at issue is that these images are offensive and are mentally disturbing and sickening to almost anyone who sees them."[48]

The editorial staff of the *Lariat* had gotten the point—and missed it all at the same time. Of course the killing of a little human being is grotesque.

If killing unborn babies was a pleasant business, there would be nice family portraits taken with the aborted fetus. It's not a pleasant thing, and Bears for Life was making a strong point: if you can't stand to look at the pictures, then how can you go through with the actual act of abortion?

In the same issue, columnist Steven Dove wrote that the display might even serve to open up the Baylor campus to the views of more liberal students—views that traditionally went against the grain of Baylor's mission. But Dove's column also carried accounts of an amazing dichotomy—the difference in how the more conservative students approached the controversy as opposed to the liberals: "Some students and community members stopped to pray in front of the graphic display of aborted fetuses while other passersby hurled obscenities as they denounced the efforts of the anti-abortion student group . . ."[49]

Even though it's a Christian (Baptist) institution, the students at Baylor seemed to be split along the same lines you'd find at some big state-supported school. The students who supported the display (and there were many) wrote lucid, well-thought-out letters to the *Lariat*. Those who opposed the display were almost unanimous in their belief that such a display should never have been allowed.

The incidents of free-speech suppression at Baylor are tame compared to the story of author David Horowitz when he dared to take a conservative message to not one but dozens of campuses.

Horowitz is the author of several books, president of the Los Angeles–based "Center for the Study of Popular Culture," and a former campus radical himself. In the spring of 2001, he made an attempt to voice his opposition to reparations for slavery by placing ads in college newspapers. In his book *Uncivil Wars*, Horowitz tells the story of how he was demonized, accused of racism, and shouted down on campus after campus—even to the point that he was forced to hire bodyguards.

The beginning of the story is simple enough. Horowitz saw a rising tide for the issue of reparations for slavery and he thought the idea was a bad one. So he put together an ad entitled "Ten reasons why reparations for blacks is a bad idea for blacks—and racist too."[50] His idea was to place the ad in college newspapers and get a dialogue going.

The ad copy was based on research that Horowitz had done, but in the end, it all boiled down to Horowitz's opinion. There was nothing in the copy that was the least bit objectionable from the standpoint of race—except that the opinions expressed ran contrary to approved campus-think. Like Ward Connerly, Bill Dembski, and the Bears for Life, David Horowitz had committed the sin of independent thought.

Just so you'll know, the ten reasons were spelled out as sub-headlines with short blocks of copy to support them. They concerned such "controversial" points as "there is no single group responsible for the crime of slavery," "only a tiny minority of white Americans ever owned slaves and others gave their lives to free them," "America today is a multi-ethnic nation and most Americans have no connection to slavery," and "the reparations claim is one more attempt to turn African Americans into victims." Though a lot of people disagree with these and the other points he made, nothing that Horowitz said was out of the mainstream; in fact, much of the rhetoric in the ad was quite complimentary toward blacks. But that didn't matter on campus.

Horowitz explained that once the ad appeared in campus papers, all hell broke loose: "On campus after campus, protests erupted and indiscriminate rage spilled over into every corner of the public space. It was a breathtaking display of intolerance for an academic community. In their anger, my critics showed little regard for fairness or facts, or common decency."[51]

At the University of California, Berkeley, the ad ran in the *Daily Californian* on February 28, 2001, and it received a swift reaction. Forty angry black students, accompanied by a professor of African-American studies, stormed the paper's offices and held a "raucous finger-wagging session" with editor Daniel Hernandez. They pointed out to Hernandez that he, too, was an oppressed minority, and they demanded an apology. It appeared on the front page the next day.[52]

Other campuses saw similar incidents. In Madison, angry students at the University of Wisconsin formed a chanting mob to attack the offices of the *Badger Herald*. The demonstrations were organized by a group known as the "Multicultural Student Coalition." They demanded the resignation of editor Julie Bosman and wanted the *Herald* to be banned from campus newsstands.[53]

When the student newspaper at Brown University, the *Brown Daily Herald,* printed the ad without comment on March 13, student radicals responded by organizing a group called the "Coalition of Concerned Brown Students" (including the Black Student Union, Third World Action, the Asian-American Student Association, the Young Communist League, and the International Socialist Organization) and made two key demands. They wanted the money that Horowitz had paid for the ad ($580) to be forked over to the Third World Center, and they wanted free space on the front page for a message of their own. The *Brown Daily Herald* said no. The group then fanned out across the campus and stole the entire run of the March 16 edition.[54]

When Horowitz showed up in Austin for a campus forum, angry students lined up to challenge him, but again, the attacks were more personal than factual. Robin Citizen referred to Horowitz's views as "disgusting and condescending." Nakia Hillary worried that by just being on campus, Horowitz had "degraded" the University of Texas.[55] There were no incidents, but the discussion was peppered with applause and boos from supporters and detractors. Horowitz noted that UT had posted about half a dozen security guards.

Understand that what you have just read is a much-abbreviated version of what happened to David Horowitz; for the full story, you'll need to read his book. His original intent—to provide an opposing viewpoint on college campuses—was completely overshadowed by the most amazing display of closed-mindedness the United States has seen in recent years. Even papers at such bastions of education as Penn, Columbia, Virginia, Harvard, Notre Dame, and the University of Washington rejected the ad outright.

In the mainstream press, pundits were talking about the ad, too. Like most of the student protestors, liberal columnist Richard Cohen couldn't find factual errors in the ad. But that didn't matter; he still didn't like it. "Word for word, the ad makes sense," he wrote. "Something about it, though, is wrong. What's wrong is the message between the lines." Cohen goes on to say that if he had been a college editor, he would have rejected the ad.[56]

Conservative columnists like William Murchison weren't trying to read between the lines. They were framing the debate as a freedom-of-speech issue and finding college campuses lacking in that respect. Murchison wrote that while it's all right to ridicule Republicans and heterosexual men, you can't "bruise the feelings" of any member of a pre-1964 outsider culture: "Yes, reparations for slavery is a nutty notion. But—shhhhh—we're not supposed to say so when Johnnie Cochran finally gets around to filing his federal lawsuit demanding big bucks for what folks in Charleston did a century and a half ago."[57]

Cohen and Murchison had nailed the issue, though from opposite sides of the political spectrum. To Cohen, the ad just felt wrong. To Murchison, it was obvious that it had caused bruised feelings. There's that word again—"feelings"!

If the emotions of today's college students are so fragile that campus newspaper editors must walk on eggshells, then how are these students challenged in the rigorous environment of a classroom?

It's time to take back our schools

The problems discussed here are very entrenched and institutionalized, and it will take a major movement to effect change. That is to say, it will take a movement of the people; the schools themselves may very well be incapable of recognizing that anything is wrong.

Chester E. Finn, saying that the schools need a major overhaul, simply doesn't believe that it can happen from within: "The public school system as we know it has proved that it cannot fix itself. It is an ossified government monopoly that functions largely for the benefit of its employees and interest groups rather than that of children and taxpayers."[58]

Finn is correct. Teachers' unions don't exist for the benefit of children; they work to increase teachers' pay and other benefits and seem to oppose every meaningful reform that might be proposed. Union members have a great deal of influence within the Democratic Party and often make up more than 10 percent of the delegates at the Democratic National Convention. Whatever they want, the Democratic Party will fight to deliver.

One thing the unions are dead-set against is school choice—allowing parents to take their kids out of failing government schools and use some of their own tax money to send them elsewhere. So when was the last time you saw a Democratic congressman or senator come out in favor of school choice or vouchers?

The unions have made it impossible for Democrats to back any real reform, but the crazy ideas all seem to take root. *Investor's Business Daily* put it this way: "The public schools seem to have no defense mechanism, no way to stop the most absurd, goofball ideas from becoming the norm."[59]

It has become a vicious circle. The education establishment in the form of the unions has become very powerful; the Democratic Party depends on the teachers' unions as a key constituency; the Democratic Party supports the Department of Education and other federal government meddling in the public schools; goofy left-wing ideology becomes entrenched in the schools; and Republicans eventually give in and agree to sink more money into a failing system, expecting different results.

We've just seen this happen again with the George W. Bush expansion of the Education Department, while school choice was expelled from the new legislation.

Hiring better teachers and better school superintendents and electing better school board members won't help much, either. The good teachers—the ones who actually recognize the wacky education fads for what they are—can't speak out, for fear of losing their jobs. School superintendents are equally trapped, hampered by so many state and federal rules and regulations that they are all virtually the same. School boards may vote to expel a disruptive student (if he's not a member of a protected group) or decide the scope of a bond issue, but that's about it. The public schools are so set in their ways that individuals have little effect on them.

But individual administrators and boards do have a major effect on private schools that don't accept government funding. The late James Coleman of the University of Chicago did some studies and found that students in Catholic schools were more likely to stay in school and earn higher test scores. He found that part of the answer was simply high academic expectations; part was that Catholic schools spend their money more wisely. But Coleman found that the most important factor in the success of the Catholic school is that it "strengthens families and provides for many children the caring, stability, community and discipline that used to come from parents."[60]

Parents and local administrators should take this as a lesson. High expectations and discipline have been replaced in the public schools by self-esteem and diversity, and consequently, Johnny can't read. So the question becomes, "How can the public schools become more like the private schools before the education fads move into the private schools?"

The answer is simple, but will be hard to implement. The unions and the Democrats have killed school choice for the time being, but that doesn't matter; the solution must go far beyond school choice. First, the federal government has got to go. The Department of Education is a failure and it must be eliminated. Then the fifty states can make their decisions: either run the schools with state and local control, or go one step further.

That final step is complete privatization. Columnist Linda Bowles says that privatization should be accomplished "with a high wall of separation between state and education. This will subject schools to that tried-and-true, all-American marketplace competition, which demands results, instills discipline and accountability, relentlessly drives toward excellence, and puts customers (parents and children) first."[61]

This idea would diminish the power of the unions, rid the schools of most of the nutty education fads, give parents full choice over where their kids attend school, make schools as good as local taxpayers want them to be, get the politicians out of the way, and eventually send a new generation of students and professors to our colleges and universities. Grade school kids—and eventually even college kids—would learn to think again and maybe even consider opposing points of view.

Taxpayers in some school district in some community will have to start the ball rolling. One success story and it's all over for government schools.

CHAPTER 10

Acknowledge Right from Wrong

*We must declare that there is a discernable dif-
ference between the concepts of right and wrong,
and good and evil, and that America cannot survive under a system of moral relevance.*

Admitting that there is a difference between right and wrong is a difficult
prospect for some people. After all, in the animal kingdom, there really
isn't such a concept; animals kill for food or for self-protection. To them, there
is no right and wrong. But human beings are supposed to be different. We are
supposed to know better. In the Declaration of Independence, Jefferson used
the term "self-evident," referring to a truth so basic that it is patently obvious.

For centuries, humankind has recognized that the difference between
right and wrong is self-evident. After all, how could a civilized society survive without a system of ethics? In business, in politics, and in day-to-day
human relationships, we simply could not function without such a system.
But in modern society, that logic has been challenged, primarily by academics on the Left. They argue that all things are relative and that society should
be tolerant and nonjudgmental.

This system, known as "moral relevance," holds that "wrong" and "evil"
are simply in the eyes of the beholder and that there are far more important
things to worry about in this country—such as diversity and the environment.

So has moral relevance taken hold in the boardrooms and classrooms of
the United States? You might think so by looking at the corporate accounting
scandals that began with Enron and spread to Global Crossing, WorldCom,
and others. But what if you went to college campuses and checked on the attitudes of seniors who will soon be working for many of those companies and
who will be running them—and the country—someday?

181

An organization called "The National Association of Scholars" did that, hiring Zogby International to poll 401 seniors, selected at random. The study found that three-quarters of all college seniors believe that "right and wrong" depend on "differences in individual values and cultural diversity." Only about a fourth of the students responded that their professors were teaching "clear uniform standards of right and wrong by which everyone should be judged."[1]

The students were asked to prioritize various business practices, based on what they had learned in class. Thirty-eight percent of the students chose as most important "recruiting a diverse workforce in which women and minorities are advanced and promoted." Only 21 percent chose "providing clear and accurate business statements to stockholders and creditors." If you find that result amazing and somewhat disturbing, you should know that another 18 percent chose "minimizing environmental pollution by adopting the latest anti-pollution technology and complying with government regulations." The Zogby poll makes it clear: Diversity is all-important to college students, and environmental issues are not far behind.

The ethics—or lack of ethics—being taught in our schools is taking its toll. Stop for a moment and think of all the stories that have made news in recent years, where right and wrong have been trumped by some other interest that took precedence:

- In the O. J. Simpson murder trial, jurors felt that racial issues were more important than a true verdict.
- In the impeachment trial of Bill Clinton, the United States Senate thought political issues were more important than the removal of a corrupt president.
- In the Gary Condit case, the U.S. representative from California thought his congressional seat was more important than being candid about his relationship with the murdered intern.
- In the corporate accounting scandals, CEOs felt that appearing to be profitable was more important than providing accurate financial numbers.

Imagine how each of these stories might have turned out different had all the players been steeped in the kind of traditional ethics that America was built on. Unfortunately, in today's mixed-up society, right and wrong are often based simply on what someone believes he can get away with.

A classic case is that of a hardened Texas hate criminal named Gary Graham. As we go through the litany of crimes that Mr. Graham is known to have committed, keep this question in mind: Is it possible to characterize Mr. Graham as a victim—or is evil his only legacy?

On June 22, 2000, Gary Graham was executed in Huntsville, Texas, for the murder of Bobby Grant Lambert in the parking lot of a Houston grocery store. He was convicted largely on the testimony of just one eyewitness, Bernadine Skillern, who saw his face for just a split second in the parking lot from a distance of thirty to forty feet. Ms. Skillern testified that she honked her horn in an attempt to stop the assault, but that Graham glanced at her and then shot Lambert anyway.[2] She never wavered from her testimony.

Death penalty opponents cried foul. They said that a man should not be put to death on the strength of a single witness and other evidence that they found to be lacking. But our purpose here is not to argue that case; if indeed Mr. Graham was executed for a murder that he did not commit, that would be a miscarriage of justice. But let's take a look at what we know for certain that Mr. Graham did.

The murder was committed on May 13, 1981. On May 20, Mr. Graham was arrested following a weeklong crime spree that included twenty armed robberies, three kidnappings, a rape, and three attempted murders. There were twenty-eight victims of this spree and nineteen eyewitnesses who fingered Graham.[3]

Gary Graham's own words, culled from eyewitness reports, also give a clear impression of what kind of person he was. To a rape victim, fifty-seven-year-old Lisa Blackburn, he said, "I have already killed three people and I'm going to kill you. You don't mean nothing to me, bitch." To David Spiers, a shooting victim: "After I kill you, I am going back to kill your fiancé and her parents so they can go with you to honky hell. Before I kill your fiancé, I'm going to rape her." And to Richard Carter after forcing him to kneel and placing a shotgun in his mouth: "Blowing away another white mother f——r don't mean nothing to me."[4]

By now, you may have decided that even if Ms. Skillern was wrong, there's still plenty of evidence to conclude that Gary Graham was a bad person. With all the testimony, the eyewitness accounts, and Mr. Graham's own words, no one could possibly believe that he was anything but evil. Well, if you're the Reverend Jesse Jackson, you can believe anything you want.

Jackson, who had been a witness at the execution, acted as if Mr. Graham was something of a saint who should be fitted for a halo. "Sleep on, prince," said the reverend at Graham's funeral. "You've done your job. You organized us. Because you sleep, we are awake."[5]

The "celebration" of Mr. Graham's life lasted three hours, during which time he was compared to Moses, Jesus, Nelson Mandela, Malcolm X, Martin Luther King Jr., and other religious and historical figures. Big-screen monitors flooded the sanctuary with images of Mr. Graham, with the music of "Wind Beneath My Wings" in the background.

Jesse Jackson did not speak of hate crimes. Instead, he handed out voter registration cards so that mourners could be sure and go to the polls to turn aside the real criminal in this case: George W. Bush.[6]

To this day there is still some doubt that Gary Graham was the man who killed Bobby Lambert. But how could anyone—even someone as racially motivated as the Reverend Jackson—truly believe that Mr. Graham was a "prince"? Such a belief defies all logic, and yet the papers were full of stories about people who felt that Mr. Graham was a victim.

If people could believe that, could they also find excuses for people who would deliberately fly airplanes into buildings or people who would send their own children into crowded marketplaces to blow up themselves and others?

You bet they could.

Right and wrong on the world stage

When the United States was brutally attacked on September 11, 2001, there were plenty of apologists standing by to take the side of the attackers. Even with four airplanes crashed, two skyscrapers destroyed, a wing of the Pentagon in flames, and almost three thousand people murdered, some on the Left still sought to blame the United States.

The reasons for this are varied—everything from our support of Israel to exploiting the Middle East for its oil to our military missions overseas. In reality, many on the Left just couldn't admit that there is evil in the world. The moral relativists simply believed that while the attacks were despicable, they were the direct result of the United States' own crimes against humanity.

Robert Jensen, a journalism professor at the University of Texas at Austin, wrote that he was angry about the attacks but his primary anger was directed at the leaders of the United States. The attacks were "reprehensible and indefensible," he wrote in an op-ed piece in the *Houston Chronicle* just three days after September 11. But Jensen also believed that they were no more horrific than what the U.S. has perpetrated on the people of Vietnam, Cambodia, Laos, Indonesia, East Timor, Chile, Central America, Iraq, or Palestine: "For more than five decades throughout the Third World, the United States has deliberately targeted civilians or engaged in violence so indiscriminate that there is no other way to understand it except as terrorism."[7]

Jensen's column did not offer evidence that the United States had deliberately targeted civilians in any of its military excursions. Even so, his greatest fear was that we would retaliate for 9/11 without any regard for innocent lives.

As if in response, William Bennett offered a contrary opinion—that the

United States was attacked simply because it has been a force for good. Writing in the *Dallas Morning News*, Bennett called the 9/11 attacks a moment of moral clarity. "For almost forty years, we have been a nation that has questioned whether good and evil, right and wrong, true and false really exist. Some—particularly those in our institutions of higher learning and even some inside our own government—have wondered whether the United States really is better than its enemies around the world. After the events of September 11, we no longer should be unsure of such things."[8]

Bennett wrote that the United States' support for human rights and democracy is "our noblest export to the world" and that time after time, we have acted well and honorably.

"Despite what Saddam Hussein, Osama bin Laden and, shamefully, some American clerics have said," Bennett wrote, "the United States wasn't punished because we are bad but because we are good."[9] Bennett went on to say that we have been engaged in a "frivolous dalliance" with dangerous theories of relativism, historicism, and values clarification that were all proven to be empty by the events of 9/11.

Not everyone thought so; especially not everyone in the business of gathering and disseminating the news. Some TV news organizations announced that anchors would not be wearing American flag lapel pins, so that their coverage of the attacks would not seem slanted toward the American point of view. And the Reuters News Service went so far as to announce that it would not refer to the attackers as "terrorists" because that would call for a judgment on its part.

Reuters' position attracted the attention of U.S. Representative J. C. Watts, R-Okla., who wrote a pithy letter to Tom Glover, the wire service's CEO, and Geert Linnebank, its editor in chief: "I write you today to ask you to reverse this decision and grant your writers and editors the freedom to use words including 'terrorist' that best characterize those who attacked the United States on September 11, 2001. I am not asking you to be Radio Free Afghanistan. Rather, I am merely requesting that you not sever the word 'terrorist' from your stylebook. I fail to see how the aforementioned noun is not an accurate portrayal of the aggressors who committed the acts of violence witnessed by the entire world last month."[10]

For his part, President Bush began the War on Terrorism with near-total moral clarity. He established what became known as the Bush Doctrine: Every nation must decide—"Either you are with us or you are with the terrorists." And in his first State of the Union Address, the president put three rogue nations on alert: "The United States will not permit the world's most dangerous regimes to threaten us with the world's most destructive weapons," he said.[11]

Mr. Bush's statement that the three countries—Iraq, Iran, and North Korea," formed an "Axis of Evil" rocked the world. The three nations wasted little time in firing back, with Iranian Foreign Minister Kamal Kharrazi proclaiming that Mr. Bush's "arrogant" statements were nothing more than a pretext for the U.S. to continue its support of Israel. "Bush is attempting to divert public opinion from the Middle East issues by raising up a new subject and thereby pave the ground for the U.S. to continue support for Israel in suppressing the Palestinian nation," he said.[12]

Kharrazi was attempting to use words to muddle the Bush message. Without a doubt, he chose to inject the Israeli-Palestinian conflict into the argument because Mr. Bush had not approached that issue with the same moral clarity. The Iraqis, even less tactful, called the United States "the sole evil on earth" in the official *Al-Iraq* newspaper. Iran's supreme leader, Ayatollah Ali Khamenei, joined the chorus by saying it was an honor to be singled out by "the most hated Satan in the world."[13] Iran further protested the president's remark by pulling its foreign minister out of a scheduled economic forum in New York.

If any of this bothered Mr. Bush, he did not show it. Instead, he began to ratchet up the rhetoric about a possible preemptive strike against Iraq, a nation he was sure was developing weapons of war. In June 2002, he told future army officers at West Point that the United States could not use threats of retaliation in the new War on Terrorism. He said we have to be ready to strike our enemies first. "If we wait for threats to fully materialize, we will have waited too long," he said. "The War on Terror will not be won on the defensive."[14] This was a direct reference to his plans for a regime change in Iraq. The president spoke frankly about first strikes, punishing those who engage in terror, and imposing a universal standard of moral clarity between good and evil.

Our European allies, and Saddam's Arab neighbors, were having a great deal of difficulty in seeing things as clearly as Mr. Bush. The Europeans, in fact, were flat-out uncooperative in some ways. Germany said it wouldn't turn over some documents that might link the so-called "twentieth hijacker" Zacharias Moussaoui to al-Qaeda because we might impose the death penalty. Writing in the *Washington Times*, Bill O'Reilly said the entire European Union is being problematical. "The E.U. has told the Bush administration that it has a 'problem' with trying captured terrorists in front of military tribunals. Well, pardon me, E.U., but blank you."[15] O'Reilly noted that there are killers living in Europe whose only goal is to destroy Western civilization.

But like United States liberals, much of Europe was far too embroiled in political correctness—mostly about the rights and feelings of suspected terrorists—to be of any real support. President Bush pressed on. It was only on the Israeli-Palestinian question that he appeared to waver. While promising to root out terrorism wherever it existed, Mr. Bush nonetheless seemed willing (at least for a long while) to work with Yasser Arafat even while terrorist groups such as Hezbollah and Hamas were sending suicide bombers to take out as many Israelis as possible—including children and other civilians.

That would seem to brand the tactics of those who support the Palestinian cause as evil. But the fact remains that much of Europe and practically all Arab states support the Palestinians—and that's even though the Israelis have made a number of viable offers for peace. The history of those peace opportunities goes back before there even was a Yasser Arafat and is tied to the overall history of the land—which both sides claim.

The Jews say it is God-given, dating back to the time of Abraham and Moses. After 1,500 years, the Jews were expelled by the Romans in A.D. 135. The Romans renamed the area "Palestine." In A.D. 638, the land fell under the control of the new Islamic religion and stayed so for 1,300 years.

For a long time, Jews didn't have a homeland and faced religious persecution no matter where they tried to locate. So they began a movement in the nineteenth century and early twentieth century to form a state in their former homeland—partly because of growing anti-Semitism in Eastern Europe. But by 1911, the Palestinians had formed organized opposition to the new Jewish settlements. As early as 1922 there was an opportunity for an agreement, as the League of Nations was mandated to "facilitate" Jewish immigration. However, Palestinian Arabs opposed this move, wanting all the land to be under Arab control.

World War II was a turning point in the conflict. The Nazis killed about six million European Jews, and those who survived were living as refugees in other countries. Britain was trying to limit those people from emigrating to Palestine, but the Jews protested. In 1947, Britain asked the United Nations to step in.

On May 14, 1948, the Jews finally got their home back. The UN divided the area into a Jewish state and a Palestinian state, with the agreement calling for Jerusalem to be placed under international control. Here was the perfect opportunity for peace. The Jews accepted it. But on the very next day, neighboring Arab states invaded, intending to destroy the new Israel. The Jews rallied and won the battle. In the process, they picked up some additional land. There was another war in 1955, and then came the Six-Day War in 1967. Egypt, Syria, and Jordan planned an attack to destroy Israel. The Israelis discovered the plan, struck first, and took the Golan Heights, the West Bank, and Gaza.[16]

In each case, when the Arabs have tried to completely destroy Israel, the Israelis have won and have assumed control of more land, and that's why we have the so-called "occupied territories"—land that would not be in question had the Arabs embraced peace.

So those Americans who support Israel are looking at a people who have the world's longest history of oppression. Most Americans may not be fully cognizant of the anti-Semitism that has existed in Europe over the decades, but they certainly recall the Holocaust, the death camps, and the Jewish refugees. They also consider all the missed chances for peace dating back to the 1920s and including such modern opportunities as Oslo and the Ehud Barak offer that would have given the Palestinians about 97 percent of what they wanted, including the Temple Mount and a divided Jerusalem.

Those who support Israel watch their television screens each night and see a constant onslaught of stories about a bitter people—the Palestinians—who will blow themselves up just to kill a few Israelis and who have rejected every opportunity for an agreement. They remember Palestinian street celebrations on 9/11. And they see the Israelis as an oppressed people throughout all of history, who have been willing time and again to accept peace.

Of course, not all Americans see it that way, and neither does much of Europe. But those who do would like to see the violence stop. They want to know why terrorist organizations that target Israel aren't included under the Bush Doctrine.

Cal Thomas complained in his newspaper column that "all it takes is another meaningless statement from Yasser Arafat 'condemning' terrorism for Secretary of State Colin Powell to get a meeting and shake the PLO leader's bloody hand."[17] Thomas echoed the words of former Israeli Prime Minister Benjamin Netanyahu in saying that Bush's inconsistency could hurt the ultimate war with Iraq. The Bush administration later began to say that they could not work with Arafat. Still, the suicide bombings continued, and the United States still failed to go after Hezbollah and Hamas.

So, what can we make of the two world conflicts we've discussed?

Instead of wiping out thousands of people, why didn't the September 11 terrorists use a civilized means to bring their grievances before the world? Why not call for an international summit, or send their leaders to meet with President Bush, or even go before the United Nations? They didn't because those are the things that civilized people do and because they had no desire to make peace with those they considered to be "infidels." They simply wanted to destroy us.

Instead of sending in suicide bombers, why don't the Palestinian leaders accept a peace plan? The Israelis have made it clear time and again that they are willing to trade "land for peace" and do what it takes to coexist with the

Palestinians. But the Palestinians will never accept any peace plan, because they hate the Israelis. They simply want to drive the Israelis into the sea.

The bottom line is this: On these two major events now playing out on the world stage, there is a right and wrong—a side that works for good facing the other side that represents evil. There is no moral relativism here at all.

Right and wrong: there really is a difference

Part of the problem in defining the difference between right and wrong is that so many people don't seem to care. The lines are so blurred that what used to be considered "pornography" or simply "smut" is now mainstream popular culture.

In her 1987 book *Raising PG Kids in an X-Rated Society,* Tipper Gore took on the recording industry, saying that no one seems to ask about content anymore, or what the effect of a product will be on kids; they just ask how well it will sell. In the introduction to her book, Mrs. Gore issued an apology for the profanity and imagery that her book would necessarily have to contain if she were to provide actual illustrations of what is happening in popular culture. This sequence from chapter one is a prime example, explaining what Mrs. Gore saw when she first paid attention to MTV:

"I sat down with my kids and watched videos like Mötley Crüe's *Looks That Kill,* with scantily clad women being captured and imprisoned in cages by a studded-leather-clad male band. In *Photograph* by Def Leppard, we saw a dead woman tied up with barbed wire. The Scorpions' *Rock You Like a Hurricane* showed a man tied to the walls of a torture chamber and a singer being choked by a woman. These images frightened my children; they frightened me! The graphic sex and the violence were too much for us to handle." [18]

Just in this one passage you find instances of partial nudity, necrophilia, bondage, and torture. But as Mrs. Gore points out later in her book, nothing sells like sex, including masturbation, intercourse, and sexual sadism. Mrs. Gore wrote:

"It is a quantum leap from the Beatles' 'I Want to Hold Your Hand' to Prince singing: 'If you get tired of masturbating . . . /If you like, I'll jack you off.' It's a long way from the Rolling Stones' 'Let's Spend the Night Together,' which drew protests in its day, to Sheena Easton's 'Sugar Walls': 'You can't fight passion when passion is hot/Temperatures rise inside my sugar walls.'" [19] And where Elvis Presley merely sang about an attraction to his girlfriend's "Little Sister," Tipper points out that Prince openly sings of making love to his own sister.

Mrs. Gore concluded that in a free-speech society such as ours, parents would have to fight back, enlisting the aid of responsible industry executives and artists. She listed Smokey Robinson, former Beatle Paul McCartney, and

Mike Love of the Beach Boys as artists who have helped to make a difference. But in the years since Mrs. Gore's book was published, there hasn't
been much if any improvement.

Rap music has become the rage, and along with it graphic images of
killing policemen and homosexuals and sexual exploitation of women. Even
sports networks like ESPN have pushed the bounds of respectability with
such offerings as a profanity-laced TV movie about basketball coach Bobby
Knight.

It is now a fact that ratings are so important—and often difficult to get
and to maintain—that TV and radio will resort to almost anything to build
an audience. Television is famous for reality shows like *Survivor* and
Temptation Island that often place real people in sexual situations, with the
Fox Network's *Who Wants to Marry a Millionaire?* considered by many to be
an all-time low. And today's comic books—mostly aimed at young males—
are populated with women sporting missile-like breasts that have no relation
to true human anatomy.

On radio, so-called "shock jocks" like Howard Stern lace their shows
with profanity and sexual references (usually about the size of women's
breasts) and seem to take delight in seeing how vulgar they can be.

A syndicated duo out of New York, "Opie and Anthony," decided to
boost their ratings with a little stunt called "Sex for Sam" that involved people "doing it" in risky locations. Having sex in a church would get you 25
points; sex with a police officer or a firefighter would net you 100 points. The
contest drew entries, and eventually, a Virginia couple was arrested for public lewdness after fulfilling the terms of the contest in St. Patrick's Cathedral.
Comedian Paul Mercurio, who was providing an on-air play-by-play account
of the couple's activities, was also arrested.[20] The "Opie and Anthony" program had been cited as "indecent" and fined by the Federal Communications
Commission three times before.

The sad part of this story is not the depravity of Opie and Anthony, or
Howard Stern, or for that matter any of the profane and outrageous stars of
radio, TV, movies, and records. The sad part is very simply this:

None of these people would be stars—and their shows, movies, and
recordings would not be seen and heard on a daily basis—if the American
people didn't accept the depravity.

We might even say that the American people demand the depravity.
Opie and Anthony are far from being the only male duo in radio's "hot talk"
format that pushes the envelope. They know, and so do their corporate
bosses, that the more outrageous they get, the more audience they're likely
to pull from competing shows. MTV, from lewd videos to *Beavis and Butt-
Head,* runs programming that its adolescent audience wants to see. And

today's movie audiences seem willing and eager to see films that feature graphic violence coupled with explicit sex.

But why?

Does anyone really believe that *The Maltese Falcon* would have been a better movie if Sam Spade had bedded Brigid O'Shaughnessy? Would *The Longest Day* have been a better movie if it had been more graphic like *Saving Private Ryan*? Almost certainly not. The great classics of all forms of popular culture relied more on good writing, plot development, and showmanship; they could be good without being graphic. Today, while there is still a lot of excellent writing and moviemaking going on, it's more often than not laced with profanity, violence, and sexual content—because the public seems to want it.

The same is true in the political arena, where elected officials seem able to get away with just about anything while the public yawns and says "who cares?" Knowing this, the officials in question put their spin teams to work and tell us that the president "needs to get back to what the American people elected him to do," or that "this doesn't rise to the level of impeachment," or simply that "mistakes were made."

Author Phillip Hubbell says this passive-voice statement relating to mistakes is a favorite trick of corrupt officials who want you to believe that their character flaws (or crimes, as the case may be) are no worse than day-to-day slip-ups of normal people. You get to "move on" after a mistake, he says, while you may go to jail if you've committed a crime. "A mistake is when you show up for a movie an hour before it starts," says Hubbell. "It isn't a mistake when you lie to the police during a missing-person investigation. It isn't a mistake when you take money for an action and then perform the action for which you took the money. It isn't a mistake when you drive off with furniture that doesn't belong to you."[21] Everyone makes mistakes, says Hubbell, but not everyone commits felonies.

In the old days, we were told that "crime does not pay," but in the real world of politics, President Bill Clinton was able to characterize his crimes as "mistakes" or "snafus" and avoid paying any price. Gary Condit failed to get reelected to his California congressional seat but paid no other price. Hillary Clinton, who made "mistakes" with the Rose Law Firm billing records, the pillaging of White House lawyer Vince Foster's office after his death, and the firing of the White House travel office, was elected senator from New York and will almost certainly run for president of the United States.

As a whole, the American people don't care.

If we're going to change the moral direction of the country, we have to change this attitude. Parents are going to have to set an example for their children; schools are going to have to teach character; we're going to have to hold our politicians accountable for their actions, just as we're going to do with CEOs. We're going to have to turn off the TV and radio and stay home from the movies if we don't think the product is appropriate for human consumption. We have to be able to look evil in the face and call it what it is.

As Tipper Gore said in her book, censorship is not the answer; morality is. There is a "right" and a "wrong," and even though our moral compasses have grown weak, most of us can still tell the difference.

CHAPTER 11

Respect the Judeo-Christian Ethic

We must declare that we are a nation under God, reaffirming the relevance and validity of the Judeo-Christian Ethic as the underpinning of our moral compass.

If there is indeed a difference in right and wrong, there must be something—some foundation—that makes it so. Here in America, we're fortunate to have become the greatest nation the planet has yet seen, largely because of great traditions that are based on religious beliefs.

There is, of course, a difference between "ethics" and "morals," with ethics being more of an academic study of the genre of right and wrong and morals being more concerned with the reasons why people and nations behave as they do. Old sayings to the contrary, our governmental bodies are in the business of legislating both ethics and morals every day. Laws set down basic rules, often called "regulations," and they set moral standards by making it illegal to steal, assault, or murder. Such laws could be enacted in a society with no moral foundation—but what would compel the people of such a society to obey them? Only the threat of swift and severe punishment.

The United States of America was founded upon more than secular law. Even a casual glance at our two great founding documents provides ample evidence. Thomas Jefferson wrote in the Declaration of Independence, "We hold these truths to be self-evident, that all men are created equal, that they are endowed by their Creator with certain unalienable Rights ..."

It is clear from this statement that Jefferson and the others who pledged "our Lives, our Fortunes and our sacred Honor" by signing the declaration believed in a superior force, referred to in the opening paragraph as "Nature's God." According to the declaration, it is from this creator—not government—that basic rights such as life, liberty, and the pursuit of happiness flow. Governments, then, are only instituted to secure these rights.

In the Constitution, the framers were careful not to create a theocracy, but there are clues in the document that they believed in a superior force. For example, in the preamble, one of the things deemed necessary to form a more perfect union was to "secure the Blessings of Liberty to ourselves and our Posterity…" The dictionary definition of the word "bless" is "to hallow or consecrate by religious rite or word." And in the much-debated so-called "establishment clause" of the Bill of Rights, the framers not only banned any law "respecting an establishment of religion" but also forbade Congress to pass any law "prohibiting the free exercise thereof."

Clearly, the framers wanted to make sure that no national religion would ever be established. But it is just as clear that they believed it to be "self-evident"—what today's slang would call a "no-brainer"—that basic truths come from the Creator.

Did the framers know something that modern-day liberals can't seem to recognize? You bet they did! Modern Americans should ask themselves the same question that may well have been pondered back in 1776: Is it possible to have a generally moral society in the absence of all religious conviction?

Again, the answer is self-evident. Just as a computer requires an operating system to make its programs work, so does the human psyche require something more than rules and laws. In other words, it requires some underlying reason to do the right thing when no one is watching—when there is little chance that fraud or immorality might be discovered. The Left will tell you that human beings are inherently good, but the Left is naïve. Ethics and morals do not spring into being spontaneously; they require a foundation that is usually a belief in God or even the possibility that there might be a God.

But many religions believe in God, and some believe in more than one god. It is not our purpose here to pit any of the world's religions against each other, nor to suggest that government should officially adopt the particular teachings of any religion that do not pertain to morality. That would be establishing a state religion. Rather, the intent here is to examine those teachings that have arisen from two great religions—Judaism and Christianity—that became the basis for our laws and our moral compass. Commonly referred to as the "Judeo-Christian Ethic," it has proven to be far superior to the moral codes found in other religions.

Essentially, the Judeo-Christian Ethic can be summed up in six of the Ten Commandments—the ones that deal with relationships among people:[1]

· Honor thy father and thy mother.
· Thou shalt not kill.

- Thou shalt not commit adultery.
- Thou shalt not steal.
- Thou shalt not bear false witness against thy neighbor.
- Thou shalt not covet thy neighbor's house, thou shalt not covet they neighbor's wife, nor his manservant, nor his maidservant, nor his ox, nor his ass, nor anything that is thy neighbor's.

The other four commandments deal with man's relationship to God and therefore are outside the scope of what the Constitution allows government to endorse. But of the six listed above, at least two are against the law—three, if you interpret "bear false witness" as perjury. The other three—parental respect, adultery, and envy—go right to the heart of what is thought of as morality.

Now let's back up and take a look at the first four commandments:[2]

- I am the Lord thy God. Thou shalt have no other Gods before me.
- Thou shalt not make unto thee any graven image, or any likeness of any thing that is in heaven above, or that is in the earth beneath, or that is in the water under the earth.
- Thou shalt not take the name of the Lord thy God in vain.
- Remember the sabbath day, to keep it holy.

These are the laws that the Left objects to the most, because they deal with religious beliefs in a direct way. But liberals take their objections even further. To them, none of the commandments should be posted in a government school or other public place, because of their source.

The Ten Commandments are from the Hebrew Bible—referred to by Christians as the Old Testament—specifically from the Torah, the first five books that laid down the basic teachings of Judaism. Christianity, which developed from Judaism, embraced its morality.

The commandments are so steeped in religious belief and tradition that no self-respecting true believer in the separation of church and state could ever condone their appearance in any public place. And yet, the fact that our present-day system of morals and laws flows directly from them is inescapable. Then don't we have an obligation to our children to instill them with basic morals and to tell them exactly where those morals came from?

The Left certainly doesn't think so.

The Supreme Court goes to school

"The first half of my life I thought I was living in a Christian nation." So began a speech by State District Judge Oliver Kelley.[3] Judge Kelley was mystified by the changes he was seeing in a nation that used to regularly invoke the name of God. The more religion was deemphasized, the more he saw the nation slip into moral decline. He suspected that a lot of the problem could be traced to a series of momentous decisions by the Supreme Court.

There were a few key rulings that got the ball rolling toward a full-fledged separation of church and state in the context of public schools. They included:

- *Illinois ex rel. McCollum v. Board of Education* (1948): The Court ruled that there could be no religious instruction in a public school.
- *Engel v. Vitale* (1962): In this case, the Court banned the practice of public schools requiring the recitation of prayers.
- *Abington School District v. Schempp* (1963): This time the Court went even further, banning school prayers and Bible readings even if they were voluntary.

All of this was in the name of adherence to the First Amendment.

Judge Kelley believed that the decision amounted to a "reinterpretation" of the First Amendment, ignoring the part about "nor abridging the free exercise thereof." As redefined by the High Court, he said that the First Amendment now meant that anything the government does must have an underlying secular purpose and nothing the government does can advance the cause of religion. Judge Kelley was particularly concerned about *Abington*. "In one of these cases, *Abington School District v. Schempp*, two dissenters warned that this new concept of neutrality toward religion could lead to . . . not simply noninterference and noninvolvement with the religious as the Constitution commands, but a brooding and pervasive devotion to the secular and a passive, or even active, hostility to the religious. This series of decisions placed an interpretation on the Establishment Clause the Framers never intended."[4]

Old traditions began to vanish. The school day no longer began with a short devotional and prayer delivered by a member of the Student Council. First grade students no longer sang in unison, "All things bright and beautiful, the Lord God made them all." Textbook publishers began to make changes to avoid lawsuits.

Judge Kelley saw a decline in the quality of our schools, and to him, it was no coincidence. "Despite the best efforts of dedicated teachers and school administrators, our educational system is failing. Coincidentally, the SAT score slide started the year after the school prayer decision. Before that, as has often been said, the problems in school were talking and chewing gum in class, passing notes, and smoking in the boys' room. Now they are murder, rape, armed robbery, arson, and drug dealing."[5]

Judge Kelley supported a school prayer amendment as a first step toward restoring morality to the schools and the nation. Little did he know that the Left had something else in mind.

New fronts in the battle: the pledge and vouchers

The whole concept of separation of church and state reached its logical conclusion in late June 2002. A federal appeals court in San Francisco, acting on a lawsuit brought by atheist Dr. Michael Newdow on behalf of his second-grade daughter, ruled that the Pledge of Allegiance to the flag is unconstitutional because of the words "under God."

Let the record state that there can be no doubt that these words refer to religion. They were added in 1954 while the Cold War with the Soviet Union was raging. But why? Did the Congress want to impose upon young students and others who would recite the pledge that they should join the Catholic Church or the Methodist Church? Was the Congress insisting that Americans be baptized by immersion or by sprinkling? Did the words "under God" force any religious action at all upon the public? Of course not.

The amendment to the pledge followed a campaign by some religious leaders, including the Knights of Columbus, who wanted to show the world that the United States was different from atheistic Communists. In other words, the phrase "under God" was specifically intended to distinguish the United States as a nation of morals. In 1954, many Americans, including President Dwight Eisenhower, who signed the legislation, still equated morality with religious beliefs.

But a three-judge panel of the left-leaning 9th U.S. Circuit Court of Appeals produced a three-to-one majority that leaned toward a more liberal interpretation of the First Amendment. Judge Alfred T. Goodwin, a Nixon appointee, wrote the majority opinion: "A profession that we are a nation 'under God' is identical, for Establishment Clause purposes, to a profession that we are a nation 'under Jesus,' a nation 'under Vishnu,' a nation 'under Zeus,' or a nation 'under no God,' because none of these professions can be neutral with respect to religion."[6]

Not exactly. If the word "God" is taken as a practical synonym for "morality," and stipulating that practically all religions worship something referred to as "God," then the only slighted group would seem to be atheists. Even so, the great majority of atheists believe in morality. And since the words "under God" provide no religious instruction whatsoever, they establish no state religion.

Perhaps for some of these reasons—and with an election coming up in November—members of the political class reacted to the decision with outrage. White House spokesman Ari Fleischer, who was with President Bush during a Canadian summit, said: "The President's reaction was that this ruling is ridiculous." Back in Washington, Senate Majority Leader Tom Daschle called the decision "just nuts." House Majority Leader Dick Armey was more specific: "A judge who believes the Pledge of Allegiance is unconstitutional doesn't belong on the bench. I hope the court returns all the taxpayer money they have been paid in currency marked 'In God We Trust.'"[7]

House members gathered on the Capitol steps to recite the Pledge in unison while members of the Senate stopped debate on a defense bill to cast a unanimous vote denouncing the decision.

It seemed that everyone was blasting the 9th Circuit Court. On the Fox News Channel, the Reverend Jerry Falwell said, "It's a nutty ruling by a nutty court."[8] Former House Speaker Newt Gingrich said the two judges who ruled in favor of the ban should be removed from office: "These two judges are so out of touch with reality that they should be kicked off the bench."[9]

The pundits spoke out, too, but here, there were voices on both sides of the issue. Cal Thomas said that ruling pretty well sums up what most Americans think is wrong with the country: "We tolerate and protect those who wish to take God's name in vain, but we penalize anyone who dares speak well of God." Thomas Sowell was unhappy that such a momentous decision was made in a courtroom: "It is denying us the right to fight it out among ourselves by judicial fiat that is the real danger." E. J. Dionne took the other side, remembering a situation in which Newt Gingrich had once blasted then–front runner for the Democratic nomination Michael Dukakis because Dukakis had rejected a bill that would have required Massachusetts students to recite the Pledge. Dionne remembered that the Dukakis camp wasn't concerned about the issue: "Mr. Dukakis, after all, was on strong constitutional ground in defending the rights of religious minorities who rejected the pledge. But what Mr. Gingrich grasped that Mr. Dukakis' lieutenants didn't was the deep resonance of patriotism and its traditional forms of public expression."[10]

What Mr. Dionne was saying is that Mr. Dukakis failed to recognize the political danger of appearing to come out against patriotism. That is why, he said, Tom Daschle and Dick Gephardt came out in support of the Pledge and against the ruling. The political future of the Democratic Party—especially in light of the upcoming elections—was at stake.

The Democrats had a pretty good idea that the vast majority of the American people thought the ruling was hogwash, but they weren't getting pounded like Dr. Newdow was. The news media camped out in his front yard, and he had to buy an additional telephone line because of the volume of calls—mostly negative. Message after message crammed into his answering machine, and some of them weren't pretty: "You atheist [expletive deleted]. If you don't like the way this country is, take yourself and your family and get the hell out," one woman told him. Newdow said he never saw this type of reaction coming. "I wasn't prepared," he said. "And I was stupid not to be prepared." [11]

Judge Goodwin wasn't prepared, either, and just one day after the initial ruling, he put the decision on hold pending a rehearing of the case before either the same three-judge panel or an eleven-judge panel. At the same time, Attorney General John Ashcroft said the Justice Department would "defend the ability of our nation's children to pledge allegiance to the American flag." [12]

In the most bizarre twist in the case, it turned out that the little girl at the center of the case—Dr. Newdow's eight-year-old daughter—had no problem whatsoever with reciting the Pledge. That information came from her mother, Sandra Banning: "I was concerned that the American public would be led to believe that my daughter is an atheist, or that she has been harmed by reciting the Pledge of Allegiance, including the words 'one nation under God,'" Ms. Banning told the Associated Press. "We are practicing Christians and are active in our church." [13] It was revealed that Ms. Banning and Dr. Newdow were never even married and Ms. Banning had hired lawyers to see if she could help in getting the ruling reversed.

The bottom line for Democrats is that the words "under God" offend only a very few people, with most Americans equating the Pledge with patriotism. Democrats don't like any mention of God in a religious or moral sense in the classroom, and they never will. But this is a battle they cannot win, and so they will turn their attention to another issue that is more important to them anyway. The Pledge issue is, after all, a dispute about words. But the question of vouchers concerns the wishes of a Democratic Party core constituency—teachers' unions—and money!

As in the case of the pledge, the vouchers issue was thrust back into the headlines in late June 2002 when a court ruling—this time the United States Supreme Court—ruled that they are constitutional. It was a 5–4 decision allowing parents to use taxpayer money to send their children to private schools—even religious ones—as long as they retain a wide choice of schools. President Bush was elated: "The Supreme Court has offered the hope of an excellent education to parents and children throughout our country," he said. "This decision clears the way for other innovative school programs so that no child in America will be left behind." [14]

The case, *Zelman v. Simmon-Harris,* arose out of a program in inner-city Cleveland, Ohio, that gives parents a tuition subsidy of up to $2,250 per child. The Cleveland district is recognized as perhaps the worst in the nation, and this program was designed to help the children of poor parents escape into better schools.

It's interesting to note here that on the front page of newspapers all over America, there was a photograph of a young black girl holding up a pro-vouchers sign on the steps of the Supreme Court. This is part of what makes this case difficult for Democrats. The Democratic Party claims to be the party of the poor and downtrodden, but the very people who benefit most from school voucher programs are poor minorities—a key Democratic constituency. But the teachers' unions are much more powerful than poor people, and so, when forced to choose, the Democrats will go with the powerful.

There's a simple reason why teachers' unions don't like school choice. Vouchers break up the government monopoly and create more competition. The unions don't want any additional competition; they want tax money collected for schools to stay with the government schools. In addition to that, those within the education community, including the unions, are scared to death that private schools will succeed and undermine most of the social experimentation and education fads that have permeated public schools. If that happens on any large scale, public schools will be forced to implement real reforms in order to survive. The last thing the education establishment wants to see is a market-based school system.

So regardless of the *Zelman* ruling, this is a fight that isn't over.

The arguments start with those made by the dissenting judges. Justice David Souter announced his problems with the decision from the bench, saying that parents really don't have much choice: "There is, in any case, no way to interpret the 96.6 percent of current voucher money going to religious schools as reflecting a free and genuine choice by the families that apply for vouchers." And Justice John Paul Stevens was somehow able to connect his dissent to religious unrest in Northern Ireland and the Middle East: "Whenever we remove a brick from the wall that was designed to separate religion and government, we increase the risk of religious strife and weaken the foundations of our democracy," he said.[15]

So, in Justice Stevens' mind, allowing poor minority parents to pull their kids out of the nation's worst school district and place them in a private school of their choice is going to make the United States end up like Northern Ireland. If you can buy into that logic, you can probably agree with the other implication of Justice Stevens' remarks—that it's much better for the future well-being of our country to keep poor students in a failing school system rather than provide a means to a good education.

Justice Stevens—and his three liberal compatriots on the Court—are part of the radical separation-of-church-and-state crowd that believes strongly in the first half of the Establishment Clause but totally ignores the second half. The Reverend Barry Lynn, executive director of "Americans United for the Separation of Church and State," called the ruling the worst church-state decision in fifty years: "The Supreme Court has taken a wrecking ball to the wall of separation between church and state," he said.[16]

However, in the majority opinion, Chief Justice William Rehnquist wrote that the Cleveland program is religion-neutral. He's right. School vouchers are a freedom issue, pure and simple. Will poor people—who presumably pay at least some school taxes—be forced into having their kids attend crummy public schools, or is it right and proper for them to use some of their own tax money and the tax money of others who are concerned about the poor quality of education to choose some other alternative? After all, when American servicemen use tax money for college tuition, schools such as SMU, Baylor, and Notre Dame are not automatically excluded.

In fact, says William Bennett, the former secretary of education, it is impossible for the Cleveland program to violate separation of church and state, even if all the parents there opted for religious schools. "Cleveland's school choice program allows parents—and not the government—to choose what school their child attends," he wrote. "And parents, as far as I know, are not bound by the First Amendment."[17]

Once you get by the church-state zealots, you run straight into the other main group of voucher opponents—those who have the most to lose from competition.

Interestingly, as the Supreme Court decision was being handed down, the National Education Association, the nation's largest teachers union, was having its convention in Dallas. Bob Chase, the NEA's president, wrote an op-ed piece for the *Dallas Morning News* with the theme that the public doesn't really want vouchers at all. He mentioned every setback for school choice that he could find, such as the defeat of a pro-voucher gubernatorial candidate in [liberal] New Jersey, insinuating that it was the voucher issue that decided the race.

You had to wonder if Mr. Chase had seen the photos of young minority students holding their signs in front of the Supreme Court or read the quotes of poor inner-city parents in Cleveland who were praying for a favorable ruling when he wrote: "Ronald Reagan pitched tuition tax credits as a fairness issue. But no amount of fireworks and bunting could distract from the reality that the tuition tax credits were designed to be a subsidy for affluent parents who send their children to Sidwell Friends or Phillips Andover."[18] Mr. Chase was in deep denial.

In fact, he was wrong on all of his points. Not only are vouchers a program that will primarily benefit the poor (the rich can send their kids wherever they please), but voucher proponents have put together an impressive string of wins. "It was the seventh consecutive defeat in the court for the enemies of choice," wrote George Will, "whose tenacity is inversely proportional to the morality of their cause."[19]

It was a big win for vouchers, effectively keeping the movement alive and allowing President George W. Bush the opportunity to go back to Congress and ask it to reconsider the school choice element that was removed from his education bill.

If the Congress does consider a broader voucher plan for the nation, there will be a new battle to fight. Already there are calls for any private school that accepts voucher money to adhere to all the rules and regulations that have made our public schools what they are today. That will not be an improvement. The worst thing that could happen is that private schools, in accepting kids on vouchers, are remolded in the image of failed public schools.

But two things will be most interesting to watch, should a voucher system become widely used. First, if a significant number of American students wind up in private schools of a religious nature, will that have a positive effect on the overall morality of our nation? Second, will public school advocates find a way to instill some Judeo-Christian morality of their own without violating the separation of church and state that they believe in so strongly?

Let's be a nation "under God"

Most of the time, we never make it as far as the fourth verse of our National Anthem, "The Star-Spangled Banner." But if we did, we'd be singing some lines that would run afoul of the church-state radicals. The words, written by Francis Scott Key during the War of 1812, may have actually given an idea to members of Congress: "And this be our motto: 'In God is our trust.'" In 1956, Congress took Key's advice and made the motto official. It had appeared on our coinage since 1864.

It's facts like these that make it tough for the Left. In their arguments on separation of church and state, they have half of a constitutional amendment. Those who believe that we must be a nation under God in order to remain great have the other half of the same amendment and more than 200 years of tradition.

In his seminal book *The De-Valuing of America,* William Bennett writes, "Everyone, including 'First Amendment' liberals, agnostics, and atheists, must concede that the Judeo-Christian tradition is a major formative influence on American life, on our law, ideals, and principles as a free people. Even a rudimentary knowledge of history makes that clear."[20] Bennett notes the words of some of our most beloved founding fathers:

"Of all the dispositions and habits which lead to political prosperity, religion and morality are indispensable supports," said George Washington in his farewell address. "And let us with caution indulge the supposition that morality can be maintained without religion."

The man who followed Washington into the presidency agreed. "Our Constitution was made only for a moral and religious people," said John Adams. "It is wholly inadequate to the government of any other." James Madison said, "Before any man can be considered as a member of civil society, he must be considered as a subject of the Governor of the Universe." And Thomas Jefferson asked, "Can the liberties of a nation be thought secure when we have removed their only firm basis, a conviction in the minds of the people that these liberties are the gift of God?"

Much later and 143 years to the day before the attack on America, Abraham Lincoln also talked about freedom as it relates to the Supreme Being: "It is not our frowning battlements, our bristling sea coasts, our Army and our Navy ... Our reliance is in the love of liberty which God has planted in us."[21]

It could not be clearer that those who built and shaped our nation believed that it was all worthwhile because of a higher power. They felt that if that higher power—God—was removed from public discourse that all of our morals, and eventually our nation, would collapse.

Modern church-state radicals believe that morality does not flow from God, but rather from basic human instincts. Columnist William Murchison says it isn't true—you just can't construct a system of secular virtue: "Who says I have to keep promises, tell the truth, spurn dubious accounting practices or abstain from burning down a national forest? What's it to you anyway, bub?"[22] Religionless morality, says Murchison, is purely personal; each person decides just how honest to be. It is, in effect, no morality at all.

And it is what we are teaching in our schools. In today's religion-free school environment, kids learn about things that never showed up in a classroom in the 1960s: environmentalism, self-esteem, diversity, and tolerance. And while all this is going on, the popular culture is feeding them a strict diet of violence, sex, and profanity. And we wonder why we have high crime, a soaring divorce rate, an epidemic of out-of-wedlock pregnancies, and corporations that cheat on their books?

The Left has been very successful at removing any mention of God from public places. They've attacked the Pledge of Allegiance, and they've fought school vouchers tooth and nail. They are going after public displays of the Ten Commandments, and they will try to have "In God We Trust" removed from our money. If they are completely successful in what they seek, we will no longer swear to tell the truth in court or to uphold the Constitution "so help me God," we will no longer sing "God Bless America" in public places, and city-sponsored Christmas parades will feature Santa Claus—but not the baby Jesus.

And yet, the Constitution does not prohibit religion. No matter what the Left tries to tell you, there is no constitutionally mandated separation of church and state. What the Congress is prevented from doing is "respecting an establishment of religion."

So why can't we be a nation "under God," meaning that we, as a people, recognize that our country was built on religious traditions that, to this day, form the bedrock of our society? Without teaching religious doctrine in schools, why can't students learn that our morals and even our legal system stem from the Judeo-Christian ethic?

A United States "under God" should not be a nation that proselytizes in the classroom, the courtroom, or even the boardroom. But we should accept that without recognition that there is a God, we have no basis for the kind of morality that must be present if a democracy is to succeed. Over the past three decades, we've seen the results of a religion-free morality, and those results have not been good. We must change back to what we once were—a nation that embraces the morality that comes with being "under God."

That is the only way to turn our country around and to secure the blessings of liberty to ourselves and to our posterity.

CHAPTER 12

Return to the Constitution

We must declare a reaffirmation of the Constitution and the Bill of Rights as the very basis for our limited government and our precious freedoms.

They argued; they haggled; some of them walked out. At last, they compromised, and in so doing, they created the greatest document of governance known to humankind—the Constitution of the United States of America.

That the Constitution is a great document is generally accepted by Americans these days—even by those who utilize it to create rights or powers that simply aren't there. But at the time of its creation, the document was not in great favor with all of the people, the states, or even the men who framed it. The final document, after all, is a collection of compromises designed to satisfy an assemblage of statesmen with differing views on what the new nation should be. Benjamin Franklin, for example, was not entirely pleased, but he was willing to accept the document: "I doubt ... whether any other Convention we can obtain, may be able to make a better Constitution ... Thus I consent ... to this Constitution because I expect no better, and because I am not sure, that it is not the best."[1]

It was with some urgency that Alexander Hamilton organized the convention; after all, the United States was in danger of falling apart, and several statesmen, including George Washington, were calling for a drastic revision of the government.

So the delegates met in Philadelphia on May 25, 1787, originally to rewrite the Articles of Confederation. It became apparent to a majority that a rewrite was not enough and that a new document was needed. It's interesting to note that John Adams and Thomas Jefferson were out of the country on government business and did not attend, while Patrick Henry and Samuel Adams refused to participate because they opposed the creation of a strong central government. The State of Rhode Island declined to send a delegate because it was afraid that its trade would suffer under national regulations.

Fifty-five delegates were present for the near-continuous debates, and thirty-nine of them signed the Constitution on September 17, 1787, including George Washington, eighty-one-year-old Benjamin Franklin, James Madison, Alexander Hamilton, and Gouverneur Morris, who did much of the writing. Madison is known as the "Father of the Constitution" because of his negotiations and extensive records of the debates.

In some areas, the Constitution was precise in framing the basic laws of the land. But in other areas it was vague, perhaps an indication that the framers purposefully were setting up the document to endure through the ages. A contributing factor to the vagueness of certain sections is surely the wide range of views that the framers brought to the table about what form of central government the United States ought to have.

Had the Articles of Confederation endured, today's United States would be very different, since the Articles recognized the sovereignty of the individual states. In the end, the view of a national, centralized government won out, but there can be no doubt that the Constitution is designed to place severe limits on that government's powers. To that end, the Constitution provides for a federal system that splits powers between the national government and the states. Furthermore, it establishes a method of checks and balances by mandating three branches of government—one to create the laws (the Congress), one to enforce them (the president), and one to interpret them (the judiciary).

Even so, there was adamant opposition to the new Constitution when it was sent to the various states for ratification on September 28. Some, such as Virginia's Richard Henry Lee, a signer of the Declaration of Independence, were still against increasing the powers of Congress. "The first maxim of a man who loves liberty," said Lee, "should be never to grant to rulers an atom of power that is not most clearly and indispensably necessary for the safety and well being of society."[2] Lee thought that the convention had exceeded its powers because it was only authorized to rewrite the Articles of Confederation, and he was unhappy that the final document had not included a bill of rights. Patrick Henry, still opposed to a national government, also argued hard against ratification.

Others, such as Alexander Hamilton—even though he wasn't completely happy with the new document—worked to get it ratified. Along with Madison and John Jay, he published *The Federalist,* a collection of eighty-five essays in support of establishing a central government. In the essays, Hamilton intended to prove that a national government was absolutely necessary to the prosperity of the Union and that the present Confederation was insufficient to preserve it. "For nothing can be more evident, to those who are able to take an enlarged view of the subject," he wrote, "than the alternative of an adoption of the new Constitution or a dismemberment of the Union."[3]

Eventually, Delaware ratified the Constitution on December 7, 1787, and New Hampshire put it into effect with its ratification on June 21, 1788. Still, there were problems with the Anti-Federalists and with some of the other states, such as North Carolina—because of the lack of a bill of rights.

The first Congress convened on March 4, 1789, facing more than a hundred proposed amendments that had come from the states and minority groups—and specific bills of rights from Virginia and New York. Madison suggested fifteen amendments, Congress accepted twelve of them, and ten were eventually ratified—the Bill of Rights.

At last the Constitution contained what the Anti-Federalists had most wanted: sweeping declarations preventing the national government from taking away the most fundamental rights of the people. The Tenth Amendment also gave us something else—an elastic clause that reserved for the people or the states those powers that were not specifically delegated to the central government. Likewise, the Ninth Amendment was also purposefully vague, stating that just because certain rights are listed in the Constitution, that doesn't mean that rights not listed are automatically denied.

These amendments have resulted in decades of court cases and judicial interpretations. So have the competing segments of the so-called "Establishment Clause" in the First Amendment, and a modifying clause at the beginning of the Second Amendment. Even articles of the original document still come under dispute, especially when the three branches of government quarrel over separation of powers.

So is the Constitution a "living document," as so many people say it is, or is it a fixed law of the land? The answer lies somewhere in between. The Constitution is a living document when it wants to be, but some parts are set in concrete. Deciding which is which has become a defining issue of our times.

Momentous decisions

Sometimes, the Supreme Court makes decisions based on the fixed part of the Constitution—those clauses that seem very specific and leave little room for interpretation. For example, Article II, Section One requires that the president of the United States must be a natural-born citizen who has attained the age of thirty-five. If Congress were to pass a law making changes in that requirement, it would be instantly deemed unconstitutional. But this has never stopped Congress from making laws that conflict with the Constitution.

In 1803, the Supreme Court heard the case of *Marbury v. Madison,* in which William Marbury was trying to force through a judicial appointment that he had received from President John Adams. But Adams had left office before the appointment took effect, and Secretary of State James Madison withheld it. Marbury attempted to use Section 13 of the Judiciary Act of 1789 to force Madison's hand. Instead, the Supreme Court—saying that Section 13 granted powers to the Court not authorized by the Constitution—deemed it unconstitutional. This case set the precedent that laws passed by Congress must be constitutional and that the courts have the power to review them.

The opinion in *Marbury*—written by "the Great Chief Justice" John Marshall—paved the way for the Judicial Branch to become as powerful as the other two branches of government.

From *Marbury,* you might conclude that the Supreme Court always considers the obvious intent of the Constitution when deciding whether a law should be overturned. Your conclusion would be wrong. The Supreme Court sometimes makes rulings based on the political conditions and attitudes of the times.

The Fourteenth Amendment states quite plainly that no state shall make a law that abridges the rights, privileges, or immunities of citizens of the United States. However, in 1896, at the time of the *Plessy v. Ferguson* decision, the Supreme Court made a ruling based on current attitudes. John H. Plessy had challenged a Louisiana law that required "separate but equal" facilities for whites and blacks in railroad cars. It took fifty-eight years for the Court to revisit the issue and turn it around in *Brown v. Board of Education of Topeka.*

And yet, in today's politically correct atmosphere, that same "Equal Protection Clause" doesn't stop affirmative action and other race-based programs. There are simply too many people who view affirmative action as a moral imperative that should trump the crystal-clear intent of the Fourteenth Amendment.

It's as if the old fight between the Federalists and the Anti-Federalists is still going strong; only the names have changed. Now it's liberals and progressives against conservatives and those with a libertarian view—with moderates usually siding with those who are left of center. They align themselves, either as political parties or as interest groups, and they file lawsuits seeking to find something in the Constitution that will make their way the law of the land.

Current events and the Constitution

We've already discussed some of the best modern-day examples of Constitution-bending, such as *Roe v. Wade,* in which a so-called "right to privacy"—emerging from the Ninth Amendment (the enumeration of rights shall not be construed to deny others)—imbues women with a constitutional right to do away with their unborn children. In all probability, the framers would have looked upon such an interpretation with intense skepticism.

What would they think about some of the other contemporary issues surrounding the Constitution? Even the Federalists of the day might be taken aback at how big and bloated the central government has become— and at how much control it exerts over daily life. A case in point is the giant bureaucracy known as the Department of Education. The organization Concerned Women of America contends in its literature that there is no constitutional basis for such a department.

"The principles of federalism which America's Founding Fathers embodied in the Constitution of the United States entrust authority over education to the state and the people. A federal Department of Education is inconsistent with such principles."[4]

The fact is that the Constitution doesn't authorize a "cabinet" at all, but merely says that the president "may require the opinion, in writing, of the principal officer in each of the executive departments, upon any subject relating to the duties of their respective offices . . ."[5] At first, there were just three departments—State, War, and Treasury—plus the office of the attorney general, all established in 1789.

As time passed, more departments were added, including Agriculture; Commerce; Defense (replacing War); Health and Human Services; Housing and Urban Development; the Interior; Labor; Transportation; Energy; and the aforementioned Department of Education.

Columnist Steve Chapman writes that the government always seems to invent new bureaucracies when the country is in trouble. "When America had an energy crisis, our leaders responded by creating the Energy Department. When we perceived shortcomings in our schools, the Education Department was formed."[6] All these departments are deemed constitutional by the mere fact that the Constitution mentions "executive departments." But does that trump the language of the Tenth Amendment, which leaves to the states those powers not designated to the central government? The only departments that seem necessary to the United States government are the departments of Defense, State, and Treasury—pretty much what we had in 1789.

Modern America is facing another crisis—the threat of terrorist attacks in the wake of 9/11—and that means another major expansion of the central government. This time, it's the Department of Homeland Security. The new department consolidates twenty-two agencies—excluding the FBI and the CIA—and will have 170,000 employees and an annual budget of at least $37.5 billion.

Since the Congress created all those other departments, it can no doubt get away with creating this one; however, the president's initial proposal called for a significant transfer of power. Mr. Bush wanted the executive branch to have the ability to move money around within the department, and he preferred that its employees not be subject to civil-service regulations. Columnist Charley Reese calls the proposal an unconstitutional power grab. "The greatest threat to American freedom today is not Osama bin Laden," writes Reese, "but George W. Bush, who, if he is even aware of its existence, seems to think the Constitution is just an antiquated piece of parchment that belongs in a museum." [7]

The War on Terrorism has produced a number of other constitutional questions as the Executive Branch works to protect the country and keep certain information secret—too secret, according to some. The American Civil Liberties Union and other organizations have filed several lawsuits against the Justice Department—and they've been winning in the lower courts.

The list of practices that were being challenged included such things as the government's refusal to identify more than 1,200 detainees after 9/11; the decision to exclude the public and the media from immigration proceedings for Middle Eastern and South Asian men who were picked up during the investigation; the use of material witness warrants to detain foreigners; the use of secret evidence against Islamic charities whose assets were frozen; the denial of legal counsel for detainees; and the use of solitary confinement and prohibition of visitors for some of those arrested in the terrorism investigation. [8]

For his part, President Bush seems convinced that no rights are being trampled. "We intend to honor our Constitution and respect the freedoms that we hold so dear," he said. [9] Mr. Bush believes that these policies are necessary to protect the nation, and his opinion is shared by Richard Samp, chief counsel of the Washington Foundation. "Do I think the Justice Department is trampling on civil liberties and is going far beyond what has ever been done before?" he asked. "My answer is I strongly disagree with such a charge." [10]

What does the Constitution say? In the Bill of Rights, the First Amendment guarantees freedom of the press. The Fifth and Sixth Amendments provide the right of due process of law; the right to a speedy and public trial with an impartial jury; the right to be confronted with witnesses; and the right to an attorney. Clearly, the Justice Department was seeking to deny these things. But could the Bill of Rights be suspended in the face of a war and since many of those detained were not American citizens?

No, says columnist Steve Chapman, who complains that many of those 1,200 detained foreigners were held for months without being charged and after a year still hadn't been identified.[11] No, says a panel of the 6th U.S. Circuit Court of Appeals in ruling on a freedom-of-the-press case brought by the *Detroit Free Press*. "A government operating in the shadow of secrecy stands in complete opposition to the society envisioned by the Framers of our Constitution," wrote the panel.

The Detroit case involved the government's efforts to close a deportation hearing for an Ann Arbor Muslim activist named Rabih Haddad. The court ruled that the government might legitimately close some portions of deportation hearings against suspected terrorists—but not on a blanket basis. The justices also invoked the Fourteenth Amendment, saying that once immigrants enter the country legally and reside here, they are entitled to equal protection under the law.

And what about the USA Patriot Act, under which the American people may be spied on by our own government without much in the way of judicial review? Syndicated columnist and First Amendment expert Nat Hentoff is concerned that the FBI has the power under this law to track everything we do on a computer and can go to bookstores and libraries to get lists of what we've been reading—all in the name of fighting terrorism. "More and more American citizens, including more conservatives, are rising in concern about what is happening to the Bill of Rights," says Hentoff.[12]

Would the framers have approved of this? Not likely, writes Hentoff, pointing to James Madison's famous warning: "The accumulation of all powers, legislative, executive, and judiciary, in the same hands, whether of one, a few, or many, and whether hereditary, self-appointed, or elective, may justly be pronounced the very definition of tyranny."[13]

As a nation, we will be examining these and other cases related to legislation arising out of the terrorist attacks. Some of the cases will be settled, and some will move on to the Supreme Court. Other separation of powers issues not related to 9/11 will be the subjects of disputes between the executive and legislative branches—and some of those will go to court, too.

When the president decided to scrap the 1972 Anti-Ballistic Missile Treaty with the Soviet Union (partly because there's no more Soviet Union), thirty-one members of the House went ballistic themselves. "The Constitution of the United States is being demolished," said Representative Dennis Kucinich, D-Ohio, who was listed as the lead plaintiff in the lawsuit that the lawmakers filed.[14] The suit contended that the president couldn't withdraw from the treaty without the consent of Congress. What does the Constitution say? Not much; just that "He [the president] shall have power, by and with the Advice and Consent of the Senate, to make Treaties, provided two thirds of the Senators present concur . . ."[15] But nothing is said about withdrawing from treaties.

Early in this tome, we told the stories of a pair of President Bush's judicial appointments, Judges Charles Pickering and Priscilla Owen, both to the 5th U.S. Circuit Court of appeals, and both rejected by ten-to-nine party-line votes in the Senate Judiciary Committee. Putting partisan politics aside, were those rejections allowed under the terms of the Constitution?

Just before Judge Pickering's defeat, President Bush said the debate was about more than just the ideology of his nominee. "Under our Constitution, the President has the right and responsibility to nominate qualified judges. And the legislative branch has the responsibility to vote on them in a fair and timely manner."[16] The president was correct, but he did not go far enough.

Simply put, the Constitution makes no provision for a presidential appointment to be killed in committee. Nat Hentoff quotes Senator Arlen Specter of Pennsylvania, who is a member of the Judiciary Committee: "Article II, Section 2 of the Constitution tells us that the president 'shall nominate and, by and with the advice and consent of the Senate, shall appoint ... Judges of the Supreme Court, and all other Officers of the United States ...' Neither the text of the Constitution nor any contemporaneous or subsequent history says anything about the ability of one senator or one committee to defeat a judicial nomination."[17] But, as Hentoff mentions in his column, whichever party controls the Judiciary Committee has been ideological and partisan, committing what he calls "serial contempt" of the Constitution.

And what about war? The United States has not declared war since World War II, and yet we've been involved in major wars including the Korean War, the Vietnam War, and both Gulf Wars, plus dozens of lesser incursions into various parts of the globe. We find ourselves in an undeclared War on Terror, and President Bush insisted that he had the power to go to war with Iraq without the approval of Congress.

As the president was making his case against Saddam Hussein, two senior administration officials, whose names were not revealed, said White House counsel Al Gonzales had informed the president in August of 2002 that the Constitution gives presidents the authority to act without the expressed permission of the Congress.[18]

In this particular case, there was a variety of reasons given that President Bush could press forward with a military actions against Iraq—including the fact that a congressional resolution had authorized the first President Bush to move against Iraq in the 1991 Gulf War, and Saddam has repeatedly violated the terms of the cease-fire. Also, the unnamed officials said that the president could act under terms of the September 14, 2001, congressional resolution authorizing military action against terrorists.[19] However, the officials also said that back in 1991 Mr. Bush's father was told that he did not need congressional approval to go to war—even though he eventually sought approval anyway.

What about the Constitution? It says only that "The Congress shall have the power ... to declare war."[20] and that the president is "Commander in Chief of the Army and Navy of the United States ..."[21] However, the implication that the Congress should be involved in any decision to go to war against another nation is unmistakable.

Just to make sure, Congress passed the War Powers Act, specifically stating that its purpose is "to fulfill the intent of the Framers of the Constitution of the United States, and insure that the collective judgment of both the Congress and the president will apply to the introduction of United States Armed Forces into hostilities ..."[22] The act calls on the president "in every possible instance" to consult with Congress before using the armed forces, and to "consult regularly with Congress" until our troops are no longer engaged.[23]

In the specific case of Iraq, as George Will points out, there is no emergency that involves repelling a sneak attack and there is no intent on the part of the administration to maintain any strategic secrecy that might be ruined by an open declaration of war. That being the case, says Will, the constitutional requirement is obvious—and yet some on the Right are "construing into nonexistence the Constitution's provision for involving Congress." If those arguments are successful even in this case, Will writes, "the Constitution will have been amended without recourse to the amendment provisions."[24]

Of course the Congress could say "no" to war by refusing to fund it, but that would make it seem unsupportive of the men and women in uniform. And so presidents since World War II send our nation's military around the globe when they want to, with the Congress usually demanding to be heard. It's just the opposite of the judicial appointment procedure, where the executive branch would like to see the letter of constitutional law respected.

In the case of making war, it's the legislative branch that cries foul.

The corrupting of the Constitution: does your vote matter?

You probably think your vote—and those of your friends and neighbors—decides the outcome of the congressional race that takes place in your district every two years as called for by the Constitution. To some extent, you're right; but to a very large degree, the right of voters to select representatives to the lower house of Congress has eroded over the years.

Witness this sequence from a newspaper article about California congressional candidate Linda Sanchez: "Experts say she's a shoo-in for election to Congress in November [2002] from a new California district specifically carved out for a Hispanic."[25] Ms. Sanchez, as the article states, was indeed "a shoo-in," and yet no election had been held at the time the article was written; not one single person had voted. How can this be?

To understand how Ms. Sanchez could have won the election before it had even taken place requires a brief look back at how the Constitution intended for House members to be elected, and what has happened between then and now.

The framers thought that the election of our representatives to Congress was extremely important—so important that they outlined the procedure in the very first article: "The House of Representatives shall be composed of Members chosen every second year by the People of the several States . . ."[26] Article I goes on from there to explain more about how House and Senate members should be chosen, but most of that is technical data about age and other qualifications. The key words above are "chosen . . . by the People . . ." And that's how it was—in the beginning.

Unfortunately "the People" didn't include everyone in those early days, and it wasn't until 1869, when the Fifteenth Amendment was ratified, that the right to vote could no longer be denied on account of "race, color, or previous condition of servitude."[27] That was all well and good, but in some areas—particularly in the South—election officials still refused to allow blacks to vote. In 1965, Dr. Martin Luther King Jr. led 30,000 people on a march from Selma, Alabama, to Montgomery, where he demanded that black people be allowed to vote without unfair restrictions. The unrest in Alabama led to the Voting Rights Act of 1965.[28]

The new law strengthened and backed up the Fifteenth Amendment; recognized that "gerrymandered" districts could dilute minority voting strength; banned the use of a poll tax as a voting requirement;[29] and generally made it possible for thousands of blacks in the South to be able to vote. The act also prohibited any major changes in voting rules and regulations without approval of the federal courts or the Justice Department,[30] and it even specified that the right to vote could not be denied based "on ability to read, write, understand, or interpret any matter in the English language."[31]

And so, with the Voting Rights Act in place, the United States of America finally had a system in which all of "the People" could now go to the polls and elect their representatives fairly and squarely—right? Well, not exactly. Remember that Linda Sanchez had already won her congressional seat before a vote had been cast. The manner in which she managed to accomplish that feat is the story of how a law can go bad—how the courts can allow such a law to trump the Constitution.

There can be no doubt that the Voting Rights Act was not only well meaning but that it accomplished much for black people who had been unfairly denied the right to vote. In modern times, however, the act and subsequent court rulings are being used to socially engineer a Congress that "looks like America." While that may be an admirable goal, it cannot be found in the Constitution.

What the Constitution does say is that "Representatives shall be appor-tioned among the several States according to their respective numbers, counting the whole number of persons in each State, excluding Indians not taxed." [32]

Pay close attention to that part about "their respective numbers." That means that a state like New York could lose a seat if population figures go down, whereas a state like California might gain a few seats if the population is booming. Some districts will combine and expand; others will shrink to make way for new districts. That means that when new population figures become available—as they did in 2001 following the 2000 census—some-thing called "redistricting" takes place.

And that's where the opportunity for mischief lies.

The Constitution leaves the times, places, and manner of holding elec-tions for senators and representatives to the state legislatures, [33] and so (with the Senate locked into two senators per state), the legislatures meet to re-draw the district lines for House seats. The state politicians who are setting the new boundaries tend to favor their own interests. They engage in mas-sive fights over how many "safe" seats each party should have, and so the whole mess usually ends up before some judge or panel of judges, not men-tioned in the Constitution. The court then decides how many districts should go to Republicans and how many should go to Democrats, and (sometimes) what the ethnicity of the elected person should be.

So even though the Constitution says that "the People of the several States" will elect the representatives, the people only get to choose from within a district that is approved by partisan politicians, judges, and panels of judges. Sometimes, as in the case of Linda Sanchez, the legislatures or the courts carve out a district especially for a Hispanic; sometimes, they create one for a black.

The question then becomes: where in the Constitution—or the Voting Rights Act for that matter — does it say that anyone should be creating seats especially for blacks, whites, Hispanics, Democrats, Republicans, or anyone else? Of course, it's not in there. The Constitution laid down the rules, and the Voting Rights Act was supposed to prevent gerrymandering and make sure that the rules were enforced fairly.

Even though redistricting is not one of the bright spots of American democracy, voters do have some say in who gets elected. They decide which Republican, or which Democrat—but the winning party is often preordained. If a court sets aside a predominately minority district, then the ethnicity of the eventual House member is already decided before the voting takes place—and of course, most minority districts are safe Democratic seats.

But didn't the framers really intend for districts to be compact and kind of square or round in shape? The answer to that is probably "yes," but the Constitution is not specific. So if the court wants a safe seat for a Democrat, the court simply draws a meandering line to take in as many predominately Democratic areas as needed. The political makeup of a state's congressional delegation will eventually become what the court—petitioned by a gaggle of politicians and activist groups—thinks it should be.

The entire process is as unconstitutional as can be. Remember that the next time you vote.

A logical approach to the Constitution

In 1996, cattlemen filed a lawsuit against talk-show queen Oprah Winfrey, her production company, and a vegetarian activist who had appeared on her TV program, charging that they had violated the Texas "veggie libel" law. You read this correctly; under the "False Disparagement of Perishable Food Products Act," producers can sue anyone who knowingly makes defamatory statements about vegetables. In effect, the law extends certain protections— once reserved for human beings—to tomatoes and hamburger meat.

Ms. Winfrey ran afoul of the law when her guest, Howard Lyman, stated his opinion that U.S. beef could be at risk of spreading "mad cow disease" and Ms. Winfrey then vowed never to eat another hamburger.[34] After six plodding years, U.S. District Judge Mary Lou Robinson finally tossed the whole case out of court.

But why, if common sense had been applied, would such a ridiculous case have ever made it past opening arguments? Even if a court could accept the notion that it's possible under the Constitution to libel a hamburger, what about the freedom of speech that the First Amendment guarantees to Mr. Lyman, Ms. Winfrey, and to all other Americans? Ms. Winfrey was obviously not out to destroy the livestock business; she was producing what seemed to her to be an interesting television show. And yet the court case dragged on and cost Ms. Winfrey more than $1 million in legal fees.

The framers did not mention anything about hamburgers in the Constitution, but they did recognize that many issues would arise over the ages that they had never considered. And so the Constitution—a patchwork of compromises—was left intentionally vague in some areas. Therefore, the framers expected future generations to be logical. They vested Congress with the power to make all laws that might be "necessary and proper"[35] and expected that Congress would pass only those laws that were in accordance with the basic laws established in the Constitution.

In other words, the Constitution is the foundation; the laws are the minutiae.

Since the laws are much more detailed, we expect the court system—under a concept known as "judicial review"—to make sure that those laws are constitutional. Authorization for judicial review is assumed from the section of the Constitution that sets up the judiciary, creates the Supreme Court, and then states, "The judicial power shall extend to all Cases, in law and Equity, arising under this Constitution . . ." [36] Since *Marbury v. Madison,* the federal courts have had the power, with the final decision resting with the Supreme Court.

But when the courts are reviewing laws, do they always turn to the Constitution, applying it strictly where it is precise and using common sense where it is vague? Sometimes they do, but certainly not all of the time. As Thomas Sowell writes, "clever judges have been destroying it, bit by bit, turning it into an instrument of arbitrary judicial power . . ." [37] Sowell points out that activist judges often get away with imposing their personal view into the law because so many people look at each decision in terms of agreeing or not agreeing with the outcome.

But the common sense approach to the Constitution calls for a bias-neutral approach to judicial review. Judges should take very seriously their responsibility to be "strict constructionists"—to apply the Constitution to laws without regard to any personal point of view. Remember, one of the great functions of the Constitution is to set limits on the power of the central government, even though in *McCulloch v. Maryland* in 1918 the Supreme Court ruled that Congress possessed "implied powers" not specified in the Constitution.

Then how are we to know exactly what the Constitution is trying to tell us in establishing the basic laws of the land? One way is to look at the introduction to the document—its own preamble—which describes in broad terms just five things that the government must do in order to establish a more perfect union:

· Establish justice
· Insure domestic tranquility
· Provide for the common defense
· Promote the general welfare
· Secure the blessings of liberty

So the things that the framers deemed important were having a fair justice system; keeping the peace; making the country safe from our enemies; improving the welfare of the nation as a whole; and maintaining freedom. How far these basic goals can be stretched, while adhering to the rest of the document and the principles of common sense and logic, makes all the difference.

Clear moral objectives

Clearly the framers desired to produce a Constitution that would stand the test of time. The fact that it has been amended only twenty-seven times and is still small enough to be published in a pocket edition (unlike the voluminous Income Tax Code) is a testament to their success. And yet, for all its relevance and brilliance more than 215 years after its ratification, politicians and judges still play deadly serious games while attempting to get around it.

In this book, we've pointed out how so many of the vital issues of the day are convoluted by political spin, outright lies, and political correctness. Our goal was to set the record straight with clear, concise language, exposing the radical Left while pointing to the shortcomings of the Right as well. It's important to examine each of these issues—objectives as we have called them—in the light of the Constitution of the United States.

Preserve the Right to Life. The forces of evil have this issue well in hand. The Supreme Court reached into a vague section of the Constitution and magically extracted a "right to privacy" that cannot be seriously challenged as long as the radical Left is successful in keeping all conservative judges off the bench—and as long as even the most conservative presidents fail to make a "right to life" amendment a top priority.

Reduce the Size of Government. First the "surplus" and then the war against terrorism opened the floodgates for an already spendthrift Congress. Who can really blame them? After all, most of us want more jogging paths, museums, federal buildings, and entitlements like CHIP and a pharmaceutical benefit. After all, it states right there in the preamble that government is supposed to "promote the general welfare." If we want smaller government, we will have to hire representatives who aren't completely consumed with their own reelection.

Abolish the Income Tax Code. The bad news is that the ability of Congress to levy an income tax is right there in the Sixteenth Amendment; the good news is that it says, "Congress shall have power to lay and collect taxes on incomes," but it doesn't say that Congress "shall" exercise that power. It will not be easy to convince the Congress to abandon much of its power over the people by establishing an alternate means of taxation; we will have to insist. If we do, it could happen.

Restore the American Family. Children have no constitutional right to a family. Even so, we are a caring nation. Our compassionate government always comes to the aid of the single mother whose deadbeat husband or boyfriend has participated in the creation of a child, but then doesn't accept responsibilities. It would not be unconstitutional to pass stricter laws requiring those deadbeat parents to support their own children until the age of eighteen. After all, that would be "establishing justice" for a child, and that's the first objective mentioned in the preamble.

Foster an American Culture. The Constitution instructs us to "provide for the common defense," and yet our country is literally being overrun with waves of immigrants, changing our culture as profoundly as any invading army might do. In order to "form a more perfect union," as the framers sought, we must return to the concept of assimilation, and although we are multiheritaged, we must give up our tribal notions and become one people.

Establish English as Our National Language. The Constitution is silent on the issue of language. It does not establish a national language, nor does the Bill of Rights require the government to provide ballots for citizens who don't speak English. This has opened the way for laws such as the Voting Rights Act to require ballots and other government documents in multiple languages, and this has done considerable damage to the unity of our nation. The people of the United States should seek a constitutional amendment establishing English as the official language of our government.

End Racial Preferences. The Constitutional protection against all forms of discrimination is already in place. The "Equal Protection Clause" of the Fourteenth Amendment should be sufficient to prohibit the practice of "adversary diversity"—the use of ethnicity to obtain favors at the expense of others. So if we want to live in a society in which "the color of our skin is not as important as the content of our character," we will have to elect and appoint judges who understand the Constitution and are willing to apply it.

Keep America Strong. This is one of the basics mentioned in the preamble—the defense of our country. And yet, elected officials over the years have been willing to weaken our military forces in order to fund the social programs that make them popular in their home states and districts. Wake-up calls like Pearl Harbor and 9/11 should teach us not to become complacent. The first question we should ask any presidential or congressional candidate is, "What will you do to preserve and defend the freedom of the United States of America?"

Take Back Our Schools. You have to comb the Constitution, find the very vaguest parts, use the "implied powers" of Congress, and stretch the "general welfare" clause of the preamble to find a justification for federal involvement in the public schools. The good news on this front is that while the federal government extends its claws deeper into the education system, a certain special-interest group is mounting a counter-offensive. This special-interest group is known as "parents," and the answer to the education bureaucracy is private schools that can operate without the baggage of the federal government.

Acknowledge Right from Wrong. The preamble calls it "establishing justice." Most of the amendments—including the entire Bill of Rights—are concerned with the concept of right and wrong. And yet, in our morally challenged, politically correct country, constitutional provisions and laws can't do it all. This is one objective that the people—from parents and teachers to politicians and CEOs—must address.

Respect the Judeo-Christian Ethic. Other than the word "blessings" in the preamble, the Constitution does not invoke religion or mention the "Creator" as the Declaration of Independence does. It simply says in the First Amendment that the government cannot establish a national church. But make no mistake—the Constitution in no way prohibits the recognition that our laws and our very way of life have been shaped by principles outlined in the Bible and other religious texts. Without those principles, the United States would be nothing. The framers were well aware of that fact, as we all should be today.

And that brings us full circle to our final objective, **Return to the Constitution**. As we interpret it, stretch it, redefine it, and use it for various purposes, we have to keep in mind that this is exactly what the framers set us up to do, at least to a certain extent. They knew we'd argue about it; after all, they argued about it.

But we owe it to them to argue about the words they wrote in honesty and in truth. "Let us raise a standard to which the wise and honest can repair," said Washington.[38] But all too often, we aren't wise at all. Sometimes we ignore the Constitution altogether. And even when we don't, we spin, we obfuscate, we rummage through—and we quote those little pieces, parts, and court decisions that best live up to our own political desires.

While the framers worked to build a more perfect union, today's politicians often work to satisfy the demands of various interest groups and voting blocks. That's what Alexander Hamilton must have meant when he wrote, "The great source of all the evils which afflict republics is that the people are too apt to make choice of rulers who are either politicians without being patriots, or patriots without being politicians."[39] Hamilton was right. We need great leaders—patriotic enough to put the interests of the United States first, but with the political skills to accomplish worthy goals.

What about those of us who don't hold high office but who are subjected to the daily prattle of modern political speak? We, too, should be prepared to debate the vital issues of the day with truth and logic aforethought. Political correctness and spin are potent weapons in the fight for the soul of the United States of America. But nothing is as powerful as the truth.

So carry this book with you. Take it to the office, to parties, on airplanes, to sessions of Congress. As you use it, never lose sight of the fact that the

United States of America is still the greatest nation on Earth—a shining city on a hill, humankind's best hope for a new birth of freedom. In a strange world where up is down, black is white, and right is wrong, there is still sand left in the hourglass.

The declarations we have made within these pages transcend race, skin color, gender, creed, or societal position. They put no man or woman ahead of any other. As conservatives, we extend our hand to anyone who shares these clear moral objectives. Welcome to our tent; the door is open. If only you believe.

APPENDIX A

Clear Moral Objectives—the original op-ed

In 1999, I decided to write newspaper columns. I had been writing and voicing radio commentaries since 1995, but they were designed to last only about a minute. In the print medium, I knew that I could open up and flesh out a subject more than I could in short-form radio. Eventually, I wrote a column that I called "Clear Moral Objectives," a title taken from something Caspar Weinberger had said.

The *Dallas Morning News* accepted the column on the condition that it would be edited to about seven hundred words, which is a usual length for many newspaper op-eds. I asked if I could do the edit myself, the newspaper agreed, and even though the edited version was still more than eight hundred words long (with a wee bit of additional editing by the editor), the *News* carried the column on December 20, 1999. At that time, I had already published two books, a couple of short stories, and dozens of articles. But this was my first opinion column ever to see print.

It is still a favorite of mine and forms the basis for this book. Here is the column as it originally appeared in the *Dallas Morning News*:

* * *

Conservatives must set moral objectives

Former Secretary of Defense Caspar Weinberger says that the Cold War was won only after we finally defined a clear moral objective—when Ronald Reagan flatly declared the Soviet Union was an "evil empire." The world let out a collective gasp at the president's brash comment. But Mr. Reagan's belief was founded on conviction. His passion for freedom fueled a major shift in world opinion.

To be sure, other factors contributed to the decline of communism and the fall of the Berlin Wall. But it was Reagan and his impassioned demand to the Soviet leader—"Mr. Gorbachev, tear down this wall!"—that articulated a clear policy.

So why is it that today, those of us who call ourselves conservatives and mostly congregate in the Republican Party seem not to desire clear moral objectives? We talk of a "big tent" philosophy that welcomes any view. But what can be accomplished when the goals are so wishy-washy that they are practically nonexistent?

The Republicans should follow the example of President Reagan and state their clear moral objectives. The GOP then would be focused, and the party would be on its way toward real accomplishments.

1. Declare the sanctity of life. In our most precious documents, life even comes before liberty. We could still argue about rape, incest, and the life of the mother, but the basic idea that human beings are not disposable should be irrevocable.

2. Declare that government should be kept as small as possible. Republicans should promise and deliver real cuts in government spending, while maintaining a safety net for the deserving poor.

3. Declare that the tax code must go. Our income tax code is government's way of controlling the behavior of business and individuals. The goal should be to make April 15 just another day with no Internal Revenue Service, no deductions and no loopholes. Just a simple national sales tax.

4. Declare that "traditional families" are indispensable. The breakdown of the traditional family has done tremendous harm to our nation. Republicans should work to prevent men from abandoning their illegitimate offspring and to allow mothers to stay home with their young children.

5. Declare that America is a diverse nation under a common culture. As a nation of immigrants, our country welcomes diversity. But we should make it plain that from that polyglot of people, a distinct culture has emerged, built around concepts such as truth, justice, freedom, and personal responsibility.

6. Declare English the official language. While citizens and businesses in the private sector should be free to use any language they want, the language of government should be English. Great nations come together under a common tongue.

7. Declare all Americans equal under the law. Blatant discrimination should remain illegal, but set-asides, quotas, and affirmative action should end. No country can be truly great while pitting its people against each other because of gender or skin color.

8. Declare that America will remain the strongest nation on earth. Republicans should be unwavering in their support of our military and the

people who serve in it. We should be capable of waging two major wars at once, and we should create and deploy a high tech missile defense system.

9. Declare that our education system will be the world's best. The federal government should get entirely out of the way and let the 50 states come up with their own plans. However, at the state level, there is much that can be done. Academics should be stressed and excellent teachers should make more money. Public schools that continue to fail should be converted to charter schools.

10. Declare that there is a right and wrong. We have become a nation of moral relativism. There seems to be no shame anymore in becoming pregnant out of wedlock, committing perjury, or having an affair in the Oval Office. We have a problem, and the Republican Party should be the shining example of what is good.

11. Declare that we are a nation under God. It's still on our coinage and in our pledge to the flag, and we should reaffirm the relevance and validity of the Judeo-Christian ethic. This has nothing to do with government-sponsored religion. It has to do with our great traditions and the underpinnings of our moral compass.

12. Declare a reaffirmation of the Constitution and the Bill of Rights. Our guiding document and its first ten amendments form the very basis for our governance and our precious freedoms. Republicans should know it, live it, and work to appoint judges who will respect it.

These declarations will do more than just make a political party win; they will keep America great. They transcend race, skin color, gender, creed, or position. As conservatives, we should extend our hand to anyone who shares those lofty ideals. Welcome to our tent. The door is open. If only you believe.

APPENDIX B

A Clear Moral Bookshelf

Here are five books for suggested further reading.

Note that they are not overtly political books, but rather books that will help you to think. They have to do with advertising and marketing, positioning strategy, logical thinking, simplicity, and the potential of government. Each of these authors is a great thinker, and each of these books has taught me concepts that I use every day.

Confessions of an Advertising Man by David Ogilvy, Atheneum Publishers/Ballantine Books, 1963. While many great advertising campaigns are nothing but glitz, the acknowledged master in the field believed in the facts. "The consumer is not a moron; she is your wife," wrote Ogilvy.

Positioning: The Battle for Your Mind by Al Ries and Jack Trout, McGraw-Hill, 1986. "Every successful politician practices positioning," say Ries and Trout. "So do Proctor & Gamble and Johnson & Johnson." It's the only way to be heard above the noise in an "overcommunicated" society.

The Power of Logical Thinking by Marilyn vos Savant, St. Martin's Press, 1996. So you think you know how to think! First, Marilyn gives you difficult logic puzzles to solve; next, she teaches you how to solve them; then, she explains how politicians exploit our innocence.

The Power of Simplicity by Jack Trout with Steve Rivkin, McGraw-Hill, 1999. Trout and Rivkin shatter the myth that anything worthwhile must be complex. "Simple ideas tend to be obvious ideas because they have a ring of truth about them." This is a book about common sense.

Compassionate Conservatism by Marvin Olasky, The Free Press, 2000. The famed University of Texas journalism professor explains what government could accomplish—if it would just get out of its own way. And he explains why neighborhoods can accomplish more than all the programs of the Great Society.

ENDNOTES

Chapter 1

1. Associated Press, February 27, 1997.

2. *The New York Times*, November 6, 1995, as quoted in the newsletter of the Greater Austin Right to Life Committee, *Life Matters*, November 1995.

3. "Sustaining partial-birth abortions," the *Wall Street Journal*, September 26, 1996.

4. Associated Press, February 27, 1997.

5. Associated Press, March 16, 2002.

6. Ibid.

7. Robert Novak column, Creators Syndicate, March 12, 2002.

8. Michelle Mittelstadt, "Bush assails Senate Democrats for opposing court nominee," the *Dallas Morning News*, March 14, 2002.

9. Michelle Mittelstadt, "Senators near vote on Texas nominee to appeals court," the *Dallas Morning News*, August 30, 2002.

10. Ibid.

11. Christopher Lee, "Bush stands up for judicial nominee," the *Dallas Morning News*, July 17, 2002.

12. Michelle Mittelstadt, "Senate Panel rejects Bush nominee," the *Dallas Morning News*, September 6, 2002.

13. Sarah Weddington, op-ed, "Rights Under Seige," the *Austin American Statesman*, January 22, 1997.

14. Ellen L. McDonagh, all related quotes from op-ed, "Abortion rights' future could hinge on consent," the *Austin American-Statesman*, October 18, 1997.

15. All related quotes from "Partial birth abortion is bad medicine," the *Wall Street Journal*, September 19, 1996.

16. Julia Duin, "Abortion survivor makes case for overriding Clinton veto," the *Washington Times*, May 5, 1996.

17. Ibid.

18. "Litmus test?" the *Wall Street Journal*, January 22, 1998.

19. Ibid.

20. Ibid.

21. Ibid.

22. Ibid.

23. Associated Press, January 23, 1996.

24. Weddington, January 22, 1997.

25. Laura Meckler stories, Associated Press, February 1 and 2, 2001.

26. Cal Thomas, Tribune Media Services, May 29, 2002.

Chapter 2

1. Scott Burns, "Another take of the Bush tax cut," the *Dallas Morning News*, February 20, 2001.

2. The *Washington Post*, January 5, 2002.

3. John Lancaster article, the *Washington Post*, May 6, 2001.

4. Oliver North, "Dr. No," op-ed, January 11, 2002.

5. Rush Limbaugh, "Daschle's lose-lose agenda," the *Washington Times,* January 10, 2002.

6. "Congress raids funds for highway projects," Associated Press, February 4, 2002.

7. Ibid.

8. Ibid.

9. Eric Schmitt, "Lawmakers near record for pork," the *New York Times*, September 29, 2000.

10. Ibid.

11. News release, "Sen. Robert Byrd receives February 'Porker of the Month' Award," CAGW, February 16, 2001.

12. Ibid.

13. 2002 Congressional Pig Book Summary, "The book Washington doesn't want you to read," April 9, 2002.

14. CAGW President Thomas A. Schatz, news release, April 9, 2002.

15. Sharon Theimer article, Associated Press, November 26, 2001.

16. Ibid.

17. "Pork piggybacks anti-terrorism bill," Associated Press, December 15, 2001.

18. Ibid.

19. Senator John McCain, op-ed, "Waving the flag can be cover for looting the treasury," November 26, 2001.

20. Associated Press, January 22, 2002.

21. Ibid.

22. Ibid.

23. Associated Press, April 18, 2002.

24. Ibid.

25. *The World Book Encyclopedia*, 1993 Yearbook, p. 488.

26. *The World Book Encyclopedia*, 1994 Yearbook, p. 428.

27. Ibid, p. 143.

28. "Bill Clinton, Extremist," *Investor's Business Daily,*" 1996.

29. Julia Malone, "Clinton urges conciliation," the *Austin American-Statesman*, January 24, 1996.

30. Dob Deans, "Social Security IOU balances Clinton budget," the *Austin American-Statesman*, February 3, 1998.

31. Ibid.

32. "Surplus Alarm," the *Wall Street Journal*, June 28, 2000.

33. Ibid.

34. Robert Dodge, "Bush gets ball rolling on tax plan," the *Dallas Morning News*, February 9, 2001.

35. Ibid.

36. Scott Burns, "Another take on the Bush tax cut," the *Dallas Morning News*, February 20, 2001.

37. David Jackson, "Bush says taxpayers deserve break—Proposed cut risks future, Democrats say," the *Dallas Morning News*, February 28, 2002.

38. Ibid.

ENDNOTES 231

39. Christopher Lee, "House OKs Bush's plan for tax cuts, Democrats balk at cost," the *Dallas Morning News*, March 9, 2001.

40. Associated Press, April 9, 2001

41. Ibid.

42. Robert Dodge, "Lawmakers agree on $1.35 trillion dollar tax cut," the *Dallas Morning News*, May 2, 2001.

43. Ibid.

44. Associated Press, May 3, 2001.

45. Robert Dodge, "Tax cut clears Senate," the *Dallas Morning News*, May 24, 2001.

46. Ibid.

47. David Jackson, "Tax cuts are now a real deal," the *Dallas Morning News*, June 8, 2001.

48. Ibid.

49. Robert Dodge, "Bush takes heat as surplus shrinks," the *Dallas Morning News*, August 23, 2001.

50. Ibid.

51. Ibid.

52. Ibid.

53. Associated Press, April 9, 2001.

54. James Kuhnhenn and Ken Moritsugu, "Report: Trust fund needed," Knight Ridder Newspapers, August 28, 2001.

55. Ibid.

56. Robert Dodge, "Bush faces shrunken surplus," the *Dallas Morning News*, August 27, 2001.

57. David Jackson, "Bush says deficit may be on horizon," the *Dallas Morning News*, January 8, 2002.

58. Ibid.

59. Ibid.

60. Associated Press, January 17, 2002.

61. Richard W. Stevenson, "Agencies must make grade under Bush's budget plan," *New York Times* News Service, February 3, 2002.

62. Robert Dodge, "Bush budget heavy on defense, deficit," the *Dallas Morning News*, February 5, 2002.

63. Associated Press, February 6, 2002.

64. "Surplus talk," *Investor's Business Daily*, March 20, 1998.

65. Ibid.

66. George Melloan, "The Welfare State is being altered, not scrapped," the *Wall Street Journal*, July 29, 1996.

67. Marvin Olasky, "Welfare reform is hardly onerous," the *Austin American-Statesman*, August 7, 1996.

68. "Highlights of the new law," *USA Today*, August 23, 1996.

69. 1993 figures. "Report: 14% of Americans receive aid," *USA Today*, August 23, 1996.

70. "Apologize to Newt," the *Wall Street Journal*, May 8, 2000.

71. Ibid.

72. Michelle Mittelstadt, "Immigrant advocates rally in DC for benefits," the *Dallas Morning News*, July 7, 2001.

73. Ibid.

74. Ibid.

75. Associated Press, November 15, 2001.

76. Michelle Mittelstadt, "House supports restoring food stamps for legal immigrants," the *Dallas Morning News*, April 24, 2002.

77. Ibid.

78. Associated Press, May 17, 2002.

79. Laura Meckler, Associated Press, May 16, 2002.

80. John E. Mogk, "Nation's poor deserve care just as much as victims of 9/11," the *Detroit Free Press*, April 9, 2002.

81. Children's Special Needs Network newsletter, Temple, Texas, June 1999.

82. "Show compassion for uninsured children," the *Austin American-Statesman*, March 27, 1999.

83. Ibid.

84. Dave McNeely, "Expect Bush to sign off on full CHIP coverage," the *Austin American-Statesman*, May 5, 1999.

85. Ibid.

86. Rick Perry, "Texas children get health insurance," the *Dallas Morning News*, March 4, 2000.

87. Ibid.

88. TexCare Partnership handout, March 2001.

89. Ibid.

90. Associated Press, April 4, 2001.

91. Ibid.

92. Ibid.

93. Associated Press, July 7, 2000.

94. Associated Press, August 10, 2000.

95. Nancy San Martin, "Child health-care program promoted," the *Dallas Morning News*, January 3, 2001.

96. Ibid.

97. Robert A. Rosenblatt, the *Los Angeles Times*, January 7, 2001, with Associated Press data.

98. Bill Kidd, newspaper column, "Austin Notebook," February 2, 2002.

99. Ibid.

100. Ibid.

101. Dr. Nancy Dickey, "We must become advocates for uninsured," the *Dallas Morning News*, February 3, 2002.

102. Ibid.

103. Governor Rick Perry, "Make the most of CHIP," the *Waco Tribune-Herald*, March 9, 2002.

104. "CHIP: A major breakthrough for socialized medicine," the *Lone Star Report*, March 19, 1999.

105. Ibid.

106. Peyton Knight, "The March of Dimes-store medical coverage," the *DeWeese Report*, June 2000.

107. Patrick Poole, "Kids losing private health insurance," *World Net Daily*, July 2, 2000.

108. Ibid.

109. J. Dee Hill, "More CHIP bucks renew review," *AdWeek*, April 23, 2001.

110. "Corporate welfare isn't chicken feed," editorial, the *Austin American-Statesman*, July 21, 1999.

111. Quoted in op-ed by Sarah Eckel, Newspaper Enterprises Association, September 8, 1996.

112. Ibid.

113. Robert D. Novak, Creators Syndicate, April 30, 2002.

114. Phillip Brasher, Associated Press, May 3, 2002.

115. Ibid.

116. Ibid.

117. Dave Barry, "Farm Security: The mohair of the dog that bites you," www.MiamiHerald.com, June 23, 2002.

118. Robert D. Novak, Creators Syndicate, May 7, 2002.

119. Associated Press, May 9, 2002.

120. Ibid.

121. Associated Press, May 14, 2002.

122. Eckel, September 8, 1996.

123. Robert Dodge, "Fiscal ills leaving Medicaid in crisis," the *Dallas Morning News*, May 14, 2002.

Chapter 3

1. Steve Forbes, "Tax Reforms for Working Americans," the *Wall Street Journal*, April 14, 1999.

2. Tom Herman, "Tax professionals handled 60% of individual returns this year," the *Wall Street Journal*, June 6, 2002.

3. Herman, June 6, 2002.

4. *Forbes*, April 14, 1999.

5. Julia Malone, "Government takes a bigger bite than taxpayers realize," the *Austin American-Statesman*, April 11, 1998.

6. Ibid.

7. Julia Malone, "Tax bite is deeper, but cries are muted," the *Austin American-Statesman*, April 12, 1999.

8. Ibid.

9. Jack Anderson and Jan Moller, column, Creators Syndicate, July 20, 1999.

10. Herman, June 6, 2002.

11. "Tax report: High-income taxpayers pay a slightly larger share of U.S. income taxes," the *Wall Street Journal*, January 16, 2002.

12. Source: Citizens for Tax Justice, 1998.

13. Marvin Olasky, "Income tax had humble beginnings," the *Austin American Statesman*, April 14, 1999.

14. "The supply-side deficit myth," *Investor's Business Daily*, August 12, 1996.

15. "Tax reforms for working Americans," the *Wall Street Journal*, April 14, 1999.

16. Steve Forbes, "Tear down this Tax Code," the *Wall Street Journal*, July 15, 1997.

17. John Pisciotta, "A guided tour of the Flat Tax," the *Hankamer Business Review*, April, 1996.

18. David E. Rosenbaum, the *New York Times*, January 18, 1996.

19. Robert Eisner, "Beware of tax fads," the *Wall Street Journal*, April 23, 1996.

20. "An 'Untested' Flat Tax?" the *Wall Street Journal*, February 9, 1996.

21. Deroy Murdock, "Even Russia realizes the wisdom of a flat tax," Scripps Howard News Service, March 4, 2002.

22. David E. Rosenbaum, "Panel recommends flat tax," the *New York Times*, January 18, 1996.

23. Eisner, April 23, 1996.

24. "A comparison of the [national sales tax], the income tax, and the flat tax," Americans for Fair Taxation web site, August 2001.

25. Information available at www.fairtax.org.

26. Pamphlet, "Frequently Asked Questions," Americans for Fair Taxation, page 4.

27. Marilyn vos Savant, "Ask Marilyn," *Parade Magazine*, February 25, 1996.

Chapter 4

1. Rick Klein, "Growing number of moms choosing to remain single," the *Dallas Morning News*, November 10, 1999.

2. Source: U.S. Census Bureau, November 1999.

3. Klein, November 10, 1999.

4. Ibid.

5. "Changing Times—Are spouses really necessary these days?" the *Dallas Morning News*, August 23, 2000.

6. Associated Press, June 7, 2002.

7. Dick Stanley, "Addressing children by gender may form bias," the *Austin American-Statesman*, September 14, 1996.

8. Ibid.

9. David Jackson, "Bush, Gore tangle over child care," the *Dallas Morning News*, June 7, 2000.

10. Ibid.

11. Jenny Friedman, Ph.D, "The first three years," *American Baby*, April 1998.

12. Ibid.

13. The study was conducted by Professor Jeanne Brooks-Gunn of Columbia Teachers College and Jane Waldfogel and Wen-Jui Han, professors at Columbia's School of Social Work. The findings are published in the July-August 2002 edition of *Child Development*.

14. "Study: Mom's work affects kids' development," Associated Press, July 17, 2002.

15. Ibid.

16. James Devitt, "Teachers College, Social Work professors find association between mothers working full-time and young children's cognitive and verbal development," Columbia News web site, www.columbianews.edu, July 17, 2002.

17. Diane Ollis. "A tax on your household! Bride-to-be bemoans promise of marriage penalty," the *Austin American-Statesman*, September 16, 1997.

18. Economist Newspaper Ltd., *New York Times* Syndicate, September 26, 1997.

19. Ibid.

20. Joan Beck, Knight-Ridder/Tribune Information Services, September 16, 1997.

21. Associated Press, July 22, 2000.

22. Ibid.

23. Source: Associated Press.

24. Marc Lacey, the *New York Times*, August 6, 2000.

25. "The marriage penalty," www.concordcoalition.org, May 19, 1999.

26. Source: Congressional Budget Office (CBO), 1996 figures.

27. Ibid.

28. Bruce Bartlett (Senior Fellow), National Center for Policy Analysis, "The marriage penalty," www.ncpa.org, February 9, 1998.

29. Ibid.

30. Ibid.

31. www.concordcoaltition.org, May 19, 1999.

32. Associated Press, June 14, 2002.

33. Jim Abrams, Associated Press, November 11, 1999.

34. Ibid.

35. Ibid.

36. Dr. Sheron C. Patterson, "Welfare workers should avoid playing Cupid," the *Dallas Morning News*, March 4, 2002.

37. Leonard Pitts, the *Miami Herald*, July 17, 2001.

Chapter 5

1. Lynn Brezosky, "May she rest in peace," Associated Press, June 11, 2002.

2. Elliot Zwiebach, "Panel says ignorance major ethnic marketing pitfall," *Supermarket News,* May 27, 2002.

3. Ibid.

4. Paul Craig Roberts, "Overrun from within," the *Washington Times,* National Weekly Edition, June 26, 2000.

5. Ibid.

6. Art Moore, "Is Mexico reconquering U.S. Southwest?" WorldNetDaily.com, 2002.

7. Roger Scruton, "The Muslim next door" *National Review,* June 17, 2002.

8. Ibid.

9. William E. Simon, letter to the editor, the *Wall Street Journal,* May 1, 1996.

10. Dan Quayle, "Multiculturalism: Sounds nice, but it has dangers," *USA Today,* December 7, 1995.

11. Ibid.

12. Ibid.

13. Associated Press, January 19, 2002.

14. Kathleen Parker, "Three white guys and a flag," Tribune Media Services, January 16, 2002.

15. Ann Coulter, "The color of demagogy," from the internet, January 17, 2002.

16. "American Thanksgiving," the *Wall Street Journal,* November 17, 1998.

17. Ibid.

18. Linda Jones, "The father of Kwanzaa," the *Dallas Morning News,* December 26, 1996.

19. Paul Mulshine, "Happy Kwanzaa," *Heterodoxy Magazine,* Nov.-Dec. 1999. Also available at www.frontpagemagazine.com.

20. Ibid.

21. Ibid. Includes information from the *Los Angles Times,* May 14, 1971.

22. Jones, December 26, 1996.

23. Mulshine, Nov.-Dec. 1999.

24. Dr. Maulana Karenga, biography, from www.theblackmarket.com.

25. Ann Coulter, "Kwanzaa: holiday from the FBI," www.townhall.com, January 1, 2001.

26. Ibid.

27. Associated Press, September 9, 2001.

28. Ibid.

29. www.fightingwhites.org.

30. Linda K. Wertheimer, "Colleges debate value of required diversity classes," the *Dallas Morning News,* February 19, 2001.

31. Ibid.

32. Ibid.

33. "Reading by the numbers," *Investor's Business Daily,*" March 16, 1998.

34. "College students speak out," www.avot.org. Poll conducted by the Luntz Research Companies with a margin of error of plus or minus 4 percent.

35. David Schippers, *Sell Out: The Inside Story of President Clinton's Impeachment,* Regnery Publishing, Inc., 2000. Schippers recounts the story in an op-ed, "Abusing the INS," in the *Wall Street Journal,* August 23, 2000.

36. Ibid.

37. Associated Press, January 24, 2002.

38. Cal Thomas, Tribune Media Services, January 25, 2002.

39. Associated Press, January 24, 2002.

40. David Jackson, "Bush angry over INS visa blunder," the *Dallas Morning News*, March 14, 2002.

41. Associated Press, January 24, 2002.

42. Michelle Mittelstadt, "Legalization, amnesty, or what?" the *Dallas Morning News*, August 9, 2001.

43. Ibid.

44. Michelle Mittelstadt, "Democrats unveil plan to legalize immigrants," the *Dallas Morning News*, August 3, 2001.

45. Michelle Mittelstadt, "Latino groups warn Bush: Don't retreat on amnesty," the *Dallas Morning News*, August 23, 2001.

46. James Dale Davidson and Lord William Rees-Mogg, *The Great Reckoning*, first Touchstone edition, 1994, p. 22.

47. Georgie Anne Geyer, Universal Press Syndicate, July 3, 2000.

48. Ibid.

49. Roger Hernandez, King Features Syndicate, February 1, 2002.

50. G. Robert Hillman, "Bush's strategy to woo Latinos," the *Dallas Morning News*, August 13, 2001.

Chapter 6

1. Associated Press, January 24, 2002.

2. Gary Strauss, "Consumers frustrated by verbal gridlock," *USA Today*, February 28, 1997.

3. Ibid.

4. Ibid.

5. Associated Press, August 27, 2000.

6. Ibid.

7. Ibid.

8. Dr. Mike Moses, "Students need time to learn English," the *Dallas Morning News*, March 6, 2001.

9. Joan Beck, the *Chicago Tribune*, June 18, 1990.

10. Ibid.

11. Hal Netkin, "English not taught here," the *Wall Street Journal*, July 24, 1997.

12. Ibid.

13. K. L. Billingsley, "Hispanic parents hit bilingual classes," the *Washington Times*, February 26, 1996.

14. Lou Cannon, the *Washington Post*, July 27, 1997.

15. K. L. Billingsley, "Activist wants end to bilingual classes," the *Washington Times*, August 17, 1997.

16. K. L. Billingsley, "Latino activists sue Calif. Educators for bilingual education." the *Washington Times*, August 24, 1997.

17. Ibid.

18. Ibid.

19. "Listen to voters on bilingual education," *Investor's Business Daily*, November 7, 1997.

20. "California's unaccountable educrats," *Investor's Business Daily*, December 1998.

21. Ibid.

22. V. Dion Haynes, the *Chicago Tribune*, July 3, 1999.

23. Ibid.

24. Ibid.

25. Jacques Steinberg, the *New York Times*, August 20, 2000.

26. Ibid.

27. Charlie Brennan, "Language battle heads to Colorado," the *Dallas Morning News*, September 1, 2001.

28. "Anti-Bilingualism wins in Massachusetts," NewsMax Wires and United Press International, November 6, 2002.

29. Ibid.

30. Source: Scripps Howard Texas Poll conducted June 1–12, 1998, by Scripps Howard and the Office of Survey Research at the University of Texas. A total of 1,014 adults were interviewed by telephone in a random sample. The margin of error was plus or minus 3 percentage points.

31. A. Phillips Brooks, "Poll: Texans favor bilingual education," the *Austin American-Statesman*, June 28, 1998.

32. Ibid.

33. Ken Herman, "Bush: Judge bilingual ed by test results," the *Austin American-Statesman*, July 2, 1998.

34. Ibid.

35. Lori Price, "Translating immersion into success," the *Dallas Morning News*, August 23, 2002.

36. Mercedes Olivera, "Finally, a debate in Spanish for Latinos," the *Dallas Morning News*, January 12, 2002.

37. Sam Attlesey, "Rivals pull no punches in debates," the *Dallas Morning News*, March 3, 2002.

38. Ken Herman and Alberto Martinez, "Morales, Sanchez fire away," the *Austin American-Statesman*, March 3, 2002.

39. Attlesey, March 3, 2002.

40. Edward Rincon, "Is debate in Spanish a breakthrough? (Fluency can be asset in a state with large Latino population)," the *Dallas Morning News*, February 27, 2002.

41. William Murchison, "Is debate in Spanish a breakthrough? (Using a language other than English sets a bad precedent)," the *Dallas Morning News*, February 27, 2002.

42. Ibid.

43. Peter Applebome, the *New York Times*, December 20, 1996.

44. Ibid.

45. Nicholas Stix, "Ebonics: Bridge to illiteracy," *Liberty*, July 1997.

46. Ibid.

47. The *Liberty* article cites the research of John and Angela Rickford, "Dialect readers revisited," published in 1995 in the journal *Linguistics and Education*. John Rickford is a Stanford professor of linguistics and education, and authored a pro-Ebonics resolution passed by the Linguistics Society of America, meeting in Chicago, as covered in *Newsday*, January 5, 1997.

48. Stix, July, 1997.

49. Applebome, December 20, 1996.

50. Robert L. Steinback, *Miami Herald* column, Knight-Ridder/Tribune Information Services, December 27, 1996.

51. Leonard Pitts, *Miami Herald* column, Knight-Ridder/Tribune Information Services, December 27, 1996.

52. Neil A. Lewis, the *New York Times*, December 23, 1996.

53. Ibid.

54. Bill Cosby, "Elements of Igno-Ebonics style," the *Wall Street Journal*, January 10, 1997.

55. Ibid.

56. Ibid.

57. Tom Loveless, "The academic fad that gave us Ebonics," the *Wall Street Journal*, January 22, 1997.

58. Ibid.

59. Thomas Farragher, "English-only bill received House favor," Knight-Ridder Washington Bureau, August 2, 1996.

60. Ibid.

61. Ibid.

62. Joan Beck, *Chicago Tribune* column, Knight-Ridder/Tribune Media Services, March 7, 1997.

63. John Silber, "One nation, one language, one ballot," the *Wall Street Journal*, April 30, 1996.

64. Paul Craig Roberts, "Overrun from within," the *Washington Times*, National Weekly Edition, June 26, 2000.

65. Phyllis Schlafly, "Bush should kill Clinton's bilingual policies," *Human Events*, June 10, 2002.

66. Ibid.

67. Stix, July 1997.

Chapter 7

1. According to 1999 Labor Department figures.

2. John Leo, "Affirmative action history," *U.S. News & World Report*, March 28, 1994. Leo's article is based on an op-ed column in the *Wall Street Journal* by Gilbert Seawall, head of the American Textbook Council.

3. Ibid.

4. Dianne Solis and Alfredo Corchado, "Recession may hurt Hispanics most," the *Dallas Morning News*, January 25, 2002.

5. Sharon Jayson, "School district will chart a course toward diversity," the *Austin American-Statesman*, September 10, 1995.

6. Dan Seligman, "Mr. Diversity," *Forbes*, November 26, 2001, with information from the *New York Times*.

7. Ibid.

8. Greg Braxton and Dana Calvo, the *Los Angles Times*, December 1, 1999.

9. Donald Carty, "American underscores commitment to diversity," op-ed, the *Dallas Morning News*, April 5, 2002.

10. V. Dion Haynes, the *Chicago Tribune*, August 28, 1997.

11. Associated Press, August 29, 1997.

12. Ibid.

13. Arnold Hamilton, "Black Pledge of Allegiance 'not about separatism," the *Dallas Morning News*, January 25, 2002.

14. Ibid.

15. Paul Craig Roberts, "Is GOP losing its constituency?" the *Washington Times*, National Weekly Edition, June 10, 2002.

16. Ibid.

17. Paul Craig Roberts and Lawrence M. Stratton, *The New Color Line: How Quotas and Privilege Destroy Democracy*, Regnery Publishing, Inc., 1995.

18. Dianne Solis, "Minorities score big with arena," the *Dallas Morning News*, July 6, 2001.

19. Ibid.

20. Greg Forster, "Tax breaks for being black," the *Wall Street Journal*, November 8, 1995.

21. Ibid.

22. Bob Herbert, the *New York Times*, September 7, 1997.

23. Joan Beck, the *Chicago Tribune* and Knight-Ridder/Tribune Information Services, December 3, 1997.

24. Dianne Solis, "Contract disparity detailed," the *Dallas Morning News*, June 10, 2002.

25. Jackie Cissell, "Ugly past shouldn't overshadow future," op-ed, *USA Today*, April 19, 2002.

26. Associated Press, May 30, 1996.

27. "Justice Thomas' speech," the *Wall Street Journal*, July 31, 1998.

28. Paul Gigot, "The race card gets its moral bluff called," the *Wall Street Journal*, April 12, 1996.

29. Wallace Terry, "Racial Preferences are outdated," Parade, May 31, 1998.

30. Ibid.

31. Associated Press, April 19, 2002.

32. Leonard Pitts, the *Miami Herald,* March 19, 1999.

33. Claude R. Marx, "GOP's growing rift over race," *Investor's Business Daily*, August 22, 1997.

34. Associated Press, March 9, 1997.

35. Jim Phillips, "Minority enrollment at UT expected to decline," the *Austin American-Statesman*, July 2, 1996.

36. Ibid.

37. Christy Hoppe, "Panel removes injunction against affirmative action," the *Dallas Morning News*, December 22, 2000.

38. A. Phillips Brooks, "Texas college applications by minorities drop," the *Austin American-Statesman*, February 16, 1997.

39. Mary Ann Roser and A. Phillips Brooks, "UT reopens amid troubling racial shift," the *Austin American-Statesman*, August 24, 1997.

40. M. Michael Sharlot, "Affirmative action worked at law school," the *Austin American-Statesman*, September 5, 1997.

41. Mary Ann Roser, "Morales refuses to appeal Hopwood," the *Austin American-Statesman*, April 29, 1998.

42. "Pursue Hopwood appeal," editorial, the *Austin American-Statesman*, April 29, 1998.

43. Hoppe, December 22, 2000.

44. Christy Hoppe, "High Court lets admissions ruling stand," the *Dallas Morning News,* May 30, 2001.

45. Christy Hoppe, "High Court declines Hopwood," the *Dallas Morning News*, June 26, 2001.

46. Terrence Stutz, "Judge closes UT case on race," the *Dallas Morning News*, July 28, 1001.

47. Associated Press, February 11, 2002.

48. Christy Hoppe, "Diversity plan stirs criticism," the *Dallas Morning News*, December 13, 2001.

49. John Leo, newspaper column, February 12, 2002.

50. Associated Press, May 15, 2002.

51. Steve Chapman, column, Creators Syndicate, May 26, 2002.

52. Associated Press, February 18, 2000.

53. David Brown, the *Washington Post*, October 26, 1996.

54. Hugh B. Price, column, Copley News Service, June 22, 1996.

55. Advertisement, *USA Today*, July 17, 1996.

56. "Arkansas burning?" the *Wall Street Journal*, June 21, 1996.

57. Joyce Price and Warren R. Strobel, "President's memories disputed in Arkansas," the *Washington Times,* National Weekly Edition, June 23, 1996.

58. Lori Sharn and Gary Fields, "White churches equally subject to arson," *USA Today*, June 18, 1997.

59. Associated Press, July 5, 1996.

60. Michael Fumento, "A church arson epidemic? It's smoke and mirrors," the *Wall Street Journal*, July 8, 1996.

61. Linda Chavez and Robert Lerner, "Is the Justice System rigged against blacks?" the *Wall Street Journal*, December 4, 1996.

62. Ibid.

63. Senators Robert Torricelli, Edward Kennedy, Barbara Boxer, and Ron Wyden, newspaper column, October 26, 1998.

64. Kevin Galvin, Associated Press, April 7, 1999.

65. Osler McCarthy, "Hate crime bill expires in Senate," the *Austin American-Statesman*, May 15, 1999.

66. Associated Press, March 13, 2001.

67. Juan B. Elizondo Jr., "Perry says Texas should pass hate crimes bill," the *Austin American-Statesman*, May 6, 2001.

68. Christy Hoppe, "Hate crimes bill signed into law," the *Dallas Morning News*, May 12, 2001.

69. Associated Press, June 12, 2002.

70. Dorothy Rabinowitz, "The hate crimes bandwagon," the *Wall Street Journal*, June 27, 2000.

71. Ben Wear, "Vendor loses job over plan meant to help him,", the *Austin American-Statesman*, September 2, 1996.

72. Neal Boortz, "Hyphenated Americans," *NewsMax.com Magazine*, April, 2002.

73. "Yes or no, Mr. President?" the *Wall Street Journal*, December 5, 1997.

74. Ibid.

75. "Down in Durban," the *Wall Street Journal*, September 5, 2001.

Chapter 8

1. Judith Dupre, *Skyscrapers*, Black Dog & Leventhal, 1996, p. 67.

2. Steven Emerson, "Stop aid and comfort for agents of terror," the *Wall Street Journal*, August 5, 1996.

3. *The World Book Encyclopedia*, 1994 Yearbook, p. 56.

4. Ibid, p. 53.

5. Ibid.

6. Ibid, pp. 54-55.

7. *The World Book Encyclopedia*, 1995 Yearbook, p. 65.

8. *The World Book Encyclopedia*, 1996 Yearbook, pp. 55-57.

9. Ibid, p. 56.

10. *The World Book Encyclopedia*, 1997 Yearbook, pp. 62-65.

11. *The World Book Encyclopedia*, 1998 Yearbook, p. 66.

12. *The World Book Encyclopedia*, 1999 Yearbook, pp. 53-54.

13. Ibid, p. 54.

14. *The World Book Encyclopedia*, 2000 Yearbook, pp. 56-57.

15. *The World Book Encyclopedia*, 2001 Yearbook, p. 78 and p. 80.

16. *The World Book Encyclopedia*, 2002 Yearbook, p. 83.

17. Associated Press, August 2, 2002.

18. Associated Press, October 24, 2002.

19. "Weinberger: Clinton cut Army to less than half its Gulf War Size," *NewsMax.com Magazine*, February 15, 2002, page 26.

20. E. Thomas McClanahan, "Costs of gender-mixing," the *New York Times* News Service, March 4, 1997.

21. Ibid.

22. Scribner, 2000.

23. Stephanie Gutmann, "Men, women and war," the *Wall Street Journal*, March 24, 1999.

24. Ibid.

25. Stephanie Gutmann, "Today's Army: Warriors vs. schoolmarms," the *Wall Street Journal*, May 9, 2000.

26. Associated Press, January 24, 2002.

27. Ibid.

28. Associated Press, September 1, 2000.

29. Ibid.

30. Ibid.

31. Ibid.

32. Ed Timms, "Bush, Gore grappling over military," the *Dallas Morning News*, September 1, 2000.

33. Ibid.

34. Bob Deans, "Pentagon considers trimming 2-war doctrine," the *Austin American Statesman*, February 16, 1997.

35. Ibid.

36. David Hackworth, op-ed, King Features Syndicate, November 21, 1997.

37. Associated Press, September 28, 2000.

38. *The World Book Encyclopedia*, 2001 Yearbook, p. 78.

39. Associated Press, August 6, 2002.

40. Ibid.

41. David Jackson, "End near for ABM Treaty," the *Dallas Morning News*, December 14, 2001.

Chapter 9

1. *Sibling Revelry*, Lew Little Enterprises, Universal Press Syndicate, November 6, 1995.

2. Matthew Robinson, "Who's teaching the teachers?" *Investor's Business Daily*, November 6, 1997.

3. Ibid.

4. Thomas Sowell, column with excerpts from *Bad Teachers* by Guy Strickland, Creators Syndicate, April 20, 1998.

5. William Lutz, "Texas schools—to understand problems, talk to teachers," the *Dallas Morning News*, January 7, 2001. Lutz is a columnist for the *Lone Star Report*.

6. Associated Press, February 7, 2002.

7. Ibid.

8. Associated Press, April 4, 2001, with information from the *Bryan-College Station Eagle*.

9. "Sidwell liberals," the *Wall Street Journal*, September 8, 1997.

10. Peg Luksik and Pamela Hobbs Hoffecker, *Outcome Based Education: The State's Assault on Our Children's Values.* Huntington House Publishers, 1995, page 13.

11. Marianne M. Jennings, "MTV Math doesn't add up," the *Wall Street Journal*, December 17, 1996.

12. Luksik and Hoffecker, page 19-20.

13. Thomas DeWeese, "Mission of OBE: Modify behavior," *Media Bypass Magazine*, October, 1996.

14. Ibid.

15. George Will, *Washington Post* Writers' Group, January 6, 2002.

16. Ibid.

17. Michael Chapman, "Let 100,000 new teachers bloom—Pols and unions win, but what about the kids?" *Investor's Business Daily*, December 16, 1998.

18. Ibid.

19. Roseline Bush (editor), "Schools fail kids," *Family Voice*, September 1996.

20. Ibid.

21. Jerry Jesness, "Esteem really is delusion," the *Dallas Morning News*, August 17, 2001.

22. Editorial, "Welcome back, phonics," the *Austin American-Statesman*, May 28, 1996.

23. Dianne M. Haneke, "Balanced diet of reading approaches is best," the *Austin American-Statesman*, June 12, 1996.

24. Roseline Bush.

25. Ibid.

26. John K. Rosemond, "Feeling good, acting bad," *Hemispheres*, the United Airlines in-flight magazine, February 2001.

27. Scott S. Greenberger, "Three Rs, rote drills to return in school?" the *Austin American-Statesman*, April 19, 1996.

28. Sam Attlesey, "Bush plan wants all kids to be literate by 3rd grade," the *Dallas Morning News*, March 29, 2000.

29. Ibid.

30. G. Robert Hillman, "Bush, Democrats offer education plans," the *Dallas Morning News*, January 24, 2001.

31. G. Robert Hillman, "Education aid pledged," the *Dallas Morning News*, February 22, 2001.

32. Associated Press, May 3, 2001.

33. William J. Bennett and Chester E. Finn Jr., "Congress's virtual school reform," *The Sentinel*, May/June 2001.

34. William Bennett, "Bush already has abandoned too much of original proposal," the *Dallas Morning News*, May 5, 2001.

35. Robert D. Novak, Creators Syndicate, May 15, 2001.

36. Ibid., May 23, 2001.

37. Charles Ornstein, "Education reforms approved by House," the *Dallas Morning News*, May 24, 2001.

38. Charles Ornstein, "Education bill passes in Senate," the *Dallas Morning News*, June 15, 2001.

39. John E. Mulligan, "Accord reached on school bill," the *Dallas Morning News*, December 12, 2001.

40. Ibid.

41. Joshua Benton, "Bush signs far-reaching education bill," the *Dallas Morning News*, January 9, 2002.

42. Marvin Olasky, "Better schools can make racial preferences irrelevant," the *Austin American-Statesman*, March 31, 1999.

43. Editorial, "Connerly's message doesn't play in Texas," the *Austin-American Statesman*, March 9, 1999.

44. Fred Heeren, "The lynching of Bill Dembski," the *American Spectator*, November 2000.

45. Ibid.

46. Ibid.

47. Jeff Scheldt, "Anti-abortion display stirs debate," the *Baylor Lariat*, November 1, 2001.

48. Editorial, "BU shouldn't allow anti-abortion group's disruptive images," the *Baylor Lariat*, November 1, 2001.

49. Steven Dove column, "Door opening to liberal voices," the *Baylor Lariat*, November 1, 2001.

50. David Horowitz, advertisement copy, "Ten reasons why reparations for blacks is a bad idea for blacks—and racist too," available at www.frontpagemagazine.com.

51. David Horowitz, *Uncivil Wars*, Encounter Books, 2002, page 1.

52. Ibid, page 18.

53. Ibid, pp. 42, 43.

54. Ibid, page 56 and 59.

55. Wayne Slater, "Author, UT students argue over racial issues," the *Dallas Morning News*, March 22, 2001.

56. Richard Cohen, "Specious speech," the *Washington Post*, March 22, 2001.

57. William Murchison, "To get along doesn't mean to shut up," the *Dallas Morning News*, March 28, 2001.

58. Chester E. Finn Jr., "Why America has the world's dimmest bright kids," the *Wall Street Journal*, February 25, 1998.

59. "Public schools: Change or die?" editorial, *Investor's Business Daily*, September 30, 1996.

60. Diane Ravitch, "Why do Catholic schools succeed?" *Forbes*, October 7, 1996.

61. Linda Bowles, "What Johnny learns at school," *WorldNetDaily.com*, July 17, 2001.

Chapter 10

1. News release, "NAS/Zogby poll reveals American colleges are teaching dubious ethical lessons," www.nas.org, July 2, 2002. The National Association of Scholars is a higher-education reform group located in Princeton, New Jersey. The poll was conducted April 9-16, 2002, and has a plus or minus 5 percent sampling error.

2. Dianne Clements and Dudley Sharp, "Guilty as charged," the *Wall Street Journal*, June 28, 2000.

3. Ibid.

4. Ibid.

5. Bruce Nichols, "Leaders hail Graham as martyr during funeral," the *Dallas Morning News*, June 30, 2000.

6. Ibid.

7. Robert Jensen, "U.S. just as guilty of committing own violent acts," the *Houston Chronicle*, September 14, 2001.

8. William Bennett, "America was attacked because it is good," the *Dallas Morning News*, October 7, 2001.

9. Ibid.

10. Rep. J. C. Watts Jr., R-Okla., letter to Reuters Group PLC, October 3, 2001.

11. President George W. Bush, State of the Union Address, January 29, 2001.

12. The *Washington Post*, January 31, 2002.

13. Associated Press, February 1, 2002.

14. Mike Allen and Karen DeYoung, the *Washington Post*, June 2, 2002.

15. Bill O'Reilly, "PC Europe weakens us abroad," the *Washington Times*, National Weekly Edition, June 24, 2002.

16. Dr. Bill J. Humble, Understanding the Mideast roots of terror," *ACU Today* (Abilene Christian University), Winter 2002.

17. Cal Thomas, Tribune Media Services, April 17, 2002.

18. Mary Elizabeth (Tipper) Gore, *Raising PG Kids in an X-Rated Society*, Abingdon Press, 1987, p. 18.

19. Ibid, p. 83.

20. Philip Messing, Marianne Garvey, and Hasani Gittens, "St. Pat's shock-jock interlewd," the *New York Post* and www.nypost.com, August 16, 2002.

21. Phillip Hubbell, "Let's stop making excuses for immorality," the *Dallas Morning News*, July 17, 2001.

Chapter 11

1. Exodus 20, verses 12-17, *The Holy Bible*, King James Version. The Ten Commandments also appear in Deuteronomy 5: 6-21.

2. Ibid, verses 2-10.

3. Oliver Kelley, judge of the 169th District Court in Bell County, Texas, in a speech to the Republican Women Prayer Breakfast, January 1989, updated August 1996.

4. Ibid.

5. Ibid.

6. Associated Press, June 26, 2002.

7. David Kravets, "Pledge's 'under God' under fire," the *Dallas Morning News*, June 27, 2002.

8. Rev. Jerry Falwell on Fox News Channel, June 26, 2002.

9. Newt Gingrich, in an interview on "Hannity & Colmes," Fox News Channel, June 26, 2002.

10. Cal Thomas (Tribune Media Services), Thomas Sowell (Creators Syndicate), E. J. Dionne (The *Washington Post*), "Why remove God from our Pledge?" a summary of opinions from various columnists, the *Dallas Morning News*, June 29, 2002.

11. Scott Gold and Eric Bailey, the *Los Angeles Times*, June 30, 2002.

12. David Kravets, Associated Press, June 28, 2002.

13. Associated Press, July 11, 2002.

14. Anne Gearan, Associated Press, June 28, 2002.

15. Ibid.

16. Ibid.

17. William J. Bennett, "A victory for ordered liberty," *OpinionJournal.com*, July 4, 2002.

18. Bob Chase, "Advocates of school vouchers can't drum up public support," the *Dallas Morning News*, July 1, 2002.

19. George Will, the *Washington Post*, June 28, 2002.

20. William J. Bennett, *The De-Valuing of America*, Summit Books, 1992, p. 206.

21. Abraham Lincoln, speech at Edwardsville, Illinois, September 11, 1858.

22. William Murchison, "Only religion can form a basis for morality," the *Dallas Morning News*, July 3, 2002.

Chapter 12

1. Benjamin Franklin, from remarks made at the end of the Constitutional Convention.

2. Richard Henry Lee, as quoted in the *Annals of America*, Volume 3, "Organizing the New Nation," Encyclopaedia Britannica, Inc., 1968, p. 130. Lee wrote a series of anti-Federalist essays, some of which are reprinted here.

3. Alexander Hamilton, *The Federalist*, Number 1, 1787.

4. Pamphlet, "Eight vital reasons to abolish the Department of Education," Concerned Women for America, undated.

5. Article II, Section 2.

6. Steve Chapman column, the *Chicago Tribune*, September 7, 2002.

7. Charley Reese column, King Features Syndicate, September 9, 2002.

8. Source: *Dallas Morning News* research, June 6, 2002.

9. Michelle Middlestadt, "Bush's 9-11 policies hit legal snags," the *Dallas Morning News*, June 6, 2002.

10. Ibid.

11. Steve Chapman column, Creators Syndicate, August 22, 2002.

12. Nat Hentoff, "Sept. 11: Will we stay free?" *Jewish World Review,* Sept. 9, 2002, and at www.jewishworldreview.com. Hentoff is syndicated by Newspaper Enterprise Association.

13. James Madison, *The Federalist,* Number 47, January 1788.

14. Associated Press, June 12, 2002.

15. Article II, Section 2.

16. Michelle Mittlestadt, "Bush assails Senate Democrats for opposing court nominee," the *Dallas Morning News,* March 14, 2002.

17. Nat Hentoff column, Newspaper Enterprise Association, September 13, 2002. Senator Arlen Specter quote from *Legal Times,* July 8, 2002.

18. Associated Press, August 26, 2002.

19. Ibid.

20. Article I, Section 8.

21. Article II, Section 2.

22. The War Powers Act of 1973, SEC. 2 (a).

23. The War Powers Act of 1973, SEC. 3.

24. George Will column, *Washington Post* Writers' Group, August 29, 2002.

25. Carolyn Barta, "A House to look like America," the *Dallas Morning News,* June 2, 2002.

26. Article I, Section 2.

27. The Fifteenth Amendment, Section 1.

28. The Voting Rights Act was signed by President Lyndon Johnson on August 6, 1965.

29. The Twenty-fourth Amendment, ratified in 1964, had already banned the poll tax in elections for U.S. president and vice president, U.S. senators, and members of Congress.

30. The Voting Rights Act of 1965, SEC. 5.

31. The Voting Rights Act of 1965, SEC. 4 (e) (1).

32. The Fourteenth Amendment, Section 2.

33. Article I, Section 4.

34. Mark Babineck, Associated Press, September 18, 2002.

35. Article I, Section 8.

36. Article III, Section 2.

37. Thomas Sowell (Creators Syndicate), "Why remove God from our pledge?" a summary of opinions from various columnists, the *Dallas Morning News,* June 29, 2002.

38. George Washington, speech at the Federal Convention, 1787, as quoted by Gouverneur Morris in his funeral oration, December 31, 1799.

39. Alexander Hamilton, "for the adoption of the Constitution," letter in answer to New York Governor George Clinton, the *New York Daily Advertiser,* October 17, 1787.

INDEX

Bradley, Ann Walsh, 76
Breaux, John, 31, 32
Brooks-Gunn, Jeanne, 70
Brown v. Board of Education of Topeka, 120, 208
Brown, Oliver, 120
Brown, Ron, xi
Buchanan, 93-94
Buchanan, Pat, 90, 93-94
Bush, George W.:
   and Children's Health Insurance
      Program (CHIP), 40
   and Constitution, U.S., 210
   and culture, American, 94
   and economy, 20, 57
   and education, 162, 165, 169-173, 174, 179
   and English language, 104, 110, 111
   and farm subsidies, 47, 48
   and hate crimes, 134
   and immigration, 90, 91, 92
   judicial appointments by, 7-8, 212
   and military, 145, 149, 151-152, 154-155, 156
   and Pledge of Allegiance, 198
   and redistricting, 123
   and right to life, 12-13, 14
   and school vouchers, 202
   and tax cuts, 18-19, 21, 28, 29-35, 52, 57-58
   and terrorism, xii, 185-186, 187, 212
Bush, George H. W., 141-142, 143, 150, 212
Bush, Jeb, 130
Byrd, James, Jr., 133
Byrd, Robert, 21, 22, 35

California Association of Bilingual
   Educators (CABE), 100
California Civil Rights Initiative, 118-119
Calvert, Ken, 25
Camarota, Steven A., 91
Campbell, Lisa, 119
Canady, Charles T., 11, 125
Carter, Richard, 183
Carty, Donald, 117, 119
Carvell, Douglas, 126
Carville, James, x
Casey, Bob, 12
Castillo, John, 97
Caston-Powe, Maurice, 126

Center for the Study of Popular Culture, 176
Chapman, Steve, 130, 209, 210-211
Chase, Bob, 201
Chavez, Linda, 133
Chen Shui-bian, 154
Cheney, Dick, 31
child care, 68-71
Children's Health Insurance Program (CHIP), 39-46, 38, 49, 50
Chirac, Jacques, 81
Choctaw Erectors Inc., 121
Christie, Jack, 104
Cissell, Jackie, 123
Citicorp, 46
Citizen, Robin, 177
Citizens Against Government Waste
   (CAGW), 18, 20-21, 22
Civil Rights Act of 1964, 114
Clinton, Bill:
   and Children's Health Insurance
      Program (CHIP), 43, 45
   and church burnings, 131-132
   crimes of, 191
   and education, 165
   and English language, 111
   and government, size of, 26-29
   and hate crimes, 134
   and immigration, 94, 95
   impeachment of, 182
   and Internal Revenue Service, 64
   and Kwanzaa, 86
   and military decline, 141-145, 148, 151
   and racial preferences, 135-136
   and reelection, 49
   and right to life, 4, 5, 10-11, 12
   and school vouchers, 162
   and "spin," x-xi
   and taxes, 53, 54, 57, 72-73
   and terrorism, 140
   and welfare, 36, 37
Clinton, Hillary Rodham, xi, 19, 23, 38, 44, 191
Cochran, Johnnie, 178
Cochran, Thad, 25
Cohen, Richard, 178
Cohen, William S., 144, 149, 150
Cold War, 150
Coleman, James, 179-180
Collins, Joseph J., 149-150
Collins, Susan, 24

ABOUT THE AUTHOR

During morning drive radio in Central Texas, Lynn Woolley is the "Secretary of Logic," taking the vital issues of the day, stripping them of their emotion, and analyzing them with logic aforethought. Later in the day, he turns from talk show host to political writer, commenting on current events for such venues as the *Dallas Morning News*, the *Waco Tribune-Herald*, and the website *NewsMax.com*.

Lynn's broadcast career has included stints as a radio news anchor in Dallas and Austin, a political reporter, and a play-by-play announcer. He is the author of two prior books, both on the subject of broadcasting.

He is a past winner of the Dallas Press Club "Katie" award and has won several Associated Press awards for political commentary. Lynn has been a local TV host of the Children's Miracle Network Telethon in the Waco-Temple market since 1986. He holds a bachelor's degree from the University of Texas at Austin.

His columns are archived at www.BeLogical.com.